T0374959

A World of Fiction

DIGITAL HUMANITIES

Series Editors:
Julie Thompson Klein, Wayne State University
Tara McPherson, University of Southern California
Paul Conway, University of Michigan

DIGITALCULTUREBOOKS, an imprint of the University of
Michigan Press, is dedicated to publishing work in new media
studies and the emerging field of digital humanities.

A World of Fiction

Digital Collections and the Future of Literary History

KATHERINE BODE

University of Michigan Press
Ann Arbor

Published in the United States of America by the
University of Michigan Press
Manufactured in the United States of America
Printed on acid-free paper

First published July 2018

A CIP catalog record for this book is available from the British Library.

Library of Congress Cataloging-in-Publication data has been applied for.

ISBN 978-0-472-13085-6 (hardcover : alk. paper)
ISBN 978-0-472-12392-6 (e-book)
ISBN 978-0-472-90083-1 (Open Access ebook edition)

Digital materials related to this title can be found on
www.fulcrum.org at doi.org/10.3998/mpub.8784777

Acknowledgments

———— ৵ ————

The ideas in this book benefited enormously from the advice and feedback of generous colleagues, especially Robert Dixon, Paul Eggert, Julieanne Lamond, Glenn Roe, Kate Mitchell, Shawna Ross, and Ted Underwood. Leigh Dale deserves special thanks: as has been the case since I was a graduate student, for this book she has been my most dedicated and encouraging reader. I would also like to acknowledge Elizabeth Morrison, who was a generous reader of parts of the book and an inspiration to me while writing it. In the late 1980s, Elizabeth imagined the possibilities of an index of fiction in Australian newspapers and proposed it be held in a "computer database." In building that database and exploring that fiction I have tried to emulate the nuance and scholarly rigor of Elizabeth's work, as well as its ambitious scope.

This book would not have been possible without a Discovery Grant from the Australian Research Council. That funding enabled me to hire bibliographer Carol Hetherington. This was surely the single greatest contributor to the success of the project. I approached Carol asking for advice about whom I might hire as a research assistant; when Carol suggested herself for the job I gained a colleague and friend to share the project with. Junran Lei, development officer in the Centre for Digital Humanities Research at the Australian National University, gave invaluable technical assistance to the project. Work on this book was also supported by research travel funding from the Australian National University and by a Bicentennial Fellowship from the Menzies Centre at King's College London. While I was at King's Mark Turner kindly introduced me to a group of periodical scholars, including Laurel Brake, James Mussell, Matthew Philpotts, and Matthew Rubery. My conversations with these scholars were instrumental in shaping the book's arguments.

Chapter 1 is closely based on an article published in *Modern Language Quarterly* in 2017, which also outlines ideas I develop in chapter 2. A version of the first part of chapter 4 was published in *Book History* in 2016, and much of an earlier version of chapter 5 appeared in *Victorian Periodicals Review* in 2017. I thank the editors of these journals, particularly Marshall Brown and Alexis Easley, as well as the anonymous reviewers, for helping me to develop this work.

Finally, I want to thank my family. As always, my parents and sisters provided enormous support and encouragement. I also benefited a great deal from conversations with my mathematician brother, Michael Bode, about digital methods, and from his practical assistance with creating the decision trees used in chapter 6. My husband, Ben, and I had two children during the writing of this book—Elsa and Felix—and it is dedicated to them, and to Ben, whose understanding and support, and "actual sharing of the fatigues of the nursery" (#21693/IV), made this book possible.

Contents

———— ❧ ————

Introduction

Questions and Opportunities for
Twenty-First-Century Literary History

———— ✻ ————

This book began with a question and an opportunity. These arose, respectively, from conditions of the nineteenth century and of the twenty-first. In Australia in the nineteenth century, in contrast to the much more diversified literary markets of Britain and America, newspapers were the main local publishers as well as the major sources of fiction: local and imported. Literary historians knew much—though as this book shows, much less than we thought—about the Australian fiction published in this context. But very little was known about the fiction from elsewhere that appeared in these newspapers, even as it was estimated to comprise around 80 percent of all titles (Morrison, "Serial" 315). In asking what fiction was published in nineteenth-century Australian newspapers I wanted to know where it came from, who wrote it, when it was published, and how it got there. By association, I sought to understand the transnational conditions in which local authors wrote and were read and by which an Australian literary culture developed.

In the twenty-first century, the National Library of Australia's (NLA) *Trove* database represents the largest mass-digitized collection of historical newspapers internationally.[1] This was my opportunity: *Trove* made it possible, for the first time, to explore nineteenth-century Australian newspaper fiction in a systematic and extensive way. I devised a "paratextual method," outlined in chapter 3, that uses formal features of these digitized newspapers to automatically identify and harvest fiction. On this basis, I discovered over 16,500 works, a massively expanded record of nineteenth-century Australian literary culture and its connections with the international circulation of fiction in this period.

The titles I uncovered came from across the globe—from Britain and America as well as Austria, Canada, France, Germany, Holland, Hungary, Italy, Japan, New Zealand, Russia, South Africa, and Sweden. I found established international authors in Australian newspapers much earlier than had previously been realized, including multiple titles by Charles Dickens published prior to the mid-1850s,[2] along with fiction by Honoré de Balzac, Alexandre Dumas, Eugène Sue, William Makepeace Thackeray, Gustave Toudouze, and Ivan Turgenev. However, it was after this time that fiction in Australian newspapers really expanded. Among the thousands of titles discovered were works by other canonical American, British, and European authors, including Benjamin Disraeli, George Eliot, Thomas Hardy, Victor Hugo, Henry James, Harriet Beecher Stowe, Anthony Trollope, Mark Twain, Oscar Wilde, Émile Zola, and Heinrich Zschokke. I also found numerous stories by prolific American dime novelists such as Sylvanus Cobb, Prentiss Ingraham, Laura Jean Libbey, and Ann S. Stephens, as well as an extensive array of works by popular British authors, including Mary Elizabeth Braddon (the most published international author in colonial Australia),[3] Wilkie Collins, Arthur Conan Doyle, Robert Louis Stevenson, Ellen Wood, and many others. Alongside these international writers were a host of new Australian works and authors, with notable findings, including previously unlisted fiction by Catherine Martin and Jessie Mabel Waterhouse; a new Australian author, John Silvester Nottage, responsible for multiple full-length novels; and new titles by "Captain Lacie" and "Ivan Dexter," in addition to the discovery that both were well-developed pseudonyms for James Joseph Wright, who thereby emerges as one of, if not the most, prolific of Australia's early authors.

This greatly expanded record of nineteenth-century Australian newspaper fiction was created as a basis for what I call data-rich literary history, and what many scholars, especially in the United States, refer to in the terminology of the field's most prominent practitioner, Franco Moretti, as "distant reading."[4] This approach to literary history applies computational methods of analysis to large bibliographical and/or textual datasets—derived increasingly though not exclusively from mass-digitized collections—to explore how literary works existed, interrelated, and generated meaning in the past. By investigating the cultural and material contexts in which literature was produced, circulated, and read, data-rich literary history seeks to challenge and move beyond the literary canons that organize perceptions of past literature in the present. This, then, *was* my intention: to move from question, to opportunity, to answers and, in so doing, to advance a noncanonical, data-rich, and transnational history of the literary, publishing, and reading cultures of nineteenth-century Australia. But working with *Trove* interrupted that neat sequence. Instead of simply answering questions, that engagement produced its own, pressing questions about the nature and implications of literary history conducted with mass-digitized collections and the literary data derived from them.

While I had approached constructing a dataset of nineteenth-century Australian newspaper fiction purely as a preparatory task necessary to enable the synoptic form of literary history I sought to write, I came to realize that this supposedly precritical activity formed an extended historical argument in and of itself, in the context of a specific mass-digitized collection. And while current discussion of mass-digitization foregrounds the scale of such collections and the extensiveness of the digital access they provide, I became increasingly conscious of the gaps in *Trove*: and this is a mass-digitized collection that is among the largest, and most complete, in the world. When I looked to other data-rich literary history projects to see how they were meeting this challenge I found that the complex relationships between documentary record, digitization, data curation, and historical analysis were not fully articulated. In the highest profile work in this field— Moretti's distant reading and the "macroanalysis" of his longtime collaborator and the cofounder of the Stanford Literary Lab, Matthew L. Jockers—these relationships and their effects were essentially denied in preference for a view of large-scale literary data and mass-digitized collections as transparent windows onto the past.

The result of the questions and opportunities that led me to this project—and of the questions they, in turn, generated—is a book in two parts. The first explores limitations in existing approaches to data-rich literary history and offers an alternative in the form of a new scholarly object of analysis. My central contention in this first part is that, whatever computational methods allow us to do with ever-growing collections of literary data, the results cannot advance knowledge if the literary data analyzed do not effectively represent the historical context we seek to understand. I draw on the theoretical and practical foundations of textual scholarship to constitute what I call a scholarly edition of a literary system: that is, a model of literary works that were published, circulated, and read—and thereby accrued meaning—in a specific historical context, constructed with reference to the history of transmission by which documentary evidence of those works is constituted. In doing so, I seek to provide an appropriate foundation not just for data-rich research but for the broader discipline of literary history as it increasingly operates in a dynamic and expansive digital environment.

The second part of *A World of Fiction* demonstrates how analysis of a scholarly edition of a literary system can revolutionize knowledge of literary history as well as the frameworks and concepts through which we perceive past literature in the present. While the "transnational turn" in Australian literary studies has represented nineteenth-century Australian readers as oriented almost entirely toward British fiction, I offer a more complex picture: one where this orientation exists, but where colonial authors, publishers, and readers also forged a distinctive Australian literary culture. In the process, I describe an entirely new organization for and structures within literary culture in the colonies and demonstrate the capacity of data-rich literary history to advance understanding of major concepts and phenomena in the broader discipline, ranging from literary anonymity and pseudonymity to reception, fiction reprinting and syndication, and the nature of literary traditions.

Although terminology in the field is evolving, literary histories that employ data and mass-digitized collections still typically begin by citing Moretti's influential concept of distant reading and/or Jockers's notion of macroanalysis.[5] There is good reason for this. These scholars have dominated academic and general discussion of data-rich literary history. Not only have they written some of the only book-length contributions to the field, but remarkably for literary scholarship, Moretti's and Jockers's work is reported on in major public forums: the *Financial Times*, the *Los Angeles Review of Books*, the *New York Times*, the *New Yorker*, the *Paris Review*, and more.[6] *Distant reading* is a term routinely employed to describe the methods of computational textual analysis in general (Goldstone, "Doxa"). While the use of extensive data to investigate historical literary systems has significant antecedents, not least in book history,[7] Moretti has been highly effective in demonstrating the potential critical sophistication of this approach to the wider field of literary studies, and in thereby generating interest in digital methods.

Although influenced by both Moretti's and Jockers's work, this book begins rather differently: with a critique of their approach. Chapter 1, "Abstraction, Singularity, Textuality: The Equivalence of 'Close' and 'Distant' Reading," argues that distant reading and macroanalysis offer an inadequate foundation for data-rich literary history because they neglect the activities and insights of textual scholarship: the bibliographical and editorial practices that literary scholars have long relied on to interpret and represent the historical record. Textual scholars understand literary works as events—unfolding and accruing meaning across time and space—and the documentary record as partially and provisionally expressing that process. By contrast, distant reading and macroanalysis conceive data and mass-digitized collections as providing direct and unmediated access to the historical literary record and reduce literary works to texts, perceiving them as singular and stable entities, related to each other in history via basic categories of production. The models of literary systems that Moretti and Jockers construct on this basis are limited, abstract, and often ahistorical.

Such inattention to the historical and material nature of the documentary record is inherited from, not in opposition to, the New Criticism and its core method of close reading. Close readings are generally protected from the worst consequences of such underlying assumptions by the disciplinary infrastructure that textual scholars have produced, and by the documentary context in which such readings are enacted. The same cannot be said of distant reading and macroanalysis, which take the problematic assumptions of close reading to an extreme conclusion. The problem with these prominent approaches is not that they introduce new quantitative methods, inimical to nuanced literary-historical understanding, as has been argued. Rather, distant reading and macroanalysis construct and seek to extract meaning from models of literary systems that are essentially deficient: inadequate for representing the ways in which literary works existed and generated meaning in the past. The solution to this problem is not rejecting data-rich literary history, nor proposing new, more elaborate forms of computational analysis; it is not even integrating computational and non-computational methods, as is often proposed. These solutions define the issue in terms of the method of analysis used, when the foundational problem is the lack of an adequate object to analyze: one that is capable of managing the documentary record's complexity, especially as it is manifested in emerging digital knowledge infrastructure, and of representing literary works in the historical contexts in which they were produced and received.

Chapter 2, "Back to the Future: A New Object for (Data-Rich) Literary History," responds to this challenge by articulating the case for and describing a scholarly edition of a literary system. I begin by surveying existing projects in data-rich literary history that model literary systems differently than do distant reading and macroanalysis. Instead of treating literary works as singular and stable objects, these projects represent and explore the means by which those works connected to each other and accrued meaning in the past. I argue that explicit engagement with modeling, as the method has been theorized in digital humanities, has significant potential to enhance data-rich literary history by offering a mechanism through which to interrogate and refine conceptions of literary works and systems. But modeling alone is insufficient as a basis for the field. A data-rich model of a literary system is inevitably an argument shaped by not only the scholar's perception of cultural artifacts and phenomena but the complex history by which those artifacts and phenomena are transmitted to and by us in the present. Modeling does not provide a mechanism through which to recognize and represent the inevitably transactional nature of the documentary record: the fact that, whether analog or digital, that record never exists in a stable form but is produced in time and in our interactions with collections. Nor does modeling offer a framework for assessing and managing the inevitable, sometimes radical, disjunctions that exist between knowledge infrastructure, the historical context it is intended to represent, and the data employed in that representation.

Despite the "heavy . . . associations" the scholarly edition carries "from print culture" (Price np), it provides an effective framework through which to understand and accommodate such contingency and partiality. A scholarly edition of a literary work is sometimes perceived simply as a version with extra references, or with added historical context. In fact, it is an argument—a historical and critical but also a technical one—that offers a foundation for other literary-critical and historical arguments to build upon. It presents that argument through a curated text, one for which the content is, by definition, contested, and a critical apparatus that demonstrates and manages those contested features by describing and justifying the editor's engagement with the documentary record relating to a literary work, including with the inevitable gaps, remediations, and uncertainties that engagement exposes and creates. Another way to describe this interrelationship is to say that a critical apparatus explains the history of transmission that the editor's understanding is based upon and contributes to, while the curated text embodies the outcome of that history of transmission, including the current moment of interpretation, in the form of a stable, historicized, and publicly accessible object for analysis. While the curated text of a conventional scholarly edition embodies or models the editor's argument about a literary work, a scholarly edition of a literary system uses a curated dataset to model the editor's argument about the nature of and relationships between literary works in the past.

For this book I did not simply theorize a scholarly edition; I built one. Its curated dataset is a subset of the 16,500 titles I discovered in the nineteenth-century Australian newspapers digitized by *Trove*. This subset encompasses a little over 9,200 works of "extended" fiction. Most of these (98 percent) are extended due to serial publication over two or more (often many more) newspaper issues. A small fraction of these titles (2 percent) were completed in a single issue but amount to ten thousand or more words (sometimes considerably more, with stories identified in this project of over sixty thousand words in a single—usually a Christmas—newspaper issue).[8] The curated dataset is made available in two forms: as downloadable bibliographical and textual data from the University of Michigan Press website and through an interface for searching, browsing, partial editing, and selective or wholesale exporting through the Australian National University's Centre for Digital Humanities Research.[9]

This database also makes available the other (approximately seventy-three hundred) works of short fiction identified in nineteenth-century Australian newspapers (along with a further five thousand short and extended titles from the early twentieth-century). But I chose to focus on nineteenth-century extended fiction—to subject those titles to extensive historical and bibliographical research and representation—

because those works constitute a literary system in the form of production and reception they imply. While stories completed in a single newspaper issue suggest incidental publishing and reading—with such content often selected simply to fill column inches and likely read in a casual manner—extended fiction required deliberate sourcing and publishing by editors and implies more intensive or committed engagement from readers.

The critical apparatus for this curated dataset is composed of certain fields in the dataset that explain and justify decisions about derivation and attribution of these stories, as well as a historical introduction to the model's parameters and principles, presented in chapter 3. "From World to *Trove* to Data: Tracing a History of Transmission" describes the history of transmission by which these nineteenth-century Australian newspapers were published, and subsequently collected and remediated, ultimately as digitized documents in *Trove*, and by which I identified the fiction they contain and represented it as bibliographical and textual data. In seeking to describe the translations and transformations, as well as the gaps and uncertainties, involved in this sequence, I foreground the fact that all collections—analog and digital, those we find and those we construct—have histories. These histories fundamentally determine access to the documentary record, in conjunction with the assumptions and arguments we bring to that inquiry.

As well as a basis for the arguments presented in *A World of Fiction*, this scholarly edition of a literary system is, fundamentally, for others to use. It makes the outcomes of a rigorous engagement with a mass-digitized collection available for the benefit of all literary historians, whether they are computationally inclined or not. Accordingly, while the argument it embodies about the existence of, and the interrelationships between, literary works in the past is an outcome of analysis, it is also a basis for future exploration. As I elaborate with examples in the conclusion, like a scholarly edition of a literary work, a scholarly edition of a literary system is designed to enable and advance—rather than to decide or conclude—investigation.

In using this scholarly edition to investigate extended fiction in nineteenth-century Australian newspapers, each of the three chapters in the book's second part adapts and applies a core digital humanities method: bibliometrics in chapter 4, network analysis in chapter 5, and topic modeling in chapter 6. Each chapter begins with a critical analysis of the respective method: although it is a premise of the book that data-rich literary history should not focus on the methods of analysis used to the detriment of the object analyzed, in a field that attempts to understand literature and culture by applying techniques devised for other purposes a critical approach to methodology is essential. My focus, however, is not on trialing the newest or most innovative digital methods per se but on crafting computational approaches best suited to exploring this publishing and reading context, and to responding to the requirements of humanities inquiry. To these ends I present a form of bibliometrics that accommodates the prevalence of anonymous and pseudonymous works in the curated dataset and enables insights into reception as well as publication; I offer an application of network analysis that manages extensive gaps in the newspapers digitized and titles captured; and I devise an approach to topic modeling that creates an intelligible relationship between thematic and documentary features of individual literary works, and of the literary system in which they generated meaning.

In presenting the results of this analysis, these three chapters intervene in a prominent critical trajectory in literary studies, for Australia and internationally: the so-called transnational turn. As has been the case for many national literary fields, in recent decades Australian literary scholars have recognized that Australian literary history is not coterminous with the history of literature by Australians. Yet in Australia, this turn has arguably gone further than elsewhere, particularly for the nineteenth century, where colonial literature has been recast as marginal to the history of literature in Australia. Using various empirical sources—publishers' archives, lending library records, and reading group minutes—scholars have described an Australian literary tradition as "chronically belated" (Dolin, "Secret" 128) and have discussed colonial readers in terms of their "derivative . . . reading habits," disregard for local fiction, and marked preference for writing from elsewhere, especially Britain (Askew and Hubber 115; Lyons; Webby, "Colonial"; Webby, "Not").

While such research offers an important counterweight to the field's earlier literary nationalism, the view that Australian readers were entirely focused on overseas, particularly British, literature moves too far in the opposite direction. In investigating the main form of local publishing and source of fiction in nineteenth-century Australia—

newspapers—this book explores the profound importance of British fiction to literary production and reception in the colonies. But it denies that the relationship to British culture was one of subservience and imitation. To the contrary, I demonstrate at scale what emerging analyses of individual works and reading practices increasingly recognize: how literary forms and practices were translated and transformed by their colonial enactment.[10] More contentiously, I emphasize the distinctiveness of literary culture in the colonies, including in the forms of writing and authorship that readers valued, in how fiction was sourced, and in the themes explored in Australian stories.

Chapter 4, "Into the Unknown: Literary Anonymity and the Inscription of Reception," examines conceptions of literary and cultural value operating in colonial Australia by investigating the origins, known and inscribed, of newspaper fiction. It takes as its starting point an acknowledged characteristic of transnational literary culture in this period—anonymous, pseudonymous, and indeterminate authorship—that is nevertheless occluded by the way we study literature in the past: by extracting (predominantly canonical) works from the anonymous conditions under which they were originally published and read. Not only is this strategy impossible when dealing with thousands of works where authorship is unknown, but it treats anonymity and pseudonymity as an absence, rather than a constitutive presence, in literary culture. This approach also ignores the extensive information about authorship contained in the titles, subtitles, and other paratextual and textual components of publication events, whether or not these details align with those of the historical individuals who wrote the works. To avoid these pitfalls, I consider bibliographical designations of authorship as well as how authorship was represented—or inscribed—in newspapers.

Exploring these two models of authorship shows that cultural value in the colonies was strongly associated with men's writing, that Australian fiction was both more present and accorded more importance than has been recognized, and that newspapers privileged British, while marginalizing American, writing. With respect to colonial fiction, I demonstrate a significant shift in its promotion and publication in the late 1870s and 1880s: from metropolitan to provincial newspapers. Based on the existing understanding of provincial newspaper fiction as rare, and pirated when present, this finding would seem to have little import. In showing that these provincial newspapers published substantially more fiction than their metropolitan counterparts, this chapter reassesses the development of early Australian literature and literary culture, as well as the gendered ethos organizing this process.

Chapter 5, "Fictional Systems: Network Analysis and Syndication Networks," investigates fiction reprinting to explore the ways in which colonial literary culture both intersected with and was distinct from the global circulation of fiction in the nineteenth century. For the metropolitan context, the results challenge the existing emphasis in studies of colonial literary culture on the first and best-known British syndication agency, Tillotson's Fiction Bureau, along with the view that fiction provided by this company—and syndicated British writing generally— overwhelmed local publishing and writing. I show that Tillotson's was only one entity among many operating in Australia, that it became systematically involved with colonial newspapers a decade earlier, and by a different motivation, than has been argued, and that the involvement of colonial newspapers in publishing local writing, and in sourcing and distributing fiction, continued despite the presence of multiple international companies in the market.

Turning to provincial newspapers, I demonstrate that fiction reprinting, as well as publishing, was more common in that context than in the metropolitan one. Such reprinting was performed, in part, by editor- and author-led enterprises, of varying degrees of formality. But provincial newspapers sourced most of their fiction from an extensive array of hitherto unrecognized syndicates, operating both locally and internationally. While past histories of Australian publishing are primarily book-based, this investigation shows that a local newspaper syndication agency, Cameron, Laing, and Co., published the most Australian fiction for the nineteenth century and probably well into the twentieth. It also reveals that provincial syndicates provided more fiction to the colonies than any of the book publishers, local or global, or the metropolitan newspapers that have been the focus of previous literary and book histories.

Chapter 6, "'Man people woman life' / 'Creek sheep cattle horses': Influence, Distinction, and Literary Traditions," turns from the source and reception of fiction in nineteenth-century Australian newspapers to its content, and to the question of whether colonial writing demonstrated any distinct features. Given the transnational market in which colonial literature developed, it has been argued that a distinctive Aus-

tralian literary tradition was impossible. I show, to the contrary, thematic tendencies in colonial fiction that are clearly different from those
in American and British writing. Focusing on rural colonial spaces,
characters, and activities, such writing resonates in certain ways, including in its masculine orientation, with the primary framework through
which nineteenth-century Australian fiction was perceived prior to the
transnational turn: the bush tradition. Yet this fiction also departs from
past perceptions of that tradition, including in its presence before the
supposedly foundational decade of the 1890s, and most strikingly in
its consistent and prominent depiction of Aboriginal characters. Such
depictions refute the prevailing view that Aboriginal people were
excluded from colonial fiction and offer new perspectives on literary
engagements with colonization.

The British and American fiction in nineteenth-century Australian
newspapers tends to be characterized not by representations of identifi-
ably British or American people and places but by contrasting attitudes
toward history and time. While British fiction frequently emphasizes
the interconnectedness of past, present, and future and is ambivalent
about the capacity of individual actions to effect historical change,
much American fiction shows the opposite: a focus on the present and
optimism about the future and the individual's role in shaping it. Both
of these attitudes toward time are manifested in nineteenth-century
Australian fiction, with writing by women and in metropolitan newspapers more likely to share the prevailing British perspective and fiction
by men and in provincial newspapers more likely to demonstrate features in common with American writing. These correlations between
fictional contents and material and authorial trends suggest a fundamental cultural divide in the orientation of colonial fiction to "new"
and "old" worlds.

A World of Fiction works across, while contributing to, two fields—digital
humanities and literary history—that are in many ways closely integrated, while in others, still academic worlds apart. It may well be that
scholars who primarily align themselves with digital humanities will
gravitate to the discussion of digital knowledge infrastructure, digitization, data, remediation, and modeling in part 1 and to the critiques of
digital methods that begin the other chapters. Alternatively, literary,
book, and media historians might find more of specific interest in part

2's exploration of literary production and reception and of the transnational circulation of nineteenth-century fiction in periodical form.

While such variation in the interests of readers is perhaps inevitable, the two parts of this book fundamentally require and inform each other. Although it is often understood as such, literary history is not solely an analytical and critical enterprise; it has always been bound up in—enabled and produced by—the knowledge infrastructure that it creates and employs. Equally, although digital humanities is frequently presented as a methodological and infrastructural endeavor, it is just as much a historical and analytical one. The approaches and infrastructure developed and employed in that field have histories, just as the conceptual entities examined—including literary data and computational models—are critical and interpretive constructs. Confronting the challenges and possibilities that new digital technologies and resources bring to literary history and to the humanities broadly requires a mutually informative relationship of traditional and digital scholarship. Only such a relationship can enable the emergence and consolidation of the new forms of evidence, analysis, and argumentation required by the contemporary conditions of cultural research.

PART I

The Digital World

CHAPTER 1

Abstraction, Singularity, Textuality

The Equivalence of "Close" and "Distant" Reading

———— ❧ ————

In a blog post entitled "A Dataset for Distant Reading Literature in English, 1700–1922," Ted Underwood describes as "malarkey" the "version of distant reading currently circulating in the public imagination"—namely, that it analyzes "a massive database that includes 'everything that has been thought and said.'" He continues,

> In the early days of distant reading, Franco Moretti did frame the project as a challenge to literary historians' claims about synchronic coverage. (We only discuss a tiny number of books from any given period—what about all the rest?) But even in those early publications, Moretti acknowledged that we would only be able to represent "all the rest" through some kind of sample.

Underwood is correct in a narrow sense: Moretti engages in, and occasionally acknowledges his use of, data sampling. But it does not follow that the public imagination, or the mainstream media outlets feeding it, confected the view of distant reading as enabling direct and objective access to a comprehensive literary-historical record. Moretti's work provides more than ample grounds for this public perception, as does Jockers's closely related paradigm of macroanalysis. While claiming direct and objective access to "everything," these high-profile authors represent and explore only a very limited portion of the literary system, and do so in an abstract and often ahistorical way.

Moretti has been criticized in similar terms previously: for adopting a reductive approach to literature and associating data with comprehensive and authoritative knowledge. Those who reject any role for data in literary history maintain both of these criticisms, on the basis that data are inimical to literature, and only close reading can explore its nuance and complexity. Katie Trumpener, for instance, argues that data-based methods "violate" the "individuality" of literary works (160), while Stephen Marche insists "literature is not data. Literature is the opposite of data" (160). James English attributes such responses to the discipline's foundationally "negative relationship" to "counting," noting its intensification in the face of "ever more stringent quantification regimes of value and assessment," as well as Moretti's role in exacerbating that oppositional perspective (xii, xiii).

Those who advocate the use of data in literary studies typically deny that Moretti's approach is needlessly reductive. Echoing Moretti's account in *Distant Reading* of the method as "a little pact with the devil" (48), they acknowledge that abstracting and simplifying complex phenomena is an inevitable consequence of quantitative approaches, but one that is justified by the new forms of knowledge it enables (Love 374). Regarding Moretti's tendency to "overestimat[e] the scientific objectivity of his analyses" (Ross np) opinion is more divided. Some who support a data-rich approach to literary history perceive Moretti's claim to authoritative knowledge as an unfortunate side effect of his polemical intent to challenge literary history's reliance on close reading. As Tim Burke writes, "There is no requirement to purchase the entire methodological inventory he makes available, or to throw overboard close reading or aesthetic appreciation" (41). Others ascribe a more foundational essentialism to Moretti's work. John Frow argues that Moretti conceives of "literary history . . . as an objective account of patterns and trends" by "ignor[ing] the crucial point that these morphological categories he takes as his base units are not pre-given but are constituted in an interpretive encounter by means of an interpretive decision" ("Thinking" 142).

In my view, these critiques describe the symptoms—not the essence—of a problem, which also characterizes Jockers's macroanalysis, as well as the New Criticism's core method of close reading. Contrary to prevailing opinion, distant reading and close reading are not opposites. These approaches are united by common neglect of textual scholarship: the bibliographical and editorial approaches that literary scholars have long depended on to negotiate the documentary record. Because of this neglect, like the New Critics before them, Moretti and Jockers cannot benefit from the critical and historical insights presented by editorial and bibliographical productions. As a consequence, both authors conceive and model literary systems in reductive ways and offer ahistorical arguments about the existence and interconnections of literary works in the past.

I

Underappreciated in commentary on distant reading and macroanalysis is the shifting meanings of both terms. When Moretti originally proposed distant reading in "Conjectures on World Literature" in 2000, it was a "new critical method" for world literary studies, not for literary history (55). Distant reading aimed to overcome the focus on national canons by collating the work of multiple scholars to identify and explore "units that are much smaller or much larger than the text: devices, themes, tropes—or genres and systems" (57). With his 2005 book, *Graphs, Maps, Trees: Abstract Models for a Literary History*, the framework of world literary studies was superseded by literary history (indeed, a national formation of that endeavor, focused on eighteenth- and nineteenth-century British literature). While units smaller or larger than the text were theoretical notions in his "Conjectures" essay, in this book they are translated into data points. A systemic approach to literary history also became central, with the abstract modeling devices of the title—graphs, maps, trees—employed to explore, and to visualize, the operations of a literary history that "cannot be understood by stitching together separate bits of knowledge about individual cases, because it *isn't* a sum of individual cases: it's a collective system, that should be grasped as such, as a whole" (*Graphs* 4).

Computational methods and digital resources were in turn central to Moretti's 2013 book, *Distant Reading*, but there literary history was ceding ground to "the theory of literature" as the focus in "the encounter of computation and criticism" (Moretti, "Operationalizing" 9). Although literary data remains central, the primary object of distant reading is now less often literary systems—designated social, material, and political contexts for literary development and change—than the "concepts of literary study" (1). And while Moretti previously identified the importance of literary systems in their inclusion of the "great unread" ("Conjectures" 55), these concepts of literary study (including characterization, plot, and dramatic form) are approached predominantly through formal and computational analyses of canonical literary works.[1] Jockers's focus has remained more consistent over time. But his recent work demonstrates this same shift from literary history—his explicit concern in his 2013 book, *Macroanalysis: Digital Methods and Literary History*—to categories of literary analysis: in his case, plot and characterization.[2] Yet even as Moretti and Jockers have moved from a historical to a conceptual emphasis in their own work, distant reading and macroanalysis dominate—and limit—public, and much academic, perception of what data-rich literary history entails.

Pace Underwood's defense, in their literary-historical work both Moretti and Jockers present literary data and digital collections as pre-critical, stable, and self-evident. In conceiving data and computation as providing direct and comprehensive access to the literary-historical record, they deny the critical and interpretive activities that construct that data and digital record and make them available for analysis. In Moretti's work on literary history, literary data are consistently presented as facts rather than interpretations. Thus the first chapter of *Graphs* repeatedly references "the large mass of [literary] facts" as "ideally independent of interpretations" (3), as "*data*, not interpretation" (9), and as "useful because they are independent of interpretation" (30). On this basis, Moretti accords his arguments an unrealistic exactitude. For instance, his claim that bibliographical data "can tell us when Britain produced one new novel per month or week or day, or hour for that matter" (9) denies the inevitable gaps between the publishing context and the bibliographies he proposes to explore them with.[3] Similarly, Moretti presents data visualization as a transparent window onto history, with the idea that "graphs, maps, and trees place the literary field literally in front of our eyes—and show us how little we still know about it" (2). The same understanding of literary data appears in *Distant Reading*, where Moretti celebrates data visualization as providing "a set of two dimensional signs . . . that can be grasped at a single glance" (211). Such descriptions, which substitute seeing what is there for the interpretive acts involved in constructing literary data, organizing it, and ascribing a historical explanation to the results, underpin Moretti's contention to explore "the literary field as a whole" (67).

While this view of literary data as factual and transparent has been noted—and critiqued—such assessments miss its underlying cause: Moretti's lack of interest in the scholarly infrastructure that enables his analyses. For results derived from analog bibliographies—as in the first chapter of *Graphs* and his stylistic "Reflections on 7,000 Titles" in *Distant Reading*—parentheses and footnotes occasionally admit that comprehensive access to the facts of literary history is not achieved. For example, figure 7 in the latter study, showing the number of British novels, stops in 1836, while the other graphs extend to 1850. In a footnote, Moretti explains the discrepancy with the comment "it seems very likely that Andrew Block's bibliography significantly overstates the number of novels published after that date" (188). Yet acknowledging that his dataset arises from a ("significantly") flawed interpretive encounter affects neither Moretti's rhetoric nor his subsequent analysis. The chapter still claims to "read the entire volume of the literary past" (58), and while the data are absent from figure 7, Block's bibliography is the only source for titles published from 1836 to 1850. Moretti proceeds, in other words, by analyzing titles he knows never existed.

While literary data derived from analog bibliographies are only "ideally independent of interpretations," Moretti regards mass-digitized collections as achieving this independence.[4] With such collections becoming the rhetorical, if not the primary analytical, focus of *Distant Reading*, Moretti looks forward just "a few years," to when "we'll be able to search just about all novels that have ever been published and look for patterns among billions of sentences" (181). He notes that, while literary studies has previously experienced "the rise of quantitative evidence . . . without producing lasting effects, . . . this time is probably going to be different, because this time we have digital databases and automatic data retrieval" (212). While digital technologies are celebrated and foregrounded, beneath these claims lies the same disregard for the specifics of the disciplinary infrastructure that characterized Moretti's approach to bibliographies. This attitude is apparent in an interview in which Moretti aligns digital humanities with three elements:

new, much larger archives; new, much faster research tools; and a (possible) new explanatory framework. The archives and the tools are there to stay; they are important but not intellectually exciting. What appeals to me is the prospect of a new explanatory model—a new theory and history of literature. (Moretti, "Bourgeois" np)

In presenting digital "archives" or collections as "there to stay," Moretti disregards their status—like bibliographies—as interpretative constructs. And unlike print-based bibliographies, most digital collections are constantly changing: a dynamism with significant practical and conceptual challenges for literary history.

Asserting comprehensive access to the historical literary record is even more essential to Jockers's notion of macroanalysis. Although he sometimes presents his method as complementing rather than replacing idiographic approaches to literature (*Macroanalysis* 171), foundational to macroanalysis is Jockers's view of interpretation as methodologically defective: "Interpretation is fueled by observation, and as a method of evidence gathering, observation—both in the sciences and in the humanities—is flawed" (6). While interpretation and observation are "anecdotal and speculative," "big data" is supposedly constituted without human involvement and thus offers "comprehensive and definitive" historical facts (31). According to Jockers, literary scholars "have the equivalent of . . . big data in the form of big [digital] libraries . . . [or] massive digital-text collections," and these enable "investigations at a scale that reaches or approaches a point of being comprehensive. The once inaccessible 'population' has become accessible and is fast replacing the random and representative sample" (7–8). As Jockers says of one of Moretti's analyses, such unprecedented and supposedly uninterrupted access to the documentary basis of literary history "leaves little room for debate" (20): a perspective that overlooks the fact that all collections are selections, made according to (implicit or explicit) arguments about value, and with varying degrees of expertise and funding.

Jockers employs a number of scientific metaphors to buttress this association of scale and comprehensive access, the most explicit being "open-pit mining or hydraulicking." While "microanalysis" (including reading and digital searching) discovers "nuggets," macroanalysis accesses "the deeper veins [that] lie buried beneath the mass of gravel layered above" (9). In working with the "gravel" of literary history, employing "the trommel of computation to process, condense, deform, and analyze the deep strata from which these nuggets were born," Jockers supposedly "unearth[s], for the first time, *what these corpora really contain*" (10, my italics). This metaphor not only renders literary history as concrete an entity as a mountain: all of it can be accessed and analyzed. It also conflates analysis with the achievement of complete access. The network visualizations with which Jockers presents the cumulative results of macroanalysis reinforce this view of literary data as factual and comprehensive. As chapter 5 explores in depth, because the form and meaning of most network graphs change when new nodes and edges are added, to claim that they display the structures and relationships that organized literature in the past implies that all data are available for analysis.

While Moretti occasionally acknowledges limitations in his data (before proceeding with analyses regardless), Jockers maintains that any "leap from the specific to the general" is flawed because based on interpretation (28). Only in the book's final chapter does he admit the obvious gap between his datasets and the "population" of nineteenth-century novels, describing his largest "corpus of 3,346 texts" as "incomplete, interrupted, haphazard," and noting, "The comprehensive work is still to be done" (172). This concession generates an awkward comparison of macroanalysis with Charles Darwin's theory of evolution, which reinforces Jockers's equation of knowledge with scale and comprehensive access. While both are "idea[s]," because "there are further dimensions to explore" (171), literary scholars are advantaged over evolutionary biologists "in terms of the availability of our source material" (175). In a context where bigger is better—as Jockers says elsewhere in the book, "eight is better than one, [but] eight is not eight thousand, and, thus, the study is comparatively anecdotal in nature" (25)—his "3,346 observations and 2,032,248 data points" are seemingly indicative of knowledge in and of themselves (172). Jockers concludes by admitting one impediment to macroanalysis, but it is only legal: though almost "everything has been digitized," post-1923 publications remain (at the time he was writing) protected by copyright, leaving literary scholars dependent on legal reforms before they might realize "what can be done with a large corpus of texts" (175).

A recent collaboration of the Stanford Literary Lab, which Jockers is no longer part of, departs in one important way from the approach to literary history, data, mass digitization, and computation I have described (Algee-Hewitt et al.).[5] *Literary Lab Pamphlet 11* closely attends to the gaps between "the published" (all literary works made public in history), "the archive" (the portion of what was published that has been preserved and is now increasingly digitized), and "the corpus" (the segment of the archive selected for a research question). Although incorrectly imagining that the "convergence of these three layers into one . . . may soon be reality," in acknowledging that this state has not been achieved, the authors admit the constructed—and selective— nature of literary data. Yet *Pamphlet 11* follows Moretti's and Jockers's precedent in misconstruing the nature of our disciplinary infrastructure, in that the authors presume to overcome the selections and biases of mass-digitized collections by using analog bibliographies to generate "a random sample" of what was published (2). This strategy misses the vital point that both digitized collections and analog bibliographies are derived from "the archive," predominantly the collections of major (usually American or British) university libraries. *Pamphlet 11* also replicates Moretti's and Jockers's approach in not publishing its datasets.[6]

Moretti often references his sources of data—chapter 1 of *Graphs*, for instance, begins by listing the bibliographies it draws upon—and he advocates data sharing: "Because . . . data are ideally independent from any individual researcher, [they] can thus be shared by others, and combined in more ways than one" (5). Moretti, however, does not share his data. Jockers occasionally publishes the results of data analysis, such as the five hundred themes developed from topic modeling, presented as word clouds on his website (Jockers, "500"). But he does not provide the textual data analyzed, even at the level of word frequencies,[7] and is significantly less open than Moretti about the composition of his datasets. Although in more recent work Jockers adjusts this approach somewhat,[8] for research pertaining to *Macroanalysis* I have discovered only one instance in which he indicates the titles and authors investigated, and then, only for 106 of the total 3,346 works. These are identified almost incidentally, in reporting confusion matrices (Jockers, "Confusion").

In Moretti's case, one might suppose it possible to reconstruct his datasets from cited sources. But his account (in an appendix to *Graphs*) of creating the dataset for "British novelistic genres, 1740–1900," highlights why this is not feasible. There he describes his periodization as "not always explicit" in the bibliographies (31), thus evincing the role of his own—unpublished and therefore unspecified—interpretive decisions in data construction. And even if Jockers listed all the titles and authors he analyzed, it would be impossible to reconstruct the basis of his arguments without access to the textual data he uses, which are not just texts of literary works but highly prepared—or preinterpreted— selections from those texts. Neither critics nor supporters of Moretti's and Jockers's methods typically comment on this lack of published data. But far from an incidental oversight, this practice maintains the fiction that literary data are prior to interpretation: it removes the need either to describe the procedures for collecting, cleaning, and curating datasets or to expose the inevitably selective and limited collections resulting from that construction.

The meaning derived from a literary-historical dataset—like the interpretation of a literary work—is shaped, profoundly, by the methodological and critical frameworks through which it is approached, and by the selections and amplifications those frameworks produce. Two scholars can read the same dataset—like the same literary work— and derive different meanings. While an independent observer may be more or less convinced by the different arguments, deciding between them depends upon access to the object on which they are based. In the absence of data publication, distant reading and macroanalysis are analogous to a scholar finding a set of documents in an archive or archives, transcribing them, analyzing those transcriptions, publishing the findings, and asserting that they demonstrate a definitive new perspective on the literary field, without enabling anyone to read the transcriptions (or in Jockers's case, without revealing the titles of most of the original documents).

II

As noted in the introduction, Moretti and Jockers have been highly influential in foregrounding data-rich models of literary systems as primary units of historical analysis. Yet in not recognizing the critical and constructed nature of the bibliographies and mass-digitized collections they use to create these models, neither author can benefit from the historical insights that underpin and are translated through this scholarly infrastructure. The resulting models can be used to address certain questions. But they are ultimately reductive: these models do not represent the historical existence of literary works, including the ways in which they connect to produce literary systems.

In modeling literary systems, Moretti and Jockers define literary works as single entities in time and space, typically located as such by the date of first book publication and the author's nationality. Literary works are constituted as literary systems when they share these basic features—as in "nineteenth-century" or "British" novels—with other characteristics added within that framework (such as the author's gender or the work's genre). This basic understanding of literary systems is evident, for instance, in Moretti's analysis of "7,000 titles (British novels, 1740 to 1830)" in *Distant Reading* (179–210), discussed above, or of eighteenth- and nineteenth-century British novels defined in terms of the number of titles published, authors' genders, or fictional subgenres (*Graphs* 5–9, 26–27, 28–30). It likewise underpins Jockers's exploration in *Macroanalysis* of "758 works of Irish-American prose literature spanning 250 years" (37) or 3,346 nineteenth-century British and American novels.

Depending on the reliability of the source and the type of questions asked, datasets constructed on this basis can support insights into trends in new literary production. Jockers's study of Irish-American prose pursues an approach manifested in other digital projects—some of my own work included (Bode, *Reading*)—of using publication data to test existing perspectives on literary history. Employing a dataset with the date of first publication, as well as "the geographic settings of the works, author gender, birthplace, age, and place of residence" (36), Jockers challenges the notion of a "lost generation" of Irish-American authors from 1900 to 1930 and proposes a likely explanation for this misperception: a predominance of eastern male authors in the canon—and hence in critical assessments—of Irish-American literature (38–48). Moretti's work on new literary production extends beyond testing and revising particular arguments in literary history and is highly innovative in this respect. His study of titles, for instance, investigates a category of literary data that had not, as far as I know, been subjected to synoptic, stylistic analysis previously. More broadly, Moretti combines multiple bibliographies to challenge claims about the distinctiveness of new literary production in different historical periods, as in his discussion in *Graphs* of gender trends in British novel publication (17–20).

But literary works are not defined by a single time and place, and collecting them together in those abstract terms does not represent the interconnections that constitute literary systems. William St Clair's *The Reading Nation in the Romantic Period* aptly diagnoses the limitations of this approach. Like Moretti and Jockers, St Clair rejects what he calls the "parade of authors" convention in literary history, where canonical authors file past the commentator's box in chronological order, taken as representative of the historical period in which they wrote. But he equally dismisses the "parliament of texts" approach, where literary works first published at a particular time, and usually by authors of a particular nationality, are understood as "debating and negotiating with one another in a kind of open parliament with all the members participating and listening" (4). As St Clair notes, literary systems frequently include "texts written or compiled long ago and far away" (3), and some literary works are inevitably more widely published, circulated, read, and referenced than others.

New domestic literary production, the basis of Moretti's and Jockers's datasets, is only a subsection of the literature available at any time and place. By considering only that component—without accounting for its relative importance or acknowledging that literary systems encompass other types of works—Moretti and Jockers occlude major aspects of how literature existed in the past. The date of first book publication overlooks the differing availability of literary works in the years after they are published and that first book editions are not necessarily—and for many periods are rarely—the first time works are available. Some titles are never published as books, and many literary works—whether in book or other formats—are republished, sometimes on multiple occasions. Likewise, an author's nationality is a poor marker for the geographical existence of a literary work in a marketplace that has been globalized since at least the eighteenth century. More broadly, the construction of literary systems from the categories supplied by enumerative bibliographies—*the* title, *the* author, *the* date of publication, *the* publisher, and by association, *the* text—ignores the different titles, author names, dates and places of publication, and texts that occur as literary works are issued and reissued, and the implications of these differences for understanding production and reception.

Even for studies that focus on new book publications, this approach to modeling literary systems ignores most differences between literary works, and hence, most dynamics of those systems. Reflecting on Moretti's work, David A. Brewer notes that flattening the literary field "nicely undoes the monumentalizing that so often accompanies the literary canon," but at the expense of ignoring the varied profiles and presences of works in history (162). Brewer focuses on commercial success, arguing that the popularity of different literary works at the time they are published and in subsequent generations accords them "a massively different footprint" in history, altering their influence, and hence their meaning, for readers (163). But commercial success is not the only relevant factor. As textual scholars show by exploring the material and social dimensions of literary works, multiple issues shape their meaning, extending from the documentary forms they take to the relative positions and prestige of the individuals and institutions involved in producing them (authors, publishers, editors, illustrators, booksellers, advertisers) and the interconnected systems (economic, religious, educational, legal, geopolitical) in which they circulate.[9]

While textual scholars such as Johanna Drucker ("Entity"), Paul Eggert (*Securing*), and Jerome McGann (*New*) thereby conceptualize literary works as events—unfolding over time and space and gaining different meanings in the relationships thereby formed—Moretti and Jockers construct literary systems as composed of singular and stable entities and imagine that this captures the complexity of such systems. In fact, because their datasets miss most historical connections between literary works, their analyses rely on basic features of new literary production to constitute both the literary phenomenon requiring explanation and the explanation for it. *Macroanalysis* purports to investigate "the context in which [literary] change occurs," chiefly by analyzing words in nineteenth-century novels (156). What Jockers actually shows is the capacity of his computational method (a combination of stylistic analysis, topic modeling, and network analysis) to predict whether a work (or "bag of words" from that work) was by a man or woman, and its date of publication, genre, and national origin, from a corpus defined according to those parameters. Notwithstanding the variable accuracy of this approach for different categories,[10] the methodological demonstration is impressive for extending stylistic analysis beyond small groups of documents.

But the methodological achievement does not translate into historical insight because the study considers only an abstract amalgam of literary works. In reducing context to a few predetermined categories, Jockers is confined to stating their presence. He cannot offer any alternative influences, nor can he comment on the extent to which gender, nationality, and chronology shape literary history, except perhaps implicitly, in the proportions of titles misidentified by his models. The approach yields very general, and I would argue, self-evident statements. To give examples drawn from the conclusions to Jockers's various chapters: "the linguistic choices an author makes are, in some notable ways, dependent upon, or entailed by, their genre choices" (104); "there are both national tendencies and extranational trends in the usage of . . . word clusters" (114); "a writer's creativity is tempered and influenced by the past and the present, by literary 'parents,' and by a larger literary ecosystem" (156); and "thematic and stylistic change does occur over time" (164). The generality of these conclusions is predetermined by the dematerialized and depopulated conception of influence underpinning the analysis. The model constitutes literary works as a system based on the date of (presumably first book) publication, and any book within the dataset is understood to exert influence in a chronologically discrete manner, regardless of the actual conduits of literary influence, which require availability to readers who buy, borrow, and sometimes write literary works. Because he is modeling a diffused and generalized system, the "influence" of gender, genre, temporality, and nationality is in turn diffuse and generalized.

The inadequacy of this conception of literary systems is foregrounded when Moretti considers readers, who, as Anne DeWitt notes, "are both central to his argument and absent from his evidence" (162). Moretti takes literary data on publication and/or formal features of literary works as both expressive of and explicable by the actions of readers and the market. We can see this strategy in Moretti's discussion of the first graph in *Graphs*: the "rise of the novel" across a number of national contexts (Britain, Japan, Italy, Spain, and Nigeria) at different times. Leaving aside the question of whether his graph depicts the numbers he attributes to it,[11] Moretti ascribes the leap "from five–ten new titles per year . . . to one new novel *per week*" to "the horizon of novel-reading," the shift in the market that occurs when the novel is transformed from "an unreliable commodity" to "that great modern oxymoron of the *regular novelty*: the unexpected that is produced with such efficiency and punctuality that readers become unable to do without it" (5). The argument makes intuitive sense, but it presumes that only—and all—new titles by authors of particular nations were available to, and read by, only—and all—readers of those nations. The explanation, in other words, claims that publication data are both indicative of national reading habits and explicable in terms of that activity.

A similarly circuitous mode of argumentation characterizes "The Slaughterhouse of Literature" chapter in *Distant Reading*. Moretti proposes a framework for canon formation, wherein readers are the "butchers" of literary history

> who read novel A (but not B, C, D, E, F, G, H . . .) and so keep A "alive" into the next generation, when other readers may keep it alive into the following one, and so on until eventually A becomes canonized. Readers, not professors, make canons. (67)

Nominating formal choices as the reason readers select certain titles over others, Moretti employs the example of detective fiction and decodable clues to demonstrate this process. He identifies the presence of such clues in Arthur Conan Doyle's fiction as the reason that author was progressively selected by generations of readers to attain his now canonical status. Again, this is an interesting but circular argument. Moretti acknowledges one of the ways in which his claims are "tautological": "if we search the archive for one device only, and no matter how significant it may be, all we will find are inferior versions of the device, *because that's really all we are looking for*" (87).

Yet the same problem—of assuming the shape of the past from that of the present—occurs at a larger scale in that Moretti assumes that authors who have a canonical status in the present were selected from the time of first publication. This argument is intrinsic to his evolutionary model, and while Moretti supports it by citing an empirical study (68), others show its falsity. St Clair, for instance, demonstrates the minute early nineteenth-century readerships of five of the "big six" Romantic male poets (excepting Byron) who form the contemporary canon (660): however that Romantic canon was formed, it was not based on the poetry contemporaneous readers preferred. While in the earlier study Moretti aligns publication with reading (a title was published; ergo it was read), in this instance his argument requires titles to be published but not read. What determines if titles were read is whether they had decodable clues; thus, once again, a feature of the data (the presence or absence of decodable clues) is used both to indicate and explain the activities of readers.

Moretti has said, in defense of his method, that reducing literary works to one or two features is part of the "specific form of knowledge" that distant reading provides: "fewer elements, hence a sharper sense of their overall interconnection. Shapes, relations, structures. Forms. Models" (*Graphs* 1). My argument is not against reduction and abstraction per se. While especially obvious in data-rich studies (which rely on identifying attributes that can be represented in uniform fields), reduction and abstraction characterize all analysis. Close readings do not interpret literary works as a whole but specific, extracted instances of particular, abstracted features of those works. What I am arguing is lost in Moretti's and Jockers's approach—especially in their definition of literary systems as analogous to first book publication by authors of a designated nationality—is precisely a historical sense of "interconnection." Failing to acknowledge that the disciplinary infrastructure they use is made not given, and thus overlooking the historical information embedded in it, Moretti and Jockers model literary systems in terms of potentially, and certainly relatively, abstract categories of production. In the process they ignore the socially, spatially, and temporally specific and complex ways in which literary works exist and relate to one another in particular, historical contexts.

III

Although distant reading initially faced considerable resistance from literary scholars, now a common response to that paradigm is the call to integrate nondata- and data-based approaches. While Moretti originally suggested that distant reading should replace close reading,[12] this integrated position is the one he subsequently adopted. Describing the contrast between close attention to the canon and distant exploration of the archive in terms of "too much polyphony" on the one hand and "too much monotony" on the other, Moretti asserts, "It's the Scylla and Charybdis of digital humanities. The day we establish an intelligible relationship between the two, a new literary landscape will come into being" (*Distant* 181). Other examples of this stance abound, including from Jockers (*Macroanalysis* 26) and scholars such as Frederick Gibbs and Daniel Cohen, who argue for the profitability of "mov[ing] seamlessly between traditional and computational approaches" or between "our beloved, traditional close reading and untested, computer-enhanced distant reading" (70).

This apparent moderation in the terms of debate belies the continuing perception of close and distant reading (or micro- and macroanalysis, or nondata- and data-based approaches) as opposites. Whether close reading is presented as less "rational" than distant reading (Moretti, *Graphs* 4), or more authentic and authoritative (Trumpener), or if together, the two perspectives are understood to supplement the others' limitations, close and distant reading are conceived as antithetical in their assumptions and approaches. However, the main problems I have sought to diagnose in distant reading and macroanalysis—a disregard for textual scholarship and an assumption that literary works are stable and singular entities—are ones they share with the New Criticism and its foundational method of close reading. Distant reading and macroanalysis take the core object and premise of the New Criticism—the decontextualized text as the source of all meaning—to a conclusion rendered more abstract and extreme by the number of texts under consideration.

As is well known, the New Criticism was an early- to mid-twentieth-century movement that subordinated the historical and contextual (biographical, material, sociological) concerns of literary scholarship to "the text" itself. The critique of this movement is also well established, with the contextual focus in many subsequent forms of literary history—feminism, postcolonialism, New Historicism—explicitly rejecting the New Critical view of the text as a self-contained and self-referential aesthetic object. Despite the apparent demise of the New Criticism, the continuing centrality of close reading in literary studies, including literary history, and the rhetorical focus of such research on the text, perpetuates the earlier movement's dismissal of textual scholarship (Cain). As Eggert ("Book"), McGann ("Note"), and others have observed, assuming that literary works are texts, and that texts are single, stable, and self-evident entities, dismisses the documentary record's multiplicity, and with it the critical contributions of those endeavors—bibliography and scholarly editing—dedicated to investigating and understanding that multiplicity.

Even as contemporary enactments of close reading often foreground context, the centrality and assumed singularity of the text, and the disassociation from the literary work's complex historical existence this produces, can negatively impact the capacity of such analyses to investigate literary history. Mary Elizabeth Leighton and Lisa Surridge highlight this effect in critical discussion of Wilkie Collins's *Moonstone*. Describing the varied interpretations that contemporary critics offer of its meaning for nineteenth-century readers—from tale of "imperialist panic" to critique of colonial domination—they note that all critics assume, first, that they are "reading the same text" as readers in the past and, second, that all past readers encountered the same text as each other. In fact, as Leighton and Surridge show, *Moonstone* "took on strikingly different forms—and hence different meanings—in different markets," specifically in British and American serializations (207). In projecting textual singularity onto a historical period characterized by documentary multiplicity, the close readings these critics produce obscure the historical production and reception of this literary work even as they propose to emphasize that context.

Notwithstanding such instances, close readings are generally protected from the abstraction inherent in the notion of the text by the knowledge infrastructure in which they are embedded, and by a focus on particular documents. Scholarly editions provide critics with carefully historicized texts for consideration; when one is not available, the standard practice of bibliographical referencing ties discussion of the supposedly singular text to a version of the work. Moreover, because a close reading inevitably analyzes a version, any discussion of the text is contextualized by the information about the work's history contained in the material form that the critic assesses. Distant reading and macroanalysis do not benefit from such provisions or protections; to the contrary, as this chapter has argued, these approaches negate the interpretive nature of the disciplinary infrastructure they use, as well as their own role in constructing the meaning of the data they derive from it.

While explicitly opposing close reading, the form of Moretti's and Jockers's arguments mirrors the New Criticism's perception of the text as the source of all meaning, even as the text under consideration has expanded from a single version of a literary work to a version of bibliographical and textual data derived from multiple versions of literary works. Moretti's investigations of readers based only on data relating to first book publications enacts this view of the text as inevitably containing all that is relevant to interpreting it. In treating the literary system as a dispersed linguistic field, Jockers takes the rhetoric of text to its ultimate conclusion, proposing a literary-historical world in which there are no structures beyond the textual. "Signals" of gender, genre, or nationality, comprised entirely of word frequencies, are substituted for gender, genre, or nationality as historical and cultural constructs. Far from the opposite of close reading, the dematerialized and depopulated understanding of literature in Jockers's work enacts the New Criticism's neglect of context.

Whether literary histories are conducted in traditional or data-rich forms, the outcomes of analysis are inevitably tied to the object analyzed. When a gap exists between the contemporary object assessed and the historical object it supposedly represents—and when the critic is unaware or dismissive of that gap—no degree of nuance or care in the reading can supply that historical meaning. Herein lies the fundamental problem with proposing to integrate close and distant reading as the obvious way forward for research in literary history. Understood in terms of the different perspectives the two approaches offer, this strategy seems eminently sensible: data-rich analysis has the potential to explore large-scale patterns and connections in ways that nondata-rich research cannot; likewise, conventional textual analysis can provide insights into the meaning of literary works that quantitative studies cannot.

Yet in couching debate about the role of data purely in terms of method, this response maintains the focus on the mode of analysis employed and conceals the lack of an adequately historicized object to analyze. What data-rich literary history needs is an object capable of representing literary systems—as manifestations of literary works that existed and generated meaning in relation to each other in the past—while managing the documentary record's complexity, especially as it is manifested in new digital knowledge infrastructure. The lack of such an object, not the fundamental opposition of data and literature, is the real reason it has proven so difficult, in practice if not in theory, to integrate "traditional and computational methods" for the purposes of historical investigation (Gibbs and Cohen 70).

An appropriately historicized representation of relationships between literary works in the past would avoid the problems I have identified in Moretti's and Jockers's approach, which claims to represent everything—directly, comprehensively, and objectively—while exploring only a limited part of any given literary system. The difficulties with their approach are not the result of using data to investigate past literature. They occur because distant reading and macroanalysis adopt and perpetuate the disregard for textual scholarship foundational to the New Criticism, without benefiting from the institutional and infrastructural protections afforded to close reading. Given this source of the problem, the next chapter proposes a solution from textual scholarship. I argue that the field's foundational technology of the scholarly edition supplies both the supports and constraints necessary for data-rich literary history, while providing a framework capable of extending the insights gained from engagements with emerging digital infrastructure to the broader discipline.

CHAPTER 2

Back to the Future

A New Scholarly Object
for (Data-Rich) Literary History

———— ❦ ————

In making the case for and describing a new object of analysis for data-rich literary history, based on the scholarly edition, this chapter builds on McGann's call for "philology in a new key," most recently in *A New Republic of Letters*, and on Eggert's work on the scholarly edition as a model for conservation broadly, in *Securing the Past*. Like McGann, I propose that literary scholars respond to the challenges of digitization by employing the theoretical and practical framework through which they have long negotiated the complexity of the documentary record. I also take seriously McGann's insistence on the need to develop digital environments that demonstrate the histories of production and reception, including the current moment of interpretation, for the documentary records they model. Like Eggert, I apply this framework beyond the individual literary works that McGann maintains are the essential basis of an "object-oriented and media approach to the study of literature and culture" (*New* 3). In using the scholarly edition as a basis for modeling literary systems and for investigating the mass-digitized collections that make such historical formations amenable to analysis, I also seek to chart a path beyond the polemics of both "distant reading" and "macroanalysis" on the one hand and McGann's "new philology" on the other, and thus beyond the view of digital literary history as defined by either the multiplication of data points (in Moretti's and Jockers's work) or the elaboration of unique and ultimately unknowable philological objects (in McGann's).

Multiple projects already model historical literary systems with attention to relationships of production and reception and to the meanings these connections signify. Explicit engagement with modeling, as the method is theorized in digital humanities, is essential for data-rich literary history, but modeling alone is insufficient. Modeling recognizes data as constructed, but only by the individual scholar; it does not provide a mechanism to interrogate the history of transmission preceding and perpetuated by the scholar's engagement with the documentary record, including in its mass-digitized forms. The framework of the scholarly edition meets that challenge, presenting a structure to negotiate the incomplete and transactional nature of the documentary record and to represent the outcomes of that process. Adapted to the literary system, it offers a reliable foundation for data-rich literary history and for extending the insights gained from that field's engagement with emerging digital infrastructure to the broader discipline.

I

Although Moretti's and Jockers's work is often taken as definitive of data-rich literary history (even of digital literary studies), many projects model literary systems in significantly more nuanced ways. Far from assuming that literary works published around the same time and by authors of the same nation automatically constitute a system, these projects investigate interconnections—temporal, spatial, and social—between literary works in the past. To put this practice in the terms of textual scholarship, they depart from the ideal or regulatory category of the literary work to investigate the ways and forms in which literature has circulated and generated meaning.[1] Where Moretti and Jockers assume a relationship between what was published and what was read, these projects consider forms and relationships of production and reception. As with this book, literary data derived from periodicals is often used—and such research will be my focus in this chapter. Because periodicals are published for particular readerships at particular times, such data have clear temporal, spatial, and social dimensions; periodical collections are also increasingly and extensively digitized, making them amenable to data-rich scholarship. However, literary systems could be modeled in historically meaningful ways using any digital collection(s) or other disciplinary infrastructure, as long as a schema for production and reception is applied to sample selection and analysis.[2]

Some data-rich literary history projects use periodical data to model literary systems based on the authors and titles presented to particular readerships. Richard So and Hoyt Long employ analog bibliographies of poetry in American and Japanese periodicals—and construct their own bibliography for the Chinese context—to identify authors published together. On this basis they propose and contrast "the collaborative networks that underwrote the evolution of modernist poetry" in these countries (148). As So and Long note, because poetry periodicals served "as the institutional sites through which an expanding market for avant-garde poetry was stratified and differentiated along aesthetic, ideological, racial and even geographical lines of affiliation," data derived from them have an "inherently social dimension" that supports exploration of the historical and structural conditions under which modernist poetry emerged (158). The historical newspapers and magazines analyzed in the Viral Texts project, led by Ryan Cordell and David Smith, provide similar contextual information. Employing an algorithm to identify republished passages, the Viral Texts project discovers works in a range of genres—including many not traditionally considered by literary historians (jokes, recipes, "listicles")—where reprinting indexes popularity as well as personal and structural connections between newspaper editors (Cordell, "Reprinting").

Other projects model literary systems using more direct evidence of reception. Ed Finn explores the "public literary action" and resulting positions in the American literary field of four prominent authors—Thomas Pynchon, Toni Morrison, David Foster, and Junot Díaz—based on the authors and titles they are linked to in reviews in key American periodicals, as well as in book recommendations and reviews on Amazon. Although Internet communities are "irrepressibly international," as Finn notes, such data signifies how contemporary readers, mainly though not exclusively in the United States, position these authors and their works (48). DeWitt uses a similar approach to explore genre formation in the nineteenth century. Noting her methodological debt to Finn, DeWitt begins with seven prominent theological titles and conducts keyword searches in six mass-digitized collections to gather colocation data: titles mentioned in the same book reviews in Victorian periodicals. The resulting analysis characterizes genre as "a classification created retrospectively by readers to make sense of a field of novels" (177). Although DeWitt's model has social, temporal, and spatial parameters, she notes the potential for more detailed investigation with additional data that "differentiate between different kinds of articles, taking into account the date or location of publication as well as the sorts of periodicals in which they appear" (176).

Ted Underwood and Jordan Sellers's study of conceptions of literary prestige for poetry published between 1820 and 1919 is also based on periodical reviews: namely, 360 poetry titles reviewed in prominent American and British periodicals ("*Longue*"). But rather than investigating their contents, Underwood and Sellers use these reviews to identify a sample of reviewed poetic works. They then compare word usage in those works to that in 360 nonreviewed titles, selected randomly from the HathiTrust Digital Library. While this project—like DeWitt's—arguably conflates cultures of reviewing and constructions of literary value in two different contexts—America and Britain—its focus on titles discussed at particular times, and reviews as a marker of cultural distinction, imbues the data with clear temporal and social dimensions.

These projects recognize that literary works do not exist in a single time and place but accrue meaning in the multiple contexts in which they are produced and received. And they create models based on that understanding to investigate key issues in literary history relating to production, circulation, and reception, ranging from the nature and development of literary movements and genres to the formation of authorial identities and cultural value. In some cases they overturn core assumptions in literary history. Thus the capacity of Underwood and Sellers's machine-learning model to discern reviewed from unreviewed poetry titles enables them to demonstrate that standards governing literary prestige developed gradually over the nineteenth century, rather than changing suddenly at the end of it ("*Longue*").

If sometimes implicitly, these projects highlight the importance for data-rich literary history of the computational method of modeling. Described most fully for the digital humanities in Willard McCarty's

Humanities Computing, modeling is not simply a means of representing cultural artifacts or concepts in a form amenable to computational analysis. By foregrounding the manipulation and refinement of data, modeling produces an "experimental device" (27) or "pragmatic instrument of investigation" that supports an ongoing "process of coming to know" (36). This method enhances knowledge because these acts of representation and refinement expose the researcher's assumptions about the cultural artifact or concept under investigation and enable those assumptions to be clarified or challenged.

One contribution this book aims to make is to expand and enrich the application of modeling for data-rich literary history by connecting it explicitly to descriptive bibliography. Moving beyond basic enumerative information, this approach investigates relationships of production and reception by describing, manipulating, and refining—that is, by modeling—details of the documentary forms and historical relationships of literary works in the past. Chapter 3 presents the outcome of this practice, identifying the multiple fields I use to describe fiction in nineteenth-century newspapers. Here, two instances of features modeled—and their relationship to production and reception—will help to indicate the value of this practice for data-rich literary history.

The title changes that fiction underwent when published and republished in Australian newspapers offers a relatively straightforward example of this integration of modeling and descriptive bibliography. Collecting all manifestations of a literary work under the same title, though standard in enumerative bibliography, obscures how this documentary feature was constituted by different newspaper editors and syndicators and experienced by different reading communities. Modeling fiction with respect to the various titles used *and* the common title uniting related manifestations of a work supports insights into publication and reception: for instance, how editors altered the works they published and what this implies about their understandings of the readerships they served. It also enables analysis of the systems through which fiction circulated, in that collating multiple versions of a title indicates the works that were widely published in the Australian colonies while offering clues as to the mechanisms of that circulation: for instance, variations in a title preclude the use of certain types of (ready printed and identical) newspaper supplements as the means of distributing fiction.

Authorship was one of the most complicated features of this literary system to model. Not only were many titles published anonymously but, as chapter 4 explores in depth, some were published with attribution in one instance, and without attribution in another; some anonymously published authors remain unknown today, while others have been identified; and in many cases, the paratext of stories contained information about authorship, regardless of whether the work was published anonymously or with a named author. I embedded this information in the model through such fields as "publication author" and "author," to differentiate the form of attribution used in the newspaper from a single name uniting an oeuvre; "signature," to identify other titles described as "by the author of" the story within the publication event; and "inscribed gender" and "inscribed nationality," to depict information in subtitles and other aspects of the publication event designating the story as by a man or woman and from a particular place. Detailed modeling of authorship enabled a significantly more nuanced representation and investigation of this literary-historical phenomenon than would be possible with a single author name. It also supported analysis of reception. By indicating features of authorship highlighted by different newspaper editors and syndicators, for example, it suggests ideas about cultural value informing literary culture in the colonies.

Like other forms of textual scholarship, bibliography is often perceived as precritical and procedural. But its descriptive form has always approached bibliographical data as "capta, taken not given, constructed as an interpretation of the phenomenal world, not inherent in it" (Drucker, "Humanities" np). Modeling is likewise based on an understanding of data as contingent and constructed. Equally important, the two practices are underpinned by the same dual imperative: to enact *and* to enable critical analysis. Integrating modeling and descriptive bibliography—or more specifically, using descriptive bibliography as a framework for modeling and modeling as a method for extending bibliographical knowledge—can support detailed and nuanced representations of literary systems that explore the existence of literary works in the past and support future investigations of those works and systems. While data-based approaches to literary history are often accused of simplifying understandings of the past, this approach offers not only nuance and complexity but a means of refiguring and refining the terms in which literary history is pursued.

But however essential it is for data-rich literary history, modeling cannot be the sole foundation for the field. Models of literary systems are not simply arguments about the existence of and connections between literary works in the past; they are arguments made with reference to the disciplinary infrastructure—the bibliographies and collections, analog and digital—that transmit evidence of past works and relationships to the present. Modeling, even when integrated with descriptive bibliography as I have described, does not reflect on this transmission. Models embody a scholar's arguments, whereas disciplinary infrastructure is an effect of multiple arguments: a sequence of assumptions, decisions, representations, and remediations. Such histories of transmission shape how the researcher can explore, and what she can know of, the historical context that disciplinary infrastructure appears to represent. To adequately perform literary history, data-rich projects must investigate these histories of transmission and how they constitute the documentary record.

II

The main issues foregrounded in discussions of digital collections, particularly mass-digitized ones, are scale and access, for obvious reasons. Digital collections enable new forms of access to documentary records through novel organizations of bibliographical data and full-text searching. Often, digital collections bring a larger number of related documents together than is held in any single analog collection. Yet inevitably, digital collections of historical documents are partial representations of partial records. While many data-rich literary history projects are moving toward more critical assessments of the disciplinary infrastructure they work with, the complexity of such infrastructure and its implications for research practices are yet to be fully appreciated and answered.

The distinctions or gaps between the context signified by collections and the exemplars used in signification might partly arise from, but are not simply the consequence of, successive exclusions of documents, as the *Stanford Literary Lab Pamphlet 11* suggests. In chapter 1 I noted that, in defining "the published," "the archive," and "the corpus" as progressively smaller selections, those authors admit the constructed nature of literary data. Yet they also argue that mass-digitization largely avoids those exclusions, such that "the corpus of a project can now easily be (almost) as large as the archive, while the archive is itself becoming—at least for modern times (almost) as large as all of published literature" (Algee-Hewitt et al., 2).

Even with their account of the considerable practical challenges involved in accessing versions of specific literary works, this description of mass digitization drastically diminishes the degree of exclusion involved in constructing such collections. Digitization only captures certain features of documentary texts, and the documents digitized are only some of those that existed and some of those that were collected by an institution or group of institutions. For mass-digitized periodical collections, for instance, the documents digitized are not only those that were collected, at set times and for specific reasons, but usually those that were also microfilmed for access and preservation. Digitized collections are partial in another way, in that combining the holdings of multiple analog collections tends to obscure the individual histories of the contributing collections and their implications for the form, scope, and critical capacity of the resulting digital one.

Pamphlet 11 belies further distinctions between published, collected, and analyzed documents created by their representation and remediation: that is, by the successive acts of production and reception, critical and technical, that produce digital collections. Collections have always been constituted in this way. In analog collections, documents are represented and remediated through the cataloging systems that organize holdings and the interfaces that interpret them: the card catalogs, special collection indexes, or online library catalogs that provide a method of searching and a type, form, and detail of metadata. As Eggert notes, a library or archive, "far from acting as a neutral frame" for the documents it transmits, "wraps them up in a relationship to the intended viewer" that shapes what is discovered and how it is understood (*Securing* 13–14).[3] A key difference between analog collections and digital ones is that literary historians rarely, if ever, treat the former (a given library, for instance) as proxies for literature as it circulated and was understood in the past, whereas digital collections such as Google Books or HathiTrust are sometimes assumed to be representative in this way.

This perception persists even as the construction of digital collections constitutes a radical increase over analog ones in the degree and complexity of the representations and remediations involved. In addition to the history/ies of transmission of the analog collection(s) from which they are created, digital collections are the effects of multiple, intersecting structures and systems. Chief among an extensive array of these are the selection criteria employed in defining the digital collection and the technical workflow involved in implementing them; the metadata standards used to describe documents and how these are incorporated into the collection interface; the quality of (microfilming and) digitization and capacity of optical character recognition (OCR) to produce searchable text; the nature of the search algorithm(s) used to order results; and the interface(s) available for accessing the collection and the type(s) of access these support. The "corpus" selected from this collection and used for analysis is, in turn, shaped by the type and form of data that can be exported. All of these factors have their own constitutive effects, and all of them occur *before* the scholar begins the modeling process described in the previous section. Digital collections are also more mutable than analog ones, meaning that the results of a search conducted today might be very different from the same search conducted tomorrow.[4]

Due to their multiplicity and complex interaction, the components involved in producing digital collections expand access to the historical record in certain ways, even as they increase the likelihood of unrealized and significant disjunctions between the access we intend and the access we achieve. Digital humanities scholars recognize that digital infrastructure shapes knowledge production,[5] and digital literary historians have responded with explicitly curatorial approaches to constructing and exploring digital documents and collections. This approach is, for instance, definitive of the Text Encoding Initiative—an international consortium developing standards for the representation of texts in digital form—and of digital scholarly editing broadly.

A curatorial approach also defines projects that construct digital collections to represent particular literary works, authors, and/or publications in their historical context, including the *Rossetti Archive*, the *Orlando Project*, and the digitization of the *Western Home Monthly*.[6] Such projects attend to the specificity of collections from which documents were gathered, the different documentary manifestations incorporated, and the partiality of the digitized record, and they devise methods for representing and managing these features. These same issues are foregrounded in a growing body of research that uses these digital collections and others to historicize individual titles or authors. Recent work in this area advocates strategies for identifying and managing gaps in digital collections, including visualizing absences (Klein) and moving back and forth between digitized and analog collections (C. Robinson). In an approach similar to the one I am proposing, though focusing on particular authors and works rather than literary systems, other projects construct dedicated, scholar-built resources to circumvent the search algorithms organizing engagement with mass-digitized collections and/or to support forms of experimental and speculative analysis of literary data (Brown; Sinatra).

These digital humanities projects highlight four features that I believe should also underpin the modeling of literary systems in data-rich literary history. First is a critical assessment of the relationship between the historical context analyzed and the digital collection(s) used for analysis; second is detailed attention to the relationship between the documents included in the digital collection(s) and the terms in which they are represented; third is explicit discussion of the means by which data are extracted and modeled; and fourth is a published record of data arising from that extensive history of transmission. Existing projects in data-rich literary history often (though by no means universally) demonstrate the second and third of these features. The need for data publication, and for platforms and modes of review to support it, is also increasingly recognized and enacted.[7] But data-rich literary history projects rarely consider how the disciplinary infrastructure analyzed relates to the historical context investigated. The lack of shared standards for data publication—and, more specifically, of a framework for combining these four features in investigating and representing the transmission and transformation of historical evidence to and in the present—problematizes the field's capacity to advance historical knowledge.

To remain with the projects introduced previously, neither So and Long, nor DeWitt, nor Cordell and Smith make anything like the same polemical claims to directly represent historical fact that Moretti and Jockers do; but none of these studies adequately investigate the relationship between the historical context they explore and the disciplinary infrastructure they use to conduct this exploration. So and Long explicitly resist the view that their network model shows the evolution of modernist poetry: its nodes and edges are "an interpretation of the underlying publication data" (157). Yet in not assessing the quality of that data—or rather, in briefly noting limitations only with the bibliography they construct—So and Long do not consider the extent to which the interpretation they offer is determined by the scope and constitution of specific bibliographies.

While So and Long offer little information on data collection and construction, DeWitt extensively details this process for her study of genre formation, including the nineteenth-century periodical collections searched, the methods for extracting data from these results, and the size of the dataset gathered. Yet DeWitt similarly takes for granted that the resources she uses consistently and adequately represent the publishing context she investigates. DeWitt's datasets are derived from searching the interfaces of large, proprietary collections, and she does not discuss the manner of their construction (for instance, the reliability of the OCR-rendered text or the effects of the search algorithms used) nor the extent to which their holdings represent Victorian literary criticism. The difficulty of conducting such an analysis of proprietary collections raises an important issue for data-rich literary history, and literary history in general: the adequacy, reliability, and transparency of emerging digital infrastructure. Proprietary mass-digitized collections such as Google Books, *Early English Books Online*, and *The British Newspaper Archive* (owned by Google, ProQuest, and findmypast, respectively) are increasingly used in humanities research. But their scope and scale—let alone the histories of transmission that produce them—can be very difficult to discern; indeed, the commercial imperatives of these enterprises arguably depend on them presenting these collections as comprehensive.

Yet even when researchers use nonproprietary mass-digitized collections and move beyond the search box to export and explore the underlying data, the scope and reliability of such holdings are not ascertained. As in DeWitt's study, the Viral Texts project devotes considerable attention to describing data collection, including how its algorithm defines its object (reprinted passages), the characteristics of the resulting dataset, and the apparent and potential limitations of their method (Smith, Cordell, and Dillon; Smith, Cordell, and Mullen). While these authors note the inevitable difference between the newspapers published in the past and the mass-digitized collections used to investigate reprinting, they do not characterize the nature and extent of these gaps. Despite the undoubted technical and critical sophistication of the Viral Texts project, and the valuable insights it has produced regarding American print culture, it does not explore the relationship of the mass-digitized collections it analyses—chiefly, the Library of Congress's *Chronicling America*—to the historical contexts they are taken to represent. Even fundamental questions, such as approximately what proportion of American newspapers have been digitized by *Chronicling America*, are not addressed.

It may well be that the disciplinary infrastructure used by these projects adequately signifies the relationships of production and reception they seek to investigate, but this also might not be true, or it might be true to differing extents in the different cases. In not assessing whether and how well the data analyzed represents the historical context explored, these projects ultimately interpret the characteristics not of literary-historical systems but of particular components of our disciplinary infrastructure.

While the bibliographies and digital collections investigated by the above projects inevitably exclude multiple periodicals that existed in the past, the contemporary, born-digital collections that Finn investigates—for example, book recommendations and reviews on Amazon—embody the relationships of production and reception he seeks to explore. As well as describing the meaning of these relationships for literary culture in America, in explicitly defining his samples, Finn articulates a clear relationship between the collections he analyses and the samples he uses. For instance, with the Amazon "Customers Who Bought This Item Also Bought" category, Finn's script identifies the first ten recommendations listed for a designated author, then repeats the process for two further iterations, to gather information on a further one hundred and then one thousand links. The resulting dataset is not the reviews of an author but "the three-level network surrounding a particular author's work," as represented by Amazon at a certain time (30).

While Finn's account of data construction is exemplary, like So and Long and DeWitt, he does not publish the resulting dataset. The dataset that Finn uses to model the relationships of production and reception presented by Amazon—however representative at the time it was constructed—became different to those relationships essentially from the moment he ceased harvesting data. Accordingly, no matter how detailed his information about data construction, the basis of his study cannot be reproduced: the version of Amazon that Finn explores no longer exists. Finn's arguments refer to his own model, and with that model unpublished, no one else can engage with these arguments on the grounds on which they are made.

Data publication is integral to the Viral Texts project, which includes a searchable database of reprinted passages, including information on the periodicals encompassed by their study and locations and dates of publication for reprinted text. However, the form in which data publication occurs presents a related problem to Finn's study. We are told that the project's "database will never be a finished and polished archive, but instead an evolving and experimental space for exploring text reuse across an expanding set of corpora" (Smith, Cordell, and Mullen E14). On one level, this is an understandable response to working with (evolving and experimental) mass-digitized collections. But this approach means that the literary-historical arguments Cordell offers are not anchored in a stable and accessible dataset. The dataset he uses to explore reprinting in antebellum American newspapers, for instance, represents a stage in the development of analysis of a mass-digitized collection ("Reprinting"). With that expression subsumed into an "evolving and experimental" database, the basis of his argument no longer exists—at least, not in published form.

In chapter 1 I argued that Moretti's and Jockers's lack of data publication manifests and perpetuates their disregard for textual scholarship and the historical and interpretive meanings it offers. I do not think this is the reason for the problems with data publication—or lack thereof—in these other data-rich literary history projects. The extensive investment of time required to publish data and the lack of an established framework for doing so are the more likely culprits. But in not grounding their arguments in a stable, consistent, and freely available object of analysis, these projects manifest problematic consequences similar to those presented by distant reading and macroanalysis. Lack of access to the datasets used by these scholars makes it impossible for others to engage with their arguments in the terms in which they are made, or to reuse and repurpose the data. Because these datasets are so time-consuming to construct, lack of data publication is a significant impediment to cumulative scholarly endeavor in data-rich literary history. Without access to underlying data, visualizations and other data summaries become the only available "text" for analysis. As well as concealing the data used, this situation occludes the fact that such summaries arise from—rather than simply invite—interpretation.

Most importantly, not publishing data obscures the fundamental nature of digital collections as "transactional objects whose very identity is constituted through exchange." Drucker ("Distributed" 12) makes this point with respect to individual digital documents, but it is equally applicable to digital collections. Our inquiries to them—in conjunction with the protocols, conditions, and constraints that they enact and are enacted through—do not discover a preexisting version of the documentary past but configure and constitute one. Part of Drucker's point is that this condition is not exclusive to the digital realm, and this also is true of collections: as I maintained above, analog collections have always been produced in transactional moments of production and reception. But the multiple, interactive, and shifting instances of representation and remediation constitutive of digital collections make this situation more acute and emphasize that the historical record does not exist independently of the structures and systems through which we access it. And as Drucker notes, there is "no way to preserve or recover the phantasm whose materiality is dependent on so many contingencies and co-dependencies of distributed hardware and related software, networks and clock speeds, protocols and display capacities" (26).

But there is—and there is only—the capacity to represent the effects of engagements with particular digital collections at particular times. Herein lies the fundamental importance of data publication for data-rich literary history: in expressing a materiality that no longer exists in any other form, it offers the only possible basis for conversation on shared premises. It is not enough to point to the mass-digitized collection or bibliographical database from which data were derived. The constitutive features of that entity have almost certainly altered. And even if the digital collection has not expanded (or contracted), data-rich literary history does not analyze the collection itself. It explores the effects of scholarly engagement with and interpretation of it.

Of the data-rich literary history projects discussed in this chapter, Underwood and Sellers's work on changing standards of literary prestige most consistently enacts the curatorial elements present elsewhere in digital humanities, not least in terms of data publication. As the authors explain in an online working paper on the project, its most time-consuming element was not training their supervised model but constructing their dataset: identifying the different subgenres—poetry, prose, fiction, and drama—present in HathiTrust ("How," 6). As well as publishing the datasets and code used in their article ("Code"), in collaboration with HathiTrust Underwood takes the major, additional step of releasing the outcome of analysis of that mass-digitized collection for others to use. This takes the form of "word counts for 101,948 volumes of fiction, 58,724 volumes of poetry, and 17,709 volumes of drama" published from 1700 to 1922, as well as yearly summaries of word frequencies for each genre. Underwood refers to this dataset as a "collection" to differentiate it from a "corpus" because "I don't necessarily recommend that you use the whole thing, as is. The *whole thing* may or may not represent the sample you need for your research question" ("Dataset" np).

Signifying growing recognition of the importance of data publication, the Underwood/HathiTrust collection is an important undertaking for data-rich literary history in at least two ways. In presenting a dataset designed for literary history, it offers a shared foundation for research. Working with it, researchers can ask a range of questions based on a reliable, standardized dataset and engage with each other's arguments in terms not only of results produced but of data investigated. In characterizing that collection as the holdings of "American university and public libraries, insofar as they were digitized in the year 2012 (when the project began)," Underwood also frames a major mass-digitized collection—HathiTrust—in terms of its history of transmission ("Dataset" np). However general this framing, Underwood thus explicitly associates the dataset he publishes with a sequence of production and reception that profoundly affects its capacity to support historical analysis. In their article, Underwood and Sellers acknowledge that this history of transmission shapes their findings, noting that their model "makes more accurate" predictions for American poetry collections because HathiTrust "mainly aggregates the collections of large American libraries" ("*Longue*" 338).

This approach to data description, curation, and publication recognizes that the relationship between a collection and a historical context is never direct and transparent. But even Underwood and Sellers are equivocal in characterizing the broader relationship between literature in the past and the disciplinary infrastructure used to investigate it. Seeking to define the scope of their dataset, Underwood and Sellers note that HathiTrust "may represent more than half of the titles that were printed" because it contains "about 58% of titles recorded in standard bibliographies." Yet their own "work on fiction" with this collection belies the apparently solid basis of this estimate, finding that HathiTrust contains "many titles left out of" existing bibliographies ("How" n11). Underwood and Sellers thus indicate a significant lack of overlap between established bibliographical records and the holdings of a major digital library, although they do not highlight the significance of this finding nor explore its implications for their own study or for literary history broadly (whether conducted by computational or noncomputational means). Emphasizing that we cannot know the documentary past except through the knowledge infrastructure we create to interpret it, this disjunction that Underwood and Sellers discover highlights the potentially major gaps in all existing forms of description and interpretation: neither the analog nor the digital record offers an unmediated and comprehensive view of the documentary past; both are partial, and not necessarily in complementary ways.

III

The challenge facing data-rich literary history—of proposing a historically coherent whole (a literary system) from a collection or collections of parts (the disciplinary infrastructure and the digitized documents and literary data it transmits)—suggests the strategy for meeting it. The scholarly edition has long offered both a theoretical basis and a practical technology for demonstrating and managing the documentary record's partiality. Applied to the literary system rather than the literary work, the scholarly edition provides a framework for investigating the history of transmission constitutive of the literary system modeled, justifying the selections and decisions made in that analysis, and publishing the outcomes.

A conventional scholarly edition is not simply a version of a literary work. It is an "embodied argument about textual transmission," as

Eggert puts it (*Securing* 177) or, in McGann's words, a "hypothetical platform" for historical enquiry, one that both indicates and provides a pathway through the instability of the "textual condition" ("From" 203, 230).[8] This dual capacity inheres in the interrelationship of the edition's critical apparatus and curated text. The critical apparatus describes and justifies the editor's engagement with the documentary record constitutive of the literary work, including the inevitable gaps and uncertainties that engagement exposes and creates. The curated text represents the outcome of that extended critical encounter, offering to those who accept its tenets—or who lack the expertise to engage with the documentary record in that manner—both an argument about the nature of the literary work and a foundation for analysis of that work.

For a scholarly edition of a literary system, the critical apparatus details the history of transmission by which the existence and interconnections of literary works in the past are known. Much more than simply describing the construction of a dataset—something already offered by many data-rich literary history projects—this critical apparatus elaborates the complex relationships between the historical context explored, the disciplinary infrastructure employed in investigating that context, the decisions and selections implicated in creating and remediating the collection or collections, and the transformations wrought by the editor's extraction, construction, and analysis of that data.

A curated dataset replaces the curated text for a scholarly edition of a literary system. In the form of bibliographical and textual data, it manifests—demonstrates and, specifically, publishes—the outcome of the sequence of production and reception, including the current moment of interpretation, described in the critical apparatus. The model it provides is stable: it is published and accessible for all to use, whether for conventional or computational literary history. But that stability does not belie or extinguish its hypothetical character. Rather than showing a literary system, it presents an argument about the existence of literary works in the past based on the editor's interpretation of the multiple transactions by which documentary evidence of the past is transmitted for the present. Its suitability and reliability for literary-historical research is established by a relationship between the historical phenomena and the data model that is explicitly interpretive and contingent rather than supposedly direct or natural.

As in a conventional scholarly edition, the nature of and issues fore-grounded in any scholarly edition of a literary system will depend on what the editor or editorial team perceive as most relevant to under-standing the existence of literary works in the past and the disciplin-ary infrastructure that evidences this. My scholarly edition of a liter-ary system is profoundly influenced by the sociology of texts tradition (McKenzie). But this framework equally allows for modeling based on other theories of textual transmission. Whatever theoretical perspec-tive informs it, where "the stylistic protocols of literary criticism" mean that issues deemed methodological are often relegated to footnotes or "methodological caveats"[9]—as if they qualified rather than constituted the basis of the arguments offered—a scholarly edition of a literary system provides a dedicated format for demonstrating and justifying the foundational argument of data-rich literary history: the engage-ment with disciplinary infrastructure to effect the modeling of a liter-ary system.

In its stability, this curated dataset resembles the Underwood/HathiTrust "collection," and this feature is vital. Both publish the out-come of a critical encounter with digital disciplinary infrastructure and thus offer a consistent object for analysis that does not presume or pretend the stability of the documentary record. At the same time, a scholarly edition of a literary system differs from the word counts offered by the Underwood/HathiTrust collection, not only in pro-viding a dedicated critical apparatus to define its construction but in two other, important ways. First, and most basically, where the latter is usable only by those with programming expertise, or access to it, a scholarly edition of a literary system should be accessible to all literary scholars through an interface for searching, browsing, and exporting the curated dataset.

Second, while the Underwood/HathiTrust collection is presented as raw data from which researchers can construct a sample, a scholarly edition of a literary system explicitly embodies an argument about his-torical relationships between literary works in a set time and place, at the same time as it offers a sample of literary works for analysis. In this sense, a scholarly edition is less potentially extensible than the Under-wood/HathiTrust collection, although that collection also relates to a specific—albeit extensive—time period and collates a particular type and form of literary works. But a scholarly edition of a literary system is not designed to be applicable to all times and places. Rather it seeks to provide an interpretive intermediary between increasingly complex and extensive digital disciplinary infrastructure and the requirements of literary-historical analysis.

As noted in the introduction, for the scholarly edition of extended fiction in nineteenth-century Australian newspapers that underpins this book, the critical apparatus is comprised of two parts: fields in the curated dataset, which detail decisions and arguments underpinning specific data constructions, and a historical introduction, presented in chapter 3 and delineating the principles of the modeled literary system in terms of the history of transmission by which it is constituted. The curated dataset is published in two sites and forms—as downloadable data alongside the Open Access version of this book on the University of Michigan Press website and in a database for searching, browsing, and selective or wholesale exporting of bibliographical and textual data.[10]

This dual publication is an admittedly inelegant solution to the perpetual problems in digital humanities of sustainability and access. The first format is the most sustainable one I could devise, in that the data are held by the University of Michigan Library, in association with the press, and will be maintained by the significant resources of those institutions, I hope, well into the future. However, as with the Underwood/HathiTrust collection, in that form the curated dataset is usable only by scholars able to manipulate extensive textual and bibliographical data computationally. The database supports access for all literary scholars and permits me, and I hope others, to refer to fiction in the curated dataset in the knowledge that anyone can use the database to access the record's full bibliographical and textual data.[11] As I discuss in the book's conclusion, the database also supports ongoing research into Australian newspaper fiction and the future utility of the data underpinning this book in providing facilities for users to interact with *Trove* to identify new fiction, enhance bibliographical information, and correct textual data. Yet conceivably, that format will be sustained only as long as I remain at the Australian National University. As digital humanities scholars work toward new forms of enhanced publication, I hope that a platform for both sustainable and accessible data publication will emerge; in the interim, this is the solution I have improvised.

For some researchers, a scholarly edition of a literary system will function much as existing digital collections do: providing a site for searching or browsing the digitized documentary record. In this capacity, it also enables access to what could and I think should be a key contribution of data-rich literary history to the broader discipline: an expanded bibliographical record. While Underwood and Sellers note the presence in HathiTrust of new works not previously recorded by literary historians (who knows how many), the scholarly edition underpinning this project identifies new Australian titles and authors. For other researchers, including those currently using mass-digitized collections to locate individual authors and works in the historical context in which they operated, a scholarly edition of a literary system will offer a carefully, consistently, and—by the critical apparatus, explicitly—historicized digital collection for this task. And for researchers analyzing large-scale trends in the publication, circulation, reception, and contents of literary works, such an edition will provide a rigorously constructed and explained "shared" dataset, that could be analyzed and "combined in more ways than one" (Moretti, *Graphs* 5).

Grounding data-rich literary history in scholarly editions of literary systems emphasizes that constructing literary data is just as much an interpretive and critical activity as its analysis and that the nuance of such analyses foundationally depends on the historical knowledge embedded in those constructions. With a scholarly edition of a literary system already, in and of itself, an argument about a "collective system . . . as a whole" (Moretti, *Graphs* 4), analyses of it can attend to the multiple features and dimensions it models. Alan Liu's notion of "contingency" encapsulates the resulting analytic mode. Describing the relationship of historicism to the database, Liu notes that in neither form does one ask what is this whole, what does it mean? Rather, the question becomes how does this complex system I am investigating appear from this perspective? Although the whole is composed of parts that are explicitly defined and constrained—"chained to context," as Liu puts it—the mode of inquiry it supports is transactional, enabling unpredictable connections and insights (*Local* 262).

As with a scholarly edition of a literary work, a scholarly edition of a literary system is thus intended not to conclude but to support various forms of investigation, including those that move between the single literary work and the system in which it existed and operated, as I demonstrate in chapter 6. The issues explored in the book's second half reflect my interests, and the topics I believe are important in understanding nineteenth-century literary culture, in Australia and globally. But as I show in the conclusion, these chapters in no way exhaust— or come close to exhausting—the potential questions and arguments that this scholarly edition of a literary system might support, whether enacted through traditional or computational means.

The approach to data-rich literary history I am advocating does not take the path increasingly recommended for the field: of integrating scientific and social scientific measures of statistical uncertainty into historical analysis (Goldstone, "Distant"). Given that constructing literary data is a historical argument made in the context of a history of transmission—the effects of which are difficult to qualify, let alone to quantify—I do not see that any assessment of error is made more useful or concise by its numerical expression. Instead, in the intersection of a critical apparatus and curated dataset, the framework of the scholarly edition offers a theoretical and practical basis to model the relationships of production and reception that constitute historical literary systems, while assessing and managing the inevitable contingency of those relationships and of the documentary infrastructure through which we perceive them. As well as supplying a dedicated object of analysis for data-rich literary history, a scholarly edition of a literary system seeks to extend the insights gained from that field's engagement with emerging digital disciplinary infrastructure to the broader discipline. Conducted on that basis, data-rich literary history could transform from an unexpected, often unwelcome intruder into a vital interlocutor between literary history and the digital context in which it increasingly operates.

CHAPTER 3

From World to *Trove* to Data

Tracing a History of Transmission

———— ༤ ————

A model of a literary system is not only an argument about the historical nature and meaning of interconnections between literary works
in the past. As chapter 2 explores, inevitably, it is also the outcome
of a history of transmission: the many instances of production and
reception, including the scholar's acts of interpretation, by which evidence of those historical meanings and connections is apprehended
and represented. A history of transmission constitutes the object analyzed in data-rich literary history and, therefore, a project's capacity
to advance understanding. I ended chapter 2 by outlining an object
capable of describing that engagement and justifying and demonstrating its outcomes. Called a scholarly edition of a literary system,
it is comprised of a curated dataset, offering a stable and accessible
model of the existence and interconnections of literary works in the
past, and a critical apparatus that reveals the hypothetical nature of
that modeled literary system *and* establishes it as a reliable basis for
analysis. Along with designated fields in the curated dataset, detailing decisions and arguments underpinning individual data constructions, the critical apparatus for the scholarly edition underpinning
this book—of extended fiction in nineteenth-century Australian
newspapers—is composed of a historical introduction, describing the

broad features and effects of the history of transmission producing the modeled data.

This chapter presents that historical introduction. It elaborates the history of transmission outlined in figure 1, where each arrow signifies a process—in most cases, a series of processes—of selection, translation, and transformation of newspapers containing extended fiction, ultimately into bibliographical and textual data in the curated dataset. These processes are divided into three major sequences, explored successively in the chapter's three parts. The first concerns the historical context for the literary system I explore, with the questions marks at the top of figure 1 indicating gaps in existing knowledge that this project was designed to address. What fiction was available to colonial newspaper readers? Where did it come from? And what does it indicate about colonial literary and reading cultures and the transnational circulation of fiction?

The chapter's remaining sections describe two major sequences in the history of transmission of the documentary record. Section 2 considers the remediation of historical Australian newspapers as digitized documents in *Trove* and focuses on establishing the relationship between the newspapers in this collection and those that circulated in Australia in the nineteenth century. The final section explores the translation of parts of those digitized documents into bibliographical and textual data, explaining how I identified and harvested fiction in this mass-digitized collection, aspects of that method and of digitization that affected the outcome of this procedure, and the arguments manifested in the resulting data model. In articulating this history of transmission, including its omissions and concentrations, I aim to constitute the curated dataset as a viable foundation for literary history not by denying or concealing, but by demonstrating, its constructed and provisional nature.

I

The nineteenth century is widely recognized as a time when an expanding reading public embraced fiction, especially in its extended forms: the novel, novella, and long short story. As literary historians of Britain and the United States have demonstrated, demand for fiction occurred in the context of increased literacy and was facilitated by technological,

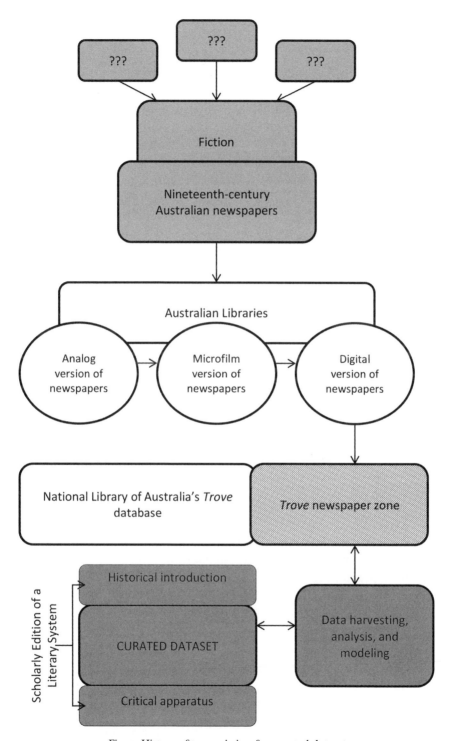

Fig. 1. History of transmission for curated dataset

legal, and cultural developments including rapid advances in printing, changes in copyright and taxation, and the emergence of celebrity authors.[1] Nineteenth-century periodical fiction has been much studied. It is generally accepted that most extended fiction of the time was published in serial form, either initially or exclusively in periodicals, including literary journals, illustrated magazines, story papers or dime novels, and newspapers. The importance of this publishing phenomenon has been established with respect to its role in shaping the history, form, and even content of nineteenth-century fiction, as well as in forming reading publics and professionalizing authorship.[2]

With people arriving in the Australian colonies from places (especially Britain) with established fiction markets, demand for such content was high. Indeed, colonial Australians—including, remarkably, those who arrived as convicts—had significantly higher literacy rates than the general British population (Nicholas and Shergold 21). Yet reading materials were significantly scarcer in Australia than in Britain, Europe, or America. Local book publishing was limited and expensive (Stewart 17); when it did occur, it was often done by job printers, with books issued in small print runs, largely or entirely paid for by authors (Webby, "Journals" 61). Imported books were expensive, and the few bookstores and lending libraries that operated were not accessible to large parts of the colonial populations. Many who lived in metropolitan centers were restricted by the high cost of buying or borrowing books, while for those who lived in rural areas, access was further restricted by the distances separating settlements.[3]

This scarcity of books increased the importance of literary journals and magazines as sources of fiction in Australia. But access to such reading material was also relatively limited. Many attempts were made to create local versions of the literary periodicals popular in Britain and America at this time, and Ken Gelder and Rachael Weaver argue that colonial journals played an "important role ... in the establishment and development of Australian literary culture" by fostering local writing (9). Yet the vast majority of these enterprises were unsuccessful. Lurline Stuart estimates that only half survived their first year, and all were plagued by financial difficulties arising from small colonial populations and the high costs of local production (1). An 1867 editorial in the *South Australian Register* attributes the short-lived nature of local literary periodicals to their inability to pay for popular authors, noting that fiction is the "backbone of our modern magazines . . . [and] also the rock on which most new enterprises make shipwreck of themselves." The editorial concludes, "If the state of their treasury will not permit them to give the fancy prices which are now paid for the names of eminent novelists, a reading public will not be tempted beyond their title-page."[4]

Local literary periodicals were also challenged by significant competition from one of the few sources of reading material available in the colonies: imported literary journals. Periodicals from Britain such as *All the Year Round, Blackwood's Edinburgh Magazine,* and the *Illustrated London News,* and from America, including the *Atlantic Monthly, Harper's Monthly Magazine,* and the *North American Review,* were imported into Australia in large quantities and could be purchased by issue or subscription. These overseas journals had higher production values than the local product, and their much larger home markets meant they could afford to secure the popular fiction authors that many readers looked for when deciding which periodicals to buy. Due to a range of factors—including lower production costs, their admission into Australia without duty, and reasonable postage rates—imported literary journals could be purchased in the colonies for not much more than was charged for them in Britain and America (Stuart 2). The popularity of overseas periodicals in Australia and the importance of the colonial market for their sales are indicated by special Australian editions of such British and American journals as *Cassell's Illustrated Family Paper, The Family Herald, Scribner's Magazine,* and *Tit-Bits* (1–2).

While popular and available, the colonial presence and circulation of these overseas literary periodicals paled in comparison to those of the "large, vigorous and thriving" local newspaper press (Morrison, "Serial" 308). Writing in 1882, Richard Twopenny described Australia as "the land of newspapers" and estimated the colonial per capita purchase of newspapers to be five times that in Britain (cited in Stewart 17). Hundreds of different newspapers were published in Australia in the nineteenth century. Each major city had multiple titles, published at various intervals (daily, bi- and tri-weekly, weekly, fortnightly, monthly); most major metropolitan dailies had weekly companions offering a compendium of news and fiction for both metropolitan and provincial readers; and even the smallest country towns frequently had a local paper. Newspapers were significantly cheaper than imported journals because local advertising offset production costs and newspaper proprietors often paid postage to rural areas. When fees were charged for postage of weekly companions, these were substantially lower than for monthly or quarterly journals (Stuart 3). The *Melbourne Age*, for instance, sold eighty thousand copies daily in 1888, at the price of a penny (the cost of postage alone for the imported literary journals), and was thus "reasonably accessible to anyone who could read" (Morrison, Introduction xxxii). Newspaper proprietors also offered inducements to readers, including competitions, products (such as free insurance), discounts, and special prices for introducing subscribers.

Nineteenth-century Australian newspapers served multiple purposes, readers, and markets. But the vast majority incorporated fiction, including what I call extended fiction. Some of these titles were full novels or novellas published in a single (often a Christmas) issue. But most were serialized over multiple installments. The prominent placement of such fiction indicates its importance to colonial literary culture. Numerous pages of Christmas issues were dedicated to single stories, with some of these special issues including multiple extended titles. Metropolitan newspapers frequently devoted two or more pages to serial fiction in every issue, while provincial newspapers (although amounting in many cases to only four pages in total) often featured at least a page of fiction. The commonplace inclusion of designated titles for women and children suggests that editors perceived fiction as a means of increasing circulation by making the content of newspapers appealing to all family members.

Multiple other features of these newspapers reinforce fiction's popularity and role in increasing circulations and ensuring reader loyalty. Editors frequently described readers' demand for fiction, with the *Barrier Miner*'s editor writing that

> The success which has attended the publication of "The Last Signal" has been so pronounced that the proprietors of the BARRIER MINER have decided to continue, for a time at least, the publication of serial stories; and have just completed arrangements wish [*sic*] Miss Adeline Sergeant for the publication of her latest brilliant dramatic serial, "Marjory's Mistake."[5]

Letters to the editor praised individual stories,[6] and authors also received readers' feedback on their work. The author of "Love and

Death" wrote in a letter to the *Naracoorte Herald*'s editor that "during the progress of the story . . . I have received so many suggestions, &c., from readers of the tale, that I shall feel obliged if you will kindly allow me a short space in your columns to answer what has been said."[7]

Stories' impending publication were signaled with effusive advertising detailing characters and events and praising the intellectual and moral qualities of the fiction as well as its entertainment value. The forthcoming "Harold Netherly" was described in the *Bowral Free Press* as "of enthralling and unsurpassed interest, and . . . replete with exciting situations and unexpected developments."[8] Of the forthcoming "Cecily's Ring," readers of the *Barrier Miner* were told, "The plot is novel, there are plenty of striking situations, the narrative is vigorous, the dialogue spirited, and there is some faithful Southern coloring."[9] Humble editorial apologies for delays in fiction installments—in suggesting readers' lack of patience with such events—also demonstrate the level of interest in fiction. The editor of the *Murrurundi Times and Liverpool Plains Gazette* wrote "to apologise to our readers for the nonappearance of the usual instalment of our Serial Tale this week, owing to the copy not having come to hand, and to request their kind forbearance in the matter, the cause of which is beyond our control."[10] The *Newcastle Chronicle*'s editor blamed the author, who was "reluctantly compelled to apologise for not having written this week's portion of his serial; but he promises to be more regular for the future, and not to disappoint his readers again."[11]

The prevalence and availability of newspapers, and their prominent and popular inclusion of fiction, made them the main source of fiction for colonial readers and major conduits for the transnational circulation of fiction in the nineteenth century. Given the scarcity of book publishers and other venues for local authors, newspapers were also the primary publishers of colonial fiction. While in Britain and America newspapers provided one site among many for publishing and reading fiction, in colonial Australia they were paramount in both respects.

Researchers have long recognized the importance of newspapers to literary culture in the Australian colonies. Multiple indexing projects—including by Victor Crittenden, Toni Johnson-Woods, Laurie Hergenhan, Elizabeth Morrison, Lurline Stuart, Cheryl Taylor, Chris Tiffin, and Elizabeth Webby[12]—have supported considerable research into colonial newspaper fiction and produced a widely accepted account of the phenomenon that is as follows. In the 1850s editors began to emphasize prose over poetry. From the late 1860s, fiction publication grew rapidly, as population growth and new print and distribution technologies combined to enable colonial editors to increase newspaper size. In the mid- to late 1880s, the entry into the colonial market of overseas, especially British, fiction syndication agencies greatly expanded the supply of newspaper fiction. But the resulting boom was short-lived, with a precipitous decline in the final years of the nineteenth century caused by fundamental changes in publishing. In particular, the transition of British publishers from expensive three-volume books to cheaper paperback editions significantly increased the availability of cheap book editions of fiction in the colonies, undermining the importance of newspaper fiction for readers.[13]

While manual indexing projects have enabled this history of Australian newspaper fiction, their usefulness is limited in respect to accessibility, interoperability, and scope. A number of projects are now only fully available as card indexes or are out of print. Where records have been collated and digitized, particularly by *AustLit: The Australian Literature Resource*, usually only Australian titles have been retained. Due to the sheer size of the archive, most previous studies have focused on major metropolitan newspapers. Accordingly, when scholars have addressed the questions highlighted in this chapter's introduction— what was published, where was it from, and what does it say about colonial and transnational literary culture—their findings have often pertained to a selective handful of examples, generalized to the literary system broadly.[14]

Morrison recognized these problems in the late 1980s and proposed an "Index to Fiction in Australian (or Australasian?) Newspapers" as the solution. To conceptualize the index's breadth, she conducted a "cross-sectional check" to explore which of the colony of Victoria's hundred or so newspapers, "issued on or about 31 August 1889, contained instalments of novels."[15] Morrison's cross-sectional analysis uncovered twenty-eight separate novels—some published multiple times—with a pattern of independent publication in metropolitan dailies and weeklies and syndicated publication in provincial newspapers. To gauge the proposed index's depth, Morrison performed "a diachronic study of serials in the *Age*"—the major daily newspaper for Melbourne, Victoria's capital city—"from April 1872 (when it began to serialise fiction) until the end of the century," identifying sixty novels in this twenty-eight-year period, mostly by English or Scottish authors, with some American and Australian titles ("Retrieving" 29).[16] In signaling its prevalence, Morrison's survey highlights the importance of studying fiction in nineteenth-century Australian newspapers at the same time as it demonstrates the practical impossibility of surveying the phenomenon using manual methods.

II

Trove's mass digitization of historical Australian newspapers provides an alternative to manually indexing fiction. But the significant possibilities this presents must be enacted with attention to the inevitable and complex ways in which collection and remediation (including digitization) translate and transform the documentary record. When using a mass-digitized collection or collections as the primary source for modeling a literary system, understanding the collection's relationship to the historical context it appears to represent is essential. To what extent do the documents digitized reflect the scope, components, and features of historical records and contexts? The transparency and detail of *Trove*'s documentation of its newspaper digitization program help considerably in assessing such representativeness. But documentation does not supplant the need for critical analysis of the amplifications and exclusions created by collection and remediation: what Bonnie Mak calls providing an "archaeology of a mass-digitization."

"Digitised newspapers" is the largest, and most heavily used, of ten "zones" in *Trove*, a freely available, online discovery service, metadata aggregator, digitized content repository, and development platform for resources relating to Australia. Newspapers are collected through the Australian Newspaper Plan (ANP), an "ambitious, ongoing program designed to collect and preserve every newspaper published in Australia, guaranteeing public access to these important historical records,"[17] and digitized under the ANP's Australian Newspaper Digitization Program (ANDP). The ANDP identifies its "long term objective" as being "to make freely available online through *Trove*, as many Australian newspapers published as possible."[18] Both the ANP and the ANDP are collaborations between Australian national, state, and territory libraries, where the NLA coordinates and provides the digital infrastructure, while other libraries take responsibility for collecting, and proposing for digitization, newspapers originating from their state or territory.[19] Newspaper digitization began in 2007, a beta service was made publicly available in 2008, and digitized newspapers were integrated into *Trove* in 2010.

On the date I ceased harvesting fiction for this project (July 16, 2015), *Trove* enabled full-text searching of 17,620,635 pages from 942 Australian newspapers[20] (this number is now significantly greater). That same day, *Chronicling America*, a partnership between the Library of Congress and the National Endowment for the Humanities, offered 9,728,249 pages; the proprietary *British Newspaper Archive*, a commercial project undertaken by findmypast in partnership with the British Library, held 11,162,283 pages; and *Europeana Newspapers*, run by a consortium of cultural institutions from twenty-three European countries, made ten million searchable pages available. Size, of course, does not define a collection's relationship to the works that circulated and were read at a particular time and place: a very large collection can be highly uneven or partial in its representation of a past literary system, just as a very small collection can be the opposite. Assessing a digital collection's relationship to historical context requires investigating the analog holdings on which it is based and the subsequent selections and translations produced by digitization.

Mass-digitization projects, particularly proprietary ones, are often opaque about the manner and outcomes of digitization. The *British Newspaper Archive* simply equates its digital collection with the British Library's newspaper holdings, and those holdings with all historical newspapers.[21] By contrast, *Trove* details the digitization process extensively. The above information about the ANP and ANDP is publicly available on the NLA's website, which also includes comprehensive selection criteria for inclusion of newspapers in *Trove*, presenting the stated aim—that content "should reflect the breadth and diversity of the Australian community and its newspaper output"—in relation to thematic, cultural, geographical, linguistic, curatorial, institutional, economic, and technical issues shaping collection practices.[22] Other information includes a detailed definition of what constitutes a newspaper for the purposes of collection;[23] full copies of annual reports;[24] a detailed workflow for digitization, encompassing the multiple stages and locations, as well as the various staff, including contractors, involved;[25] and technical features of *Trove*'s OCR, search, and storage technologies.[26]

Trove's documentation also explicitly acknowledges gaps between the historical newspapers that existed, the analog holdings of those newspapers, and the mass-digitized collection. In explaining the prioritization of certain newspapers over others, the selection criteria present digitization as selective. Although the ANDP, on at least one occasion, states its aim as complete digitization ("all Australian newspapers published prior to 1955"),[27] the ANP lists newspapers for each state and territory that are known to have existed, but for which no records, or no records for substantial durations, are available in any format, including as many as 374 New South Wales titles.[28] And in estimating the total number of historical Australian newspapers at 7,700 ,[29] while also clearly indicating the number digitized, *Trove* signals the considerable gap between its digital holdings and the newspapers published.

The 924 newspaper titles digitized when harvesting for this project ceased represent 12 percent of the estimated total of 7,700 Australian newspapers. Clearly, however, this calculation does not gauge the relationship of the newspapers in *Trove* to the production and circulation of newspapers in the Australian colonies. While that estimated total apparently refers to all newspapers published prior to 1955, the only ones I am concerned with appeared in the nineteenth century. The number of newspaper titles is also not equivalent to the number of newspapers, as banners could and did change, sometimes on multiple occasions. Of these 924 titles listed by *Trove* on July 16, 2015, 447 operated in the nineteenth century. Attending to banner changes reduces this total to 313 digitized nineteenth-century Australian newspapers.

The extent to which *Trove*'s digitized newspapers represent the newspapers that circulated in Australia cannot be assessed on a pro rata basis, because the number in operation has changed over time. But it can be estimated by determining the proportions of newspapers operating in designated years that have been digitized. While no complete record of nineteenth-century Australian newspapers exists, Gordon & Gotch—a major magazine, newspaper, and book distributor in colonial Australia (and still today)—published an *Australasian Newspaper Directory* for three select years: 1886, 1888, and 1892. Compiled for prospective advertisers, these directories aimed to supply a complete list of newspapers operating in the various Australian colonies, including information on days of publication, price, and circulation; today they offer a basis—albeit for a limited time—to gauge the representativeness of the newspapers sampled for the scholarly edition. Of those published at least weekly—the category predominantly digitized by *Trove*—Gordon & Gotch list 464, 554, and 623 titles in 1886, 1888, and 1892, respectively.[30] Comparing these totals to the number of newspapers operating in these years and digitized at the time I ceased harvesting fiction from *Trove* (135, 152, and 176, respectively) suggests that 29, 27, and 28 percent of newspapers—an average of 28 percent—are represented.

For digital research generally, this low rate of coverage should underscore the partiality of other major mass-digitized historical newspaper collections. Not only is the number of digitized newspaper pages in *Trove* significantly greater than for the *British Newspaper Archive*, *Chronicling America*, or *Europeana Newspapers*, but these other contexts encompassed more—sometimes considerably more—newspapers than the Australian colonies. For instance, compared with 623 newspapers published at least weekly in Australia in 1892, Charles Johanningsmeier identifies 15,205 operating in America in 1899: 2,226 daily and 12,979 weekly (*Fiction* 17). For my purposes, the proportional results above suggest that my analysis of *Trove* excludes around three-quarters of nineteenth-century Australian newspapers. Despite this substantial and important gap, based on further comparison of *Trove*'s holdings with historical newspaper records I feel confident describing the analyzed sample as broadly representative, albeit with areas of over- and under-representation.

Based on Gordon & Gotch's listings for the different colonies, table 1 indicates the proportion of newspapers (overall, and by type) digitized on the date I ceased harvesting fiction from *Trove*, alongside historical population statistics (Australian Bureau of Statistics). It shows that colonies with the largest historical populations (New South Wales and Victoria) have lower proportions of newspapers digitized (an average of 25 percent for the three years of the *Directory*) than colonies with the smallest historical populations (Tasmania and Western Australia, which have an average of 53 percent of newspapers digitized for these years). This outcome makes sense: smaller historical populations supported fewer newspapers, whereas contemporary state libraries have an equal capacity to contribute to the ANDP.

The middle colonies for population size—Queensland and South Australia—do not follow this pattern. Despite having similar historical populations, the proportion of nineteenth-century Queensland newspapers that are digitized is more than double that of South Australian ones (53 versus 25 percent). This disparity relates to differences in the number of provincial newspapers: similar numbers have been digitized for the two colonies, but Queensland had much fewer titles than

Table 1. Historical population statistics and proportions of newspapers digitized (July 16, 2015), based on Gordon & Gotch listings

Colony	Type/population	1886	1888	1892
New South Wales	Proportion digitized			
	Overall	26	27	28
	Metro/suburban	39	24	32
	Provincial	24	28	27
	Population	983,518	1,044,290	1,183,157
Queensland	Proportion digitized			
	Overall	53	59	61
	Metro/suburban	36	42	42
	Provincial	65	70	71
	Population	332,311	367,166	409,676
South Australia	Proportion digitized			
	Overall	26	21	28
	Metro/suburban	42	33	54
	Provincial	22	18	23
	Population	306,710	309,453	335,392
Tasmania	Proportion digitized			
	Overall	45	43	64
	Metro/suburban	33	33	43
	Provincial	60	50	100
	Population	131,190	137,877	150,212
Victoria	Proportion digitized			
	Overall	25	23	22
	Metro/suburban	31	21	18
	Provincial	23	24	24
	Population	993,717	1,079,077	1,168,747
Western Australia	Proportion digitized			
	Overall	67	55	47
	Metro/suburban	100	100	80
	Provincial	40	29	30
	Population	40,604	43,814	58,569

South Australia (for 1892, Gordon & Gotch list twenty-one and sixty-five newspapers, respectively). Table 1 also indicates *Trove*'s slight over-representation of metropolitan newspapers—another unsurprising outcome given the relative cultural importance of such publications, their proximity to collecting libraries, and the increased likelihood of their having been preserved. For New South Wales, South Australia, and Western Australia, metropolitan newspapers are more likely (in the case of Western Australia, significantly more likely) to have been digitized than provincial ones, whereas for Victoria, rates of digitization are equivalent. For Queensland and Tasmania, a greater proportion of provincial than metropolitan newspapers are digitized due to the small number of such titles in both cases (the 1892 *Directory* lists only four provincial Tasmanian newspapers).

Although overall rates of digitization are even across the period surveyed by Gordon & Gotch, the duration is relatively short. Rod Kirkpatrick's figures for provincial New South Wales, Queensland, and Victorian newspapers represent a smaller sample (*Country* 47). But the longitudinal span (every ten years from 1850 to 1890) offers a more reliable basis for assessing the curated dataset's representativeness over time. Comparing Kirkpatrick's figures with *Trove*'s holdings indicates that, on the date harvesting for this project was finalized, 100 percent of New South Wales newspapers operating in 1850 were digitized, decreasing to 66 percent for 1860, 35 percent for 1870, 31 percent for 1880, and 27 percent for 1890. Rates of digitization for provincial Victorian and Queensland newspapers show a similar pattern over time.[31] The overrepresentation of earlier titles occurs for the same reason that newspapers from colonies with smaller historical populations are more likely to be digitized: given the substantial growth in the number of Australian newspapers across the nineteenth century, digitizing a relatively small number of titles for earlier decades captures a relatively large proportion of those in operation.

Research with the scholarly edition of extended fiction in colonial newspapers should proceed with awareness of these identified areas of overrepresentation: of newspapers from colonies with smaller populations and from earlier in the century and of metropolitan titles. It is possible that undiscovered areas of variability also exist in the relationship between the newspapers in operation and those digitized. But the available historical records suggest that *Trove*'s aim to represent the "breadth and depth" of Australian newspapers, and its practice of digitizing an increasing number of titles over time, has produced a sample capable of supporting analysis of the contents of colonial newspapers, across the nineteenth century and in the range of different colonies and metropolitan and provincial locations.

III

Creating a reliable model of fiction in nineteenth-century Australian newspapers depends not only on querying a representative sample of newspapers but on identifying the extended fiction they published and translating it into data that signifies those publication events effectively. My paratextual method exploits key features of *Trove* to discover most of the extended fiction in newspapers digitized by mid-2015, again with caveats relating to limitations of that method and of collection practices. In interpreting the harvested data, I worked closely with Carol Hetherington, who brought decades of bibliographical experience to the task.

Searching for words and phrases in mass-digitized collections is a common way in which researchers seek to realize the potential of such infrastructure for historical research. This approach underpinned an article in *Science* that announced the field of "culturomics" and sought to contribute to a history of ideas by searching for and comparing the presence of n-grams (continuous sequences of words of a set number [n]) in Google Books (Michel et al.). Mass-digitized periodical collections have been similarly investigated to support historical research ranging from dictionary compilation (J. Robinson) to exploring the trans-Atlantic circulation of jokes (Nicholson, "You"). Although these studies have produced interesting findings, searching digitized documents for designated words and phrases relies upon and tends to reinforce existing perceptions of collection contents. If I sought to identify fiction in nineteenth-century Australian newspapers by searching for titles and authors I suspected were present, those are the only titles and authors I could find.

Various strategies have been devised to analyze mass-digitized collections in less predetermined ways. The Viral Texts project, discussed in chapter 2, is highly innovative in using an algorithm to identify reprinted passages in eighteenth- and nineteenth-century periodicals by detecting "clusters of reused passages . . . within much longer documents" (Smith, Cordell, and Mullen E4): it searches collections based on words drawn from passages within the mass-digitized corpus, not those predetermined by researchers. Other projects use topological features of books or newspapers—including the relationship between print, white space, and illustration—to identify such phenomena as poetry publication (Houston) or changes in the formatting and organization of newspapers (Sherratt, "4 Million"). To discover fiction in *Trove*'s nineteenth-century newspaper holdings in a way not reliant on prior assumptions I searched for specific words and phrases, but not in the contents of articles. Rather, I focused on identifying and employing search terms that recurred in the paratexts of fiction.

Paratext refers to features that surround and inform understanding of a published text.[32] In the nineteenth century, as today, different sections of newspapers—advertising, editorials, letters, news, poetry, and fiction—had unique and consistent paratextual features. This characteristic of newspapers relates to what James Mussell calls the "generic form" of periodicals, wherein

> the repetition of formal features, both across articles within an issue and then in each issue as it appears, produces an overarching set of virtual forms that regulate the miscellany, organizing content while allowing readers to anticipate what is to come. ("Elemental" 8)

These formal features, intended to support and direct readers, can serve a similar function for automatically discovering digitized content. Words consistently used to introduce and frame extended fiction in colonial newspapers, and enabling identification of those titles, were *chapter, serial and story, novelist, tales and sketches, storyteller,* and *story and teller.* These terms were identified based on those that appeared frequently in the paratext of fiction in a random selection of newspapers surveyed in preparation for automatic harvesting, supplemented by other paratextual words that recurred in relevant results for subsequent searches.

While appropriate terms were vital, this paratextual approach successfully identified fiction because it optimized three features of *Trove*'s newspaper collection: page segmentation, manual correction of title information, and the relevance-ranking algorithm. Unlike the page-level division of content employed by *Chronicling America* and much of *Europeana Newspapers*, *Trove* segments or zones newspaper pages into articles. Although more expensive, this digitization method enables targeted searching by representing newspapers as composites of articles rather than as pages of text. Manual correction of title information is an extension of page segmentation: after zoning the pages and converting each article into a full-text file using OCR software, the contractors hired by the NLA for this aspect of digitization distinguish title information (the title, subtitle, and first four lines of text) and manually correct it with the aim of achieving 99 percent accuracy. As well as separating paratextual terms from the body of articles they introduce, this feature of digitization means that OCR errors have minimal effect on representations of paratext.

Trove's relevance-ranking algorithm works in conjunction with these two features of digitization to optimize search results. It weighs more heavily (returns to the top of the list of results) articles in which search terms appear in the manually corrected title information, further increasing assumed relevance if those terms recur in the article's body. *Chapter* was the most useful term for identifying extended fiction because it was frequently used both to introduce (appearing in the title) and to segment (appearing throughout the body of) articles of this sort. In effectively combining the generic form of newspapers with the manner of their digitization, this paratextual method achieves search results in which most of the initial thousands are fiction. This method also renders concrete the point, made in the abstract in chapter 2, that historical research with mass-digitized collections engages not with a preexisting record of the documentary past but with the effect of a sequence of transactions.

Random manual checks confirmed that this paratextual method discovered most of the fiction in the newspapers digitized by mid-2015. Additional terms, including non-English terms for non-English-language newspapers, could extend the range of fiction identified, though not greatly. In one case, a word that appeared with some frequency in the paratext of extended fiction—*part*—could not be used because it returned too high a rate of nonrelevant results: *part* was frequently used to divide nonfiction publications (for instance, "Statistics of the Colonies") and often appeared in titles not relevant to this project (for example, "Women's Part," "Australia's Part," "Part Calf, Part Horse!"). Ultimately, the choice and range of search terms balanced utility against the finite time available to conduct analysis—a condition of any research, but especially relevant to the aim of publishing a stable curated dataset from an ever-expanding mass-digitized collection.

Discovery of fiction was also impacted by gaps in the analog newspaper records digitized by *Trove* and by aspects of digitization. Analog records, print and microfilm, are sparser for provincial than for metropolitan papers, meaning that even when a newspaper is included in *Trove*, some—often a substantial proportion of—issues may not be digitized. Supplements (pages sold with newspapers but created, in part or in whole, by separate agencies) were also frequently excluded from newspaper collection practices (a well-known challenge in periodical studies).[33] As discussed further in chapter 5, my analysis of *Trove* established both the high rate of exclusion of these supplements and that they were where most provincial newspaper fiction was published. Combined with the general underrepresentation of provincial newspapers discussed above, these gaps in the analog record mean that the curated dataset understates the presence of fiction published outside metropolitan areas.

Aspects of the digital remediation of newspapers also affected the discovery and representation of fiction, though in a more limited way. While *Trove*'s practice of zoning newspaper pages into articles enabled this project, it is not always conducted accurately: articles containing fiction are occasionally combined with articles immediately preceding or following them. The first instance reduces the discovery of fiction, in that paratextual information relates to the preceding article rather than the fictional installment. But this issue is more likely to affect discovery of short than extended fiction.[34] In the second instance—of a fiction title grouped with the article that follows it—the title will likely be discovered, but its representation in the curated dataset includes unrelated digitized text. Researchers who use the curated dataset to explore individual works should check for such occurrences if seeking a reliable reading text; however, due to their rarity, these zoning errors will have minimal consequences for large-scale text analysis.

Studies that explore digitized text in the curated dataset (whether using the interface to search the contents of fiction or computational methods to analyze the textual corpus extensively) should also be aware of errors in *Trove*'s OCR-rendered text. In contrast to the manually corrected title information, the accuracy of harvested textual data is highly variable.[35] Only the final chapter of this book considers textual as opposed to bibliographical data. There I have employed strategies to moderate the effects of OCR errors on results, but text in the curated dataset has not been consistently corrected.

Enacting this paratextual method—performing the queries, exporting the data, and translating it into bibliographical and textual data in the curated dataset—relied on *Trove*'s application programming interface (API)[36] and occurred via the sequence depicted in figure 2. Queries using the defined paratextual terms were made to a PHP/SQL script [1], which used *Trove*'s API to run the search [2]. The PHP/SQL script checked each article ID in the returned results against records already in the MySQL database [3] to exclude previously identified articles. Once five thousand unique article IDs were identified and their records captured, results were exported as batches in CSV format [4]. Due to the consistency of the newspaper paratext, with some experience, assessing the general presence of fiction in a batch simply involved scrolling through the returned CSV file. If a batch was mainly composed of relevant records, the query was run again. If a batch featured multiple irrelevant records, that paratextual term, in its interaction with *Trove* at that point in time, was deemed to have exhausted its usefulness. (For each term harvesting was performed multiple times over a two-year period, yielding new results as additional newspapers were digitized.)

Although most records harvested were fiction, extensive data processing was required to confirm relevance and to create rich and reliable bibliographical data. Nonrelevant results were excluded using a variety of automatic, semiautomatic, and manual methods [5]. Batches were automatically analyzed to remove multiple duplicates (records not yet in the database but present two or more times in a single batch). Identifying and searching for words and phrases likely to occur in nonrelevant records further refined results. These changed depending on the search term used. For instance, nonrelevant results for *chapter* searches included reports of meetings of a chapter of a lodge or religious association, accounts of a chapter in the life of a town or person, and public documents such as deeds of grant and regulations divided into chapters. In this latter category, identifying titles with phrases such as *land grant* or *deed of sale* facilitated exclusion of nonrelevant records.

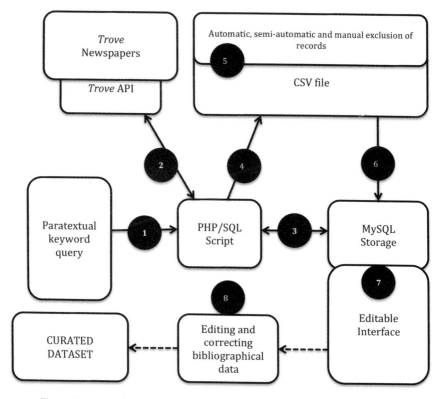

Fig. 2. Sequence for enacting paratextual method to create curated dataset

Manual checking for nonrelevant results followed these automatic and semiautomatic procedures. Sometimes, especially as the project progressed and familiar titles (in different newspapers) appeared in search results, it was possible to confirm that an article was fiction based on the information returned by *Trove*'s API. But in many cases—including the multiple records in which title information consisted only of a chapter number and/or chapter title—manual checking involved accessing the article's URL to view the digitized document and searching on and across newspaper pages to find the story's title.

Even when the API returned a full title, it was usually necessary to access—and sometimes to read—the digitized article to see if it was fiction and, if so, whether it was a short story or continued across two or more issues. Even upon reading the text, deciding if it was fiction was not always straightforward. Colonial newspapers serialized writing in a range of genres (notably history, but also geography, geology, law, politics, and travel), and the boundaries between fiction and these nonfictional genres were not as clear as today. While fictional works frequently emphasized the moral meaning and accuracy of events depicted, the nonfictional genres above often employed discursive strategies (for instance, a first-person narrator or narrative tension) that today would largely be associated with fiction. Deciding which titles were fiction and which were not was done on a case-by-case basis.

Once a batch was analyzed, CSV files were returned to the MySQL database as relevant results [6] arranged in four tables (chapter, title, author, and newspaper). An editable interface was built onto MySQL storage using the open-source software Yii [7]. Data were extensively edited and corrected through this interface [8], which also makes the curated dataset searchable, browsable, and exportable.

Investigating paratextual search results—in requiring movement back and forth between the bibliographical data extracted from *Trove* and the digitized documents that data represents—offered the necessary conditions for descriptive bibliographical modeling. As elaborated in chapter 2, one way this project aims to enhance data-rich literary history is by showcasing the critical potential of integrating modeling and descriptive bibliography. Carol and I worked to create an increasingly detailed model of extended fiction in nineteenth-century Australian newspapers by interrogating and refining representations of the historical, material, and social features of documents. This book's digital appendix 1 demonstrates the outcome of such modeling in terms of how the metadata provided by *Trove*'s API was imported, expanded, and augmented to form the fields of the curated dataset.[37]

Imported fields were employed as provided by *Trove*, with some adjustments for contextual purposes. For expanded fields, a single metadata category supplied by *Trove* became multiple fields in the curated dataset. A key area where this occurred was with *Trove*'s "heading," which represents an article's title, subtitle, and first four lines of text. To more fully model fiction in colonial newspapers, each "heading" was expanded into ten separate fields, ranging from the title and form of authorial attribution employed by newspapers to how authorial gender and nationality were inscribed in publication events and details about textual transmission (for instance, regarding copyright or translation). Although time-consuming, populating these expanded fields was greatly facilitated by data harvesting, especially as it was often possible to generalize information relevant to a single record to multiple installments (those published in the same newspaper around the same time with similar title information, excepting changes in chapter number and/or chapter title).

New fields were created for various reasons. As chapter 2 discussed, some fields highlight variation in the publication and republication of fiction: instances in which multiple author names ("publication author") were used for the same historical individual ("author") or in which different titles ("publication title") were used for a single story ("common title"). Others identify where multiple banners ("newspaper") were used for the same newspaper ("newspaper common title") or indicate whether newspapers were published in metropolitan, suburban, or provincial sites ("newspaper type"). New fields were also created for information generated from bibliographical research—for instance, authorial "gender" and "nationality"—and to categorize stories based on whether they were published in single or across multiple newspaper issues ("length"). Four newly created fields contribute to the scholarly edition's critical apparatus. "Publication sources" and "author sources" identify print and online sources by which arguments, respectively, about publication and attribution, or about authorship, were justified. "Additional information" provides further information about the fiction published, including references to other full-text records, while "nationality details" supports identification of the country of origin for fiction in complicated cases (for instance, where authors relocated during their writing career or spent extended periods in different countries).

The curated dataset publishes the bibliographical and textual data that results from this extended history of transmission [8]. It greatly expands the bibliographical record of fiction published and read in the Australian colonies. Of the 313 newspapers analyzed, 258—over 82 percent—were found to contain extended fiction. The 9,263 titles explored in the following chapters encompass over 130,000 text files and represent 6,015 individual works. As chapter 5 investigates, many of these stories were republished—sometimes on multiple occasions—in different newspapers.

Trends in extended fiction over time broadly correspond with the established account of fiction in colonial newspapers outlined earlier in this chapter. Very few titles were identified prior to the mid-1860s: only 1 in the 1820s, 8 in the 1830s, 40 in the 1840s, 55 in the 1850s, and 75 in the early 1860s. From the middle of that decade extended fiction became increasingly common, with 242 titles identified in the late 1860s, 1,093 in the 1870s, 3,241 in the 1880s, and 4,508 in the 1890s. The presence of extended fiction in Australian newspapers did decline in the final years of the 1890s—for instance, from 1,430 titles published between 1892 and 1894 to 1,340 titles from 1897 to 1899—though not with the precipitous fall that has been claimed. Indeed, and although beyond the scope of this book, a surprising discovery in analyzing *Trove* was the large amount of fiction in early twentieth-century Australian newspapers: it would seem that newspapers remained important sources of fiction in Australia even after cheap books began to be imported in large numbers.

Yet despite this general correspondence between the findings of earlier studies and the fiction discovered in this project, the account that follows differs—often radically—from the existing narrative and overturns multiple current conceptions of the influences—literary, institutional, social, political, and economic—shaping colonial literary culture and the global circulation of fiction in this period. That challenge to existing arguments is not based on access to a supposedly objective, unmediated, or comprehensive record of fiction. As this chapter demonstrates, the curated dataset on which the arguments in the second part of this book are grounded is itself an argument about nineteenth-century Australian newspaper fiction. That argument is made in the context of, and profoundly shaped by, a complex history of transmission: from the newspapers that operated in the colonies, to the documents collected, microfilmed, and digitized by the NLA, to the understanding of fiction expressed in harvesting and curating the bibliographical data. In tracing this history—including the omissions, transactions, and transformations it involves—I have sought to expose the constructed and conditional nature of the curated dataset: not in order to discount but to establish its capacity to stand as a reliable foundation for my own literary-historical arguments, and for those of others.

PART II

Fiction in the World

CHAPTER 4

Into the Unknown

Literary Anonymity and the Inscription of Reception

———— ꙮ ————

Unsurprisingly—given the ubiquity of literary anonymity and pseud-onymity in the nineteenth century—thousands of titles discovered in analyzing *Trove* were published without attribution or under an obvi-ous or discovered alias. Due to the ephemerality of newspaper pub-lication, in many cases where a title was attributed, despite the best bibliographical efforts the author's identity remains unconfirmed. Anonymous, pseudonymous, and undetermined publications pres-ent a conundrum for literary and book historians, not limited to— in fact partly produced by—the field's focus on authors: our urge to ask, as Michel Foucault put it, "From where does [this work] come, who wrote it, when, under what circumstances, or beginning with what design?" (15) We recognize that the discursive relationship of author and text (Foucault's "author function") changes over time, and that literary works have often "circulated without authors' names attached" (McGill, *American* 2).[1] Yet most literary histories, and almost all of the scholarly infrastructure they are built upon, privilege the relationship of author and text. Scholarly editions, library and collection catalogs, bibliographies, special collections, and archives all routinely organize the past, in Meredith McGill's words, by extracting "anonymous and pseudonymous texts from their disseminated condition." This paradoxically author-centered approach to literary anonymity explores "composite figures and bodies of work that did not exist and could not have existed in the era in which th[o]se texts were written" (*American* 3). It also disregards the many published works that have not been, and may never be, attached to historical individuals.

Rather than a problem that prevents analysis, the thousands of authorless works identified in this project indicate—and demand new critical approaches to understanding—the fundamentally different conceptions of literary meaning and value operating in the past. It is not simply that some stories were ascribed to authors and others were not. Exploring authorial attribution in nineteenth-century Australian newspapers reveals a spectrum of possibilities between these two poles. It also highlights the extensive information regarding authorial gender and nationality present in the publication event, whether or not these accurately describe the historical individual who wrote the work. To prevent bibliographic determinations erasing the complex ways in which authorship was represented and understood by nineteenth-century readers, this chapter considers both the authors definitively known to have published fiction in colonial newspapers and authorship as it was inscribed in these periodicals. I use these models of authorship to explore the complex ways in which authorial gender and nationality intersected with notions of cultural value in publication and reception, and the implications of that intersection for understanding the emergence and development of Australian literary culture.

The findings suggest that colonial notions of literary value were distinct from those operating in Britain and America. While women are understood to have dominated authorship of periodical fiction in these other contexts, men wrote the vast majority of extended fiction in nineteenth-century Australian newspapers and were represented as doing so. Even as British fiction was the most widely published, colonial newspapers also contained significantly more local writing than has been recognized, with the "Australian" inscription of titles implying the even greater presence of such titles. Although manifested in markedly different ways in metropolitan and provincial newspapers, in both contexts trends in authorship affirm the interest of colonial readers in British fiction (albeit a male-dominated version thereof) and suggest the cultural marginality of American writing.

While this hierarchy of value remains constant for overseas fiction, for colonial writing a significant shift occurred in the late 1870s and 1880s, when provincial newspapers became not only the major sites for publishing and promoting Australian fiction but arguably the preferred location for Australian male authors to present their work. Within the existing framework of Australian literary and book history—where metropolitan periodicals are assumed to be the major, even the only, publishers of fiction—the activities of provincial newspapers would have little import. The discovery that provincial newspapers published significantly more fiction than their metropolitan counterparts fundamentally revises that assumption. On this basis, I demonstrate the role and importance of provincial newspapers in defining early Australian literary culture, including its distinctly gendered profile.

I

Of the titles discovered in this project, 36 percent were published without attribution. While seeming to leave a clear majority of attributed titles, the representation of authorship for fiction in nineteenth-century Australian newspapers was significantly more complicated. Many stories were published under obvious pseudonyms: listed alphabetically, "A Bohemian," "A British Tourist," "A Bush Naturalist," "A Contributor," "A Correspondent," and "A Country Attorney" are the first six author names in the curated dataset. Other pseudonyms are only slightly less obvious (for instance, "A. Noble," "Mark Antony," "Sans Culottes"). Some are well known, such as "Mark Twain" for Samuel Langhorne Clemens or "Rolf Boldrewood" for Thomas Alexander Browne. Others were identified with additional research, including "Max Adeler" for Charles Heber Clark, "Johnny Ludlow" for Ellen Wood, and "Christian Reid" for Frances Christine Fisher Tiernan.

Sometimes it was comically difficult to determine if a name was a pseudonym or not. For instance, Carol Hetherington and I initially categorized "Captain Lacie" as a pseudonym before discovering an article (complete with portrait) presenting him as a historical person and "celebrated Australian writer."[2] With this evidence, and "Captain Lacie" listed as an author in *AustLit*, we designated his fiction as attributed. Only after I made this association in a published article ("Thousands" 293) did further evidence emerge supporting the first interpretation:

a story published in 1902 in the *Mercury and Weekly Courier* attributed as "By Captain Lacie (James J. Wright). Author of 'The Gem Finders,' 'In the Wake of Fortune,' 'Narratives of the Bushranging Times,' 'The Huts of Ellerslie,' &c., &c."[3] Acknowledging the uncertainty in identifying them, approximately 12 percent of fiction discovered in this project appeared under a pseudonym.

Once again, this seemingly clear statistic belies the complexity of differentiating pseudonyms and attributions for nineteenth-century Australian newspaper fiction. Should the many author names composed only of initials—"G.A.W.," "G.B.," "G.B.W.," "G.E.C."—be considered attributions? Is the use of initials intended to conceal the author's identity; to be decipherable only to certain individuals, or even to a range of readers at a designated place or time; or all of the above, in different instances? Is a woman using what is presumably her husband's name (for example, "Mrs. Walter Allingham") employing a pseudonym or following an established naming convention, one that might even make her more identifiable in a society where men tended to be the more prominent public figures? In some cases, the same form of nomenclature—such as the use of an honorific and surname, as with "Dr. Grey," "Mrs. Gurtarie," and "Miss Perry"—can have potentially different implications, for instance with respect to age or educational attainment. Because these specific author names remain unaligned with historical individuals, it is impossible to say if they are pseudonyms or not, and one can only guess at their intended meaning: are they a form of authorial discretion, an in-joke for particular readers, a way of emphasizing social standing, or again, all of the above in different instances? For some authors, the use of an honorific and surname—such as "Mrs. Oliphant"—is possible because of, and signals, the author's fame. To add to the complexity of authorial attribution, fiction was often published with signatures: a list of other works "by the author of" the title in question, whether or not that author is named. Moreover, titles that were published without attribution, or with a signature or initials only, in one instance could appear under a pseudonym or the author's legal name elsewhere. Such variability warns against interpretations that assume authors decided—or were even aware of—how their stories were attributed.

As these examples illustrate, not only were many forms of authorial attribution attached to fiction in nineteenth-century Australian newspapers, but names within the same category could have completely different—even opposite—functions and effects. Lack of attribution can also be an expression of authorial identity in itself, signifying modesty, membership in a grand collective, or insider-ship. Newspapers conventionally carried unattributed items, with bylines a mark of distinction reserved for major stories. The numerous unattributed titles identified in this project have meaning within the conventions of newspaper—as well as literary—publishing.

Taking the multiple potential implications of different forms of attribution—and nonattribution—as read, table 2 identifies seventeen author name categories employed for fiction in nineteenth-century Australian newspapers, as well as the number and proportion of titles in each. This spectrum of authorial attribution—and the fluid relationship between author and text it indicates—shows that authorship, in the sense of a definite link between a historical individual and a written text, did not provide the organizing framework for colonial newspaper fiction. As McGill says of periodical publication in antebellum

Table 2. Author name categories, 1830–99

Category	Number of titles	Percentage of titles
Attributed	2,109	23
with signature	1,338	14
Editor/translator	17	<1
with signature	2	<1
Honorific and surname	92	1
with signature	79	1
Honorific, initials, and surname	62	1
with signature	64	1
Initials and surname	463	5
with signature	253	3
Initials only	300	3
with signature	16	<1
Pseudonym	896	10
with signature	213	2
Surname only	5	<1
Unattributed	3,011	33
with signature	328	4
Total	9,247	100

America, this was a "system in which literature circulated and was read without reliable recourse to the author as originator and principle of coherence" (*American* 144).

Figure 3 explores shifts in the representation of authorship in colonial newspapers by collecting these author name categories into three broad groups. "Attributed" encompasses titles that were ascribed to an author name that has been shown or appears to be authentic, including those composed of a first name and surname, an honorific and surname (with or without initials), a surname only, or initials and a surname. "Pseudonymous" incorporates both obvious and discovered pseudonyms as well as titles attributed to an author name composed of initials only, while "unattributed" includes titles where no name, or only that of an editor or translator, was given. The figure also shows the proportion of titles in each group published with a signature. As very little fiction was discovered prior to 1865, those proportional results—and their unevenness—should be interpreted with that scarcity in mind.

The well-established nineteenth-century transition from anonymous to named authorship is apparent in figure 3, though somewhat complicated by relatively high proportions of pseudonymously authored fiction and their growth from the mid-1860s to the late 1880s: from 15 to 18 percent of all titles. And although declining significantly over this time, "unattributed" fiction still comprised 30 percent of titles in the 1890s. Notwithstanding these complications, the considerable increase in "attributed" titles—to over half (55 percent) of the extended stories in Australian newspapers by the century's end—demonstrates a clear trend toward aligning fiction with an individual author, as do trends in the allocation of signatures. Editors began routinely to assign signatures to "unattributed" and "pseudonymous" fiction in the 1860s. While emphasizing title over author, this form of attribution suggests that authors (even when not named) were increasingly understood to unite an oeuvre of works. Growth in signatures for "attributed" titles (to 24 percent of fiction in the 1890s) reinforces this association of author with oeuvre.

Despite increased attribution of fiction across the nineteenth century, and the substantial bibliographical research underpinning this project, for 38 percent of titles discovered authorial identity has not been determined conclusively.[4] With the "enigma" of literary anonymity and pseudonymity not simply a past condition that has been resolved but a continuing presence (Foucault 15), a number of possible ways forward

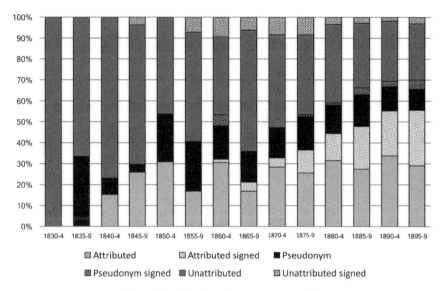

Fig. 3. Combined author name categories

suggest themselves, each with its own problems as well as recommenda-tions. The most obvious—because adopted in many literary histories—is to consider only the 62 percent of titles with authors whose identi-ties have been ascertained. Figure 4 shows this subsample of known authors (the solid line) in relation to the total number of titles (the dotted line).

In spite of the very similar shapes of these lines, known authors do not necessarily provide a reliable basis for generalizing about fiction. Authors whose names have been preserved through history or recov-ered by contemporary scholarship are, by definition, not a random sample. The reasons they are remembered might differ: perhaps their fiction was judged at the time, and/or by subsequent generations, as worth remembering, perhaps they were part of a group (such as Vic-torian women writers) whose literary talents have been reassessed in light of contemporary cultural shifts, perhaps their works were pub-lished in book editions collected by the university libraries whose col-lections formed the basis for contemporary bibliographies. Whatever the reason, these known authors have been selected for preservation or resurrection while others have not. More generally, studying litera-ture through the lens of authors whose identities are known today pre-conditions us to view the past through contemporary parameters. As

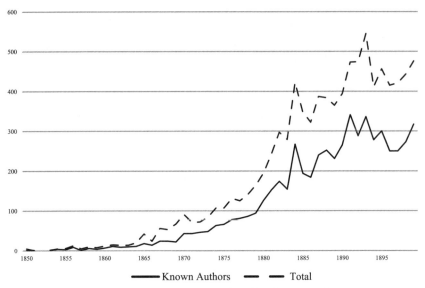

Fig. 4. Number of titles, in total and for known authors

St Clair's work and other scholarship—for instance, histories of library borrowing (Dolin, "Fiction")—attest, and as later parts of this book also demonstrate, the authors known to us today are not necessarily the same ones known to readers in the past.

Alternatively, one might deem the attribution of fiction in nineteenth-century Australian newspapers to be so distinct from contemporary formations as to render the topic of authorship irrelevant. The optimal strategy, from this perspective, would be to find new questions, categories, and approaches to elucidate the workings and values of this literary system. Rather than grouping works by authors, or author attributes (for instance, Australian or women writers), potential new arrangements might include fiction that appeared in the same newspaper or same type of newspapers (for instance, of a region, price bracket, or political persuasion), titles that were reprinted extensively, or those that were highly advertised or illustrated. One might read stories of the same genre or theme together, regardless of authorial identity, or explore networks of references established for readers by the use of signatures or by details within the publication event regarding acquisitions of copyright or sites of previous publication.

A shift away from authorship as an organizing category for reading and scholarship has benefits. Aligning fiction with aspects of its publication permits a focus on contexts of reception. It also avoids key critical impasses in contemporary literary history, including but not limited to the disproportionate power of contemporary reputation created by literary canons, the at times empowering but often ghettoizing alignment of gender with women's writing, and the continuing power of the nation to organize and limit understanding of the contours of literary, publishing, and reading culture. Certainly, the plethora of "authorless" works no doubt present in many mass-digitized collections will require non-author-centered approaches to play a greater role as literary historians increasingly investigate such records. Responding to this need, the following chapters employ some of the above strategies. But simply eschewing authorship as a category of analysis is not necessarily desirable.

For nineteenth-century Australian newspaper fiction, and literary history broadly, the author remains an important framework for at least two reasons. First, even if readers of the time did not know the identities of many authors of the fiction they read, those identities—that is, authors' backgrounds, their gender and nationality, not to mention their class, age, education, where they lived, and so on—profoundly influenced the literature produced: what they wrote and how, where and how they were published, whether and how much they were paid, and so on. For the interchange it signals between society and literature, information about authorship remains important for literary history. Second, while authorship—in the sense of a direct and unquestionable association of an individual and a body of work—was not the primary schema through which fiction in nineteenth-century Australian newspapers was published and received, this does not mean readers had no interest in the origins of stories.

In many cases, an author's gender and national or colonial origins were inscribed in publication events and functioned as important framing devices for the reception of those titles. Most obviously, a significant proportion of author names, including pseudonyms, are clearly "male" or "female," regardless of whether that gender matched that of the author. And some signatures specify an "authoress" for anonymously or pseudonymously published titles. Many pseudonyms for fiction in colonial newspapers also aligned the author with a place, either directly—for instance, "A London Man," "A Lincolnshire Clergyman," "A Mildura Lady," or "A New York Detective"—or indirectly—as with "A Bush Naturalist," "A Member of Oxford University," or "A Now Living Ex-convict." Titles and subtitles often emphasized national or proto-national origins: *Australia(n)* was the third most frequent word in titles for fiction discovered in this project (after *story* and *tale*),[5] and subtitles in the curated dataset include "A Tale of British Heroism," "A Reminiscence of the Far North-West of America," and "A Romance of the Russia of To-Day."

Information about copyright, translation, or reprinting, and frequent descriptions of stories as written "especially" for a newspaper, further associated fiction with particular national or colonial publishers, languages, or periodicals. In the absence of other indicators, prominent settings can imply that fiction originated in that part of the world. As with the gender of author names, pointers to the national or colonial origins of fiction may or may not equate to the author's actual location. Indeed, some titles or subtitles identify a story with one place, when its author is from another: "Carmeline; or, The Convict's Bride: A Romance of England and Australia Founded on Fact" is by American author Francis Durivage; "Found Guilty; or, Ralph Chandos' Fate: A Stirring Tale of the Early Days of Botany Bay" is by American Leon Lewis;[6] and "The New Editor: An Episode in the History of Warrender's Gulch, California," is by Australian author Harold W. H. Stephen. Regardless of the relationship between actual and claimed nationality, such titles clearly conveyed—and were often clearly designed to convey—messages to colonial readers about the origins of newspaper fiction.

Both actual and inscribed origins are important for understanding this literary system. Information about the historical actors who produced these stories supports exploration of the conditions under which fiction was produced and how it circulated globally; understanding how gender and nationality were inscribed in publication events enables analysis of how fiction was published and read in nineteenth-century Australian newspapers. Because these different forms of authorship can and do contradict each other—indeed, that is the premise of many feminist studies of pseudonyms—the two datasets cannot simply be combined. Either known or inscribed authorship, and hence, the conditions of either production or reception, would need to be privileged; even then, the two datasets would potentially work against each other to produce unreliable answers to either type of question.

To avoid these problems, and attend to both production and reception, I use two models of authorship. The first, for "known" authorship, represents gender and nationality only for the 62 percent of titles for which authors' identities have been verified. The second, for "inscribed" authorship, depicts gender and nationality as they were presented in nineteenth-century Australian newspapers. It does so conservatively, listing a gender only when the author name is obviously "male" or "female" and noting nationality only when it is explicitly signaled by the paratext or, in the absence of such inscriptions, is prominent in the text. For textual inscriptions, I assigned a "nationality" when the first section of a story—typically the first few paragraphs of the first harvested installment—mentioned a location or featured some detail indicating a setting (for instance, kangaroos for Australia).[7] Many stories identified in this project open with explicit geographical references. A well-known Australian example is Rolf Boldrewood's "Robbery Under Arms," which begins, "My name's Dick Marston, Sydney-side native" (#13336/I). Other textual national inscriptions, where the title was unattributed and the author's identity remains unknown, include "A Change in the Cast," which opens, "Within the walls of the substantial and convenient but withal elegant residence called Hop Villa, situated in the pleasant county of Surrey, within one hour of London Bridge terminus" (#11771/I); or "Achieving His Ransom," where the first sentence states, "Newburg was once a thriving little Missouri village, and a popular candidate for the county seat, until the Civil War stopped its growth and dwarfed its ambition" (#11770/I).

Inscribed genders and nationalities aim to model a nineteenth-century reader's initial impression, if any, about the authorship or origins of a work. While clearly it is impossible to recapture the "original meaning" of any textual event,[8] one can reasonably assume that a reader, encountering a story beginning in the "English countryside" by "John Smith" would assume a British male author. Clearly, this second dataset expresses an argument about how nineteenth-century readers interpreted publication events. For those who associate bibliometric analysis with objective historical facts, this approach will seem unreasonably speculative. Yet as earlier chapters have emphasized, this book is predicated on the view that literary data are inevitably constructed and transactional, whether they are explicitly designated so or not. Inscribed genders and nationalities represent a direct—but not exceptional—engagement with this essential condition of literary data. As with all arguments in this book, by publishing the data I make the claims and assumptions underpinning my arguments accessible to others to contest, confirm, or complement.

In total, 47 percent of titles were inscribed with an authorial gender and 79 percent with a nationality. This relatively low rate of gender inscription—more than half of all fiction is not associated with a "male" or "female" author name—emphasizes the point already made: that the author was not the primary framework through which colonial readers interpreted fiction. By contrast, national inscriptions were prevalent: paratextual associations of stories with places, and prominent geographical markers in titles, were mirrored by explicit references to place at the beginnings of stories. Establishing whether this degree of emphasis on place is unique to the stories in nineteenth-century Australian newspapers or characteristic of fiction of this period would require extensive comparative analysis. Still, this foregrounding of locations in a society in which many readers had moved from where they were born suggests a keen interest in the effects of place on experience: in remembering other locales and in narratives constructed with respect to particular spaces, including colonial ones.

Investigating this relationship between place and reception, and its implications for colonial literary culture, necessitates a note on terminology. To this point I have used, without highlighting the potential anachronism of, words such as *nation, national,* and *nationality.* Although *Australia* was a term in common use in the nineteenth century—as is reinforced by its prominence, discussed above, in the titles of newspaper fiction—the continent was not a nation until the federation of Australia in 1901. The colonies that united at this time were only six of Britain's seven Antipodean dominions. Until federation it was not inevitable that all of those colonies would come together (Western Australia was a latecomer), nor that New Zealand would be excluded. This lack of equivalence between historical and contemporary political geographies is not unique to Australia. Nineteenth-century Britain existed largely in its current form (as a nation-state composed of different countries). But America expanded from a cluster of East Coast states to occupy close to its current territory during the nineteenth century.

These histories suggest alternative geographical unities this book could have explored: English writing rather than British, for instance, or Australasian instead of Australian. Historian Alan Atkinson has proposed that the Australian colonies be understood as separate "nations," with "each of the Australasian capital cities . . . the centre of its own world. It had its own past, its own memories, its own customs, its own habits, its own hinterland, its own wealth, its own civic structure, its own ambitions" (103). As Paul Giles has done for the American context, Australian literary historians, most notably Robert Dixon, have applied this perspective to colonial fiction to explore its "intra- and inter-colonial rather than national [cartographies], albeit located within broader transnational or trans-imperial horizons" ("Before" 2). Writing this book, I was conscious that, in the colonial context, "most people who thought about their national identity were comfortably British and Victorian, or South Australian, or New South Welsh, as well as Australian" (Inglis 756).

While acknowledging the existence and importance of these layered identifications operating in Australia in the nineteenth century— and indeed, today—I use the terminology of the nation for two reasons. The first, prosaic, one is for ease of reference: I have not found a better collective term to describe where in the world the fiction in Australian newspapers came from than a range of national contexts. But I also focus on the literary production and reception of the Australian colonies as a whole, rather than primarily as separate entities or "nations," because the book's findings repeatedly align literary culture with that protonational unity. As the rest of this chapter shows, colonial newspaper editors and readers shared a preference for particular types of writing—by men, and by British and Australian authors—and the similarities between metropolitan (and between provincial) newspapers from different colonies were more marked than those between metropolitan and provincial newspapers of the same colony. The subsequent two chapters highlight, in turn, how regularly newspapers in different colonies published the same titles and thematic distinctions between the American, Australian, and British fiction published in these newspapers. Although this book considers the century, and especially the four decades, prior to Australian federation, my claim is that an Australian literary culture and tradition was already in evidence, and considerably more distinctive and independent than many transnational literary scholars envision.

II

Analyzing known and inscribed authorship indicates gender and national trends that contradict prevailing conceptions of nineteenth-century fiction, as it is understood to have appeared in colonial newspapers and more broadly. Both authorship models demonstrate substantially fewer stories by women/"women" in these newspapers than current understandings of the gendering of nineteenth-century periodical fiction would imply. There is also considerably more local writing than would be anticipated based on a core argument of the "transnational turn" in Australian literary studies: that colonial readers overwhelmingly preferred overseas, mainly British, fiction.

Numerous studies of nineteenth-century British and American fiction emphasize the dominance of women writers.[9] This situation is attributed to the perception at the time of fiction readers as women, and the subsequently devalued status of fiction, especially in periodicals.[10] Contrasting the gender trend in Britain and America, men wrote the majority (65 percent) of titles by known authors in colonial newspapers, with inscribed gender trends reinforcing this male domination. For a substantially higher proportion of titles the author name is "male" (31 percent) than "female" (16 percent), and considering only those titles where gender was inscribed, proportions of "male" and "female" authors closely resemble the results for known authors, with 67 percent of titles by "men" and 33 percent by "women."

Figure 5 presents gender proportions over time, with the solid and dotted lines indicating known and inscribed authorship, respectively. Bars depict the proportions of all titles inscribed as "male" or "female"; their relatively small size reinforces the point that the author—including the author's gender—was not the primary framework through which colonial newspaper fiction was presented or perceived, while their growth over time shows that both "male" and "female" authorship were progressively more likely to be indicated as the attribution of fiction, overall, increased.

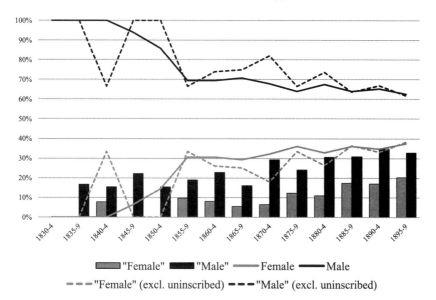

Fig. 5. Gender proportions for known and inscribed authorship

According to these results, fiction in colonial newspapers was consistently more likely to be written by men than women and, where gender was inscribed, to be presented as "male" rather than "female" authored. The first of these trends implies that, when acquiring British and American fiction, editors deliberately chose rarer, male-authored titles over more common, female-authored ones. The latter trend—especially the consistently higher rate of titles inscribed as "male" authored than known to be so—suggests that editors were keener to advertise male than female writers. Figure 5 also shows growth in fiction by women (and "women") over time. This is the opposite trend to that described in other Anglophone markets, where male authorship is understood to increase over the nineteenth century as fiction writing became more prestigious; this is a difference I return to in the next section.

If we accept that a title was more likely to be attributed to an individual when its authorship was perceived as important or prestigious, gender trends in attribution—specifically, whether authors known to be male or female were represented as such—can be used to explore editorial assumptions about readerly interest. Comparing known and inscribed gender trends reinforces the claim that editors believed their readers would be particularly interested in men's writing: fiction by known men was substantially more likely to be attributed to them (69 percent) than was fiction by known women (57 percent), and less likely to be published pseudonymously (10 versus 15 percent) or to be unattributed (21 versus 27 percent). Although the practice was surprisingly uncommon in either direction, where the gender of the author is known and a gender was inscribed, fiction by women was over ten times more likely to be published with a male pseudonym than vice versa.[11] Editors make decisions to increase the circulations of their newspapers. That these editors chose male-authored fiction, and fore-grounded its real or inscribed presence, suggests that they perceived stories by men to be of greater interest to their readers and advantageous to sales.

As with gender, national trends contradict existing accounts of nineteenth-century literary culture, in this case, the colonial relationship to Britain. Perhaps partly in reaction against the vigorous cultural nationalism of earlier scholarship, research associated with the "transnational turn" in Australian literary studies has aligned colonial literary culture predominantly with non-Australian literature. In the words of Elizabeth Webby, Sydney University's Chair of Australian Literature from 1990 to 2007, "For much of the nineteenth century and indeed afterwards, Australian readers were mainly interested in books by English authors" ("Colonial" 50). As noted in the introduction, such arguments are often based on empirical evidence of the predominance of British books in the colonies, including in the records and activities of booksellers (Askew and Hubber 115), lending libraries (Dolin, "First"; Dolin, "Secret"), and institutional reading groups (Lyons; Webby, "Not").

For the main source of reading material in the colonies—newspapers—national trends confirm the predominance, and cultural importance, of British fiction. Yet they also challenge the perception that local writing was rare and of little interest to readers. With the exception of two titles—one Australian, the other South African[12]—all of the small amount of fiction in colonial newspapers discovered prior to 1845 was British. The bars in figure 6 show the proportions of fiction by known nationalities from this time to the end of the nineteenth century, while the lines show the rates of inscription of different nationalities.

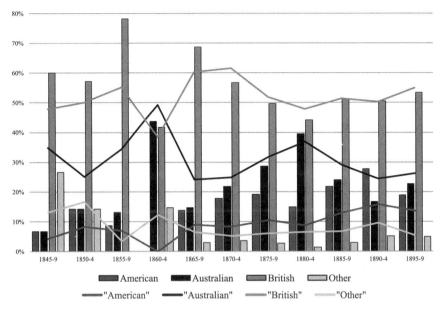

Fig. 6. National proportions for known and inscribed authorship

British fiction clearly remained dominant after 1845, representing half (51 percent) of all titles by known authors. But it was not the only fiction in colonial newspapers. Americans wrote one in every five (21 percent of) titles by known authors. Along with a small proportion (4 percent) of fiction by authors from other nations—especially France, Germany, and New Zealand—this substantial presence of American fiction shows that editors did not limit themselves to British writing when sourcing content from overseas. Australian fiction was slightly more prevalent than American, with colonial writers responsible for around one-quarter (24 percent) of titles by known authors. The population, and subsequent pool of authors, in the colonies was much smaller than in Britain or the United States, especially early in the century.[13] As late as 1891, the non-Indigenous population of all the Australian colonies was 3.24 million. The United Kingdom's population was more than ten times greater, at approximately 35 million, with America's population almost twice that again, at 63 million. Given this disparity in population sizes, the finding that colonial authors contributed half as many titles as British writers, and more fiction than American authors, reinforces the significance of their contribution to extended fiction in nineteenth-century Australian newspapers.

Referring to the 1870s and 1880s, Morrison has estimated that one-fifth of fiction published in this context was Australian ("Serial" 315). While the overall proportion reported here (24 percent) might seem to differ in only a small degree from this earlier estimate, Australian fiction was more widely published in the decades Morrison discusses, comprising 30 percent of titles by known authors in the 1870s and 1880s and as much as 40 percent in the early 1880s. Moreover, Morrison proposes a substantial decline in local fiction in Australian newspapers the 1890s, whereas the results for known authors in figure 6 indicate that a fifth (20 percent) of such titles were Australian in this decade. Finally, while Morrison's figure is an estimate based on what she acknowledges is a relatively small sample, the fiction identified in this project constitutes a substantial increase in the bibliographical record of Australian literature. As well as multiple new sites of publication for previously recorded titles, this project has uncovered new works of Australian fiction, as well as new authors, with an illustrative and selective list of these discoveries offered in digital appendix 2.

This finding that Australian fiction constituted one in every four titles by known authors in colonial newspapers could still be congruent with readers' lack of interest in such writing. In this scenario, editors published Australian writing because it was more readily accessible and/or cheaper than overseas fiction. But they did not seek to foreground its origins, and might even have concealed them, publishing colonial stories that appeared, to all intents and purposes, to come from Britain or elsewhere. Working against this interpretation is the similar shape of known and inscribed trends for Australian/"Australian" fiction in figure 6, including the higher proportion of inscribed than known titles in most periods and overall.[14] Given how the national inscription of fiction is determined—a story must appear to come from that place—these parallel trends in Australian/"Australian" fiction suggest two things: first, that colonial writing was not only present but concerned to represent new (to Europeans) Australian places, and second, that editors were interested in advertising the local origins of this fiction to their readers. These trends indicate, in other words, that editors perceived a colonial readership for fiction about Australia.

The broader argument I am proposing—that the colonial popu-

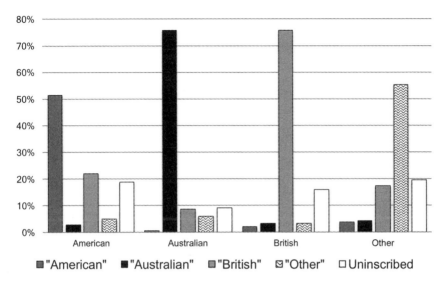

Fig. 7. Proportion of titles by authors of known nationalities as nationality was inscribed

larity of British fiction was concurrent with interest (authorial, editorial, readerly) in explicitly Australian writing—finds further support in more direct comparison of known and inscribed national trends. Figure 7 depicts the national inscription of fiction by known authors. For every national group, fiction in nineteenth-century Australian newspapers was significantly more likely to be inscribed (paratextually or textually) in accordance with the author's known nationality than otherwise. But the strength of this association varied, with the most substantial correlation between known and inscribed nationalities for British and Australian writers: 76 percent of titles by authors in both groups were inscribed in accordance with their known nationality, whereas this is the case for only 51 percent of titles by known American authors, and 55 percent by those known to be from other national contexts.

Key aspects of the results in figure 7 reinforce the interest of colonial readers in British writing. The prevalent inscription of stories by known British authors as "British" shows that, as well as sourcing much of their fiction from Britain, colonial editors were keen to make the origins of such writing apparent. Indeed, "British" origins were often presented even for fiction from other places: titles by known American and other authors were inscribed as "British" in 22 and 17 percent of cases, respectively. Such inscriptions suggest that editors were often drawn to titles that appeared to come from Britain or composed the paratext of stories to make this seem to be so.

Yet the equally prevalent inscription of known Australian fiction as "Australian" affirms the simultaneous interest of colonial editors and readers in local writing. It shows that editors were equally likely to highlight the local as the British origins of fiction. Rather than publishing Australian fiction only as a matter of convenience or commerce, editors perceived and responded to a market for writing about Australia. Although present in small proportions, the "Australian" fiction by non-Australian authors (3 percent of titles by known American and British writers; 4 percent of those by authors of other nationalities) reinforces the point that colonial editors sought to publish writing that appeared to originate locally. In some cases editors (or authors or adaptors) even appear to have modified locations and characters in non-Australian fiction to create this impression. Thus, American author Laura Jean Libbey's "Florabel's Lover; or, Rival Belles" was reprinted in multiple Australian newspapers as "The Rival Belles of Parramatta: A Charming Love Story of Intense and Thrilling Interest," and "Old Sleuth's" "The American Detective in Russia" was serialized in several Australian newspapers as "Barnes, the Australian Detective." Colonial lending libraries and literary institutions might have privileged British fiction, as authors such as Webby have argued. But these trends in known and inscribed nationality suggest that they did so in the context of an active and extensive newspaper industry where Australian fiction was both prevalent and prominent.

As chapter 2 explored, books—particularly those collected by university libraries—are more likely to enter the bibliographical record than more ephemeral forms of publication. While historical forms of publication work against the construction of comprehensive bibliographies, considering the inscription as well as the historical fact of authorship provides an important ballast for literary history: one capable, in this case, of both enlarging the record of Australian literature and indicating scope for future expansion. Although British writing undoubtedly dominated colonial newspapers, trends in known and inscribed nationality indicate that literary and book historians—arguably especially in the recent transnational turn—have underestimated the scale of Australian fiction circulating in the nineteenth century, as well as the importance of fiction from and about places in Australia to colonial publishing and reading. Combined with the general male-dominated authorship of fiction in these newspapers, these results clearly imply that literary culture in the colonies was not derivative of Britain's but had its own distinctive characteristics and preferences.

III

As would be expected from these results, considering gender and nationality together indicates that authorship was male dominated across all national groups, both as this information is known and inscribed. Of known authors, men wrote 56 percent of American fiction, 64 percent of British fiction, and 71 percent of fiction from other national contexts, and where both gender and nationality were inscribed, "men" were responsible for 75 percent of "American," 62 percent of "British," and 74 percent of "other" fiction. Local author-ship was exceptionally male dominated: 75 percent of known Austra-lian fiction in colonial newspapers was by men, with the same pro-portion by "Australian men" where both gender and nationality were inscribed. These combined trends reinforce the claim that literary culture developed differently in Australia than in Britain. But they obscure variations within the literary system. With the exception of Western Australia,[15] gender and national trends are similar regard-less of the colony in which the newspaper was published. Considering metropolitan and provincial newspapers separately, however, dem-onstrates considerable variation in gender and national trends from overall results, and between the two sites of publication.

In exploring these differences, paratextual features—including the inscription of fiction, details about copyright, and the attribu-tion of titles—support a move beyond the blunt presence of differ-ent national literatures to explore the complex frameworks of cultural value organizing literary culture in the colonies. This approach high-lights the importance of British fiction in both metropolitan and pro-vincial newspapers, particularly in contrast to the cultural marginality of American writing. It also demonstrates a profound change, in the late 1870s and early 1880s, in the publishing of Australian—especially

Australian men's—fiction. If only metropolitan newspapers are considered, the 1880s and 1890s are a period of growth in colonial women's fiction concurrent with a decline in the value of local writing. I show, instead, that Australian men's fiction shifted to provincial newspapers. Rather than being excluded from metropolitan periodicals, it seems likely that Australian male authors were drawn to the provincial promotion—even the privileging—of local fiction. These findings cast critically neglected provincial newspapers as not only the leading publishers of fiction in the colonies but major sites in the development—and gendering—of early Australian literary culture.

Figures 8 and 9 represent gender and national trends in metropolitan and provincial newspapers, respectively. The dotted black lines and secondary axes show the number of titles published in the two locations for each five-year period, solid lines indicate what proportion of known titles were by American, Australian, and British writers,[16] and the bars depict the proportions of titles in each national category written by known male authors. In exploring metropolitan and provincial publishing trends I only consider the period from 1865 to the end of the nineteenth century, as this is when the vast majority (98 percent) of fiction discovered in this project appeared.

Although some literary historians have noted the presence of fiction in provincial colonial newspapers (Law, "Savouring"; Morrison, "Contribution"; Morrison, "Retrieving"; Stewart), most have viewed the phenomenon as rare—and pirated when present. Yet comparing the number of titles in the two graphs shows that provincial newspapers published substantially more extended fiction than their metropolitan counterparts. Of the titles identified in this project, approximately thirty-eight hundred appeared in metropolitan newspapers, compared with fifty-two hundred in provincial ones.[17] And given the underrepresentation of provincial newspapers in *Trove*, and aspects of collection and digitization that limit discovery of their fictional contents (see chapter 3), it is almost certain that the disparity in rates of fiction publication was even greater.

As figure 8 shows, metropolitan newspapers were overwhelmingly dominated by British fiction: while British authors were responsible for half (51 percent) of the titles by known authors overall, this is the case for almost two in every three such titles (63 percent) in metropolitan newspapers. Multiple factors align such publishing with the perceived

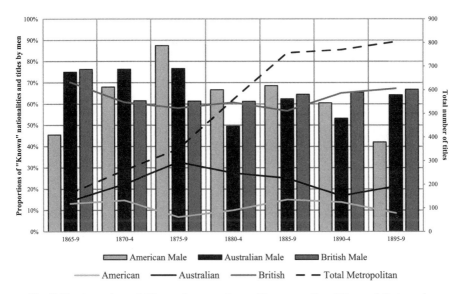

Fig. 8. Total number of titles and proportions of known nationalities and their male authorship in metropolitan newspapers

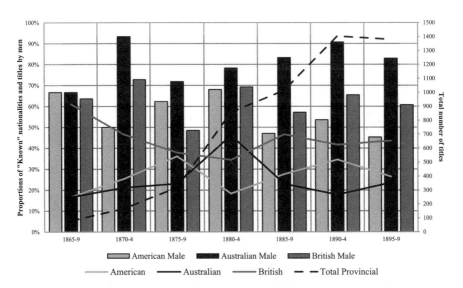

Fig. 9. Total number of titles and proportions of known nationalities and their male authorship in provincial newspapers

cultural value of British fiction, including gender trends. Reinforcing the orientation of colonial editors and readers to men's writing generally, in metropolitan newspapers men wrote the majority of fiction in all national categories. But British fiction was the most male dominated: 65 percent of known British titles were by male authors,[18] with the stable rate of such authorship suggesting that editors consistently made deliberate choices to publish British fiction by men.

Working again on the assumption that a title was more likely to be attributed to an author if that author was perceived as important or prestigious, trends in attribution reinforce this orientation toward British—and British men's—writing. British fiction in metropolitan newspapers was more likely to be attributed to a named author than was fiction from other national categories: this was the case with 76 percent of British titles, compared with 69 percent of American and 61 percent of Australian titles. And British men's fiction was more likely to be attributed to them (80 percent) than was fiction by British women (69 percent). Given the cultural prominence of metropolitan newspapers, the dominance of British men's writing in these publications emphasizes the importance of both men's and British fiction to literary value in the colonies.

Gender trends in the publication and attribution of known American fiction in metropolitan newspapers support the general focus of colonial editors and readers on men's fiction. Men wrote a majority of the American fiction in metropolitan newspapers (62 percent), and titles by American men were more likely to be attributed to them (77 percent) than were those by American women (58 percent). However, American fiction in metropolitan newspapers made up a much lower proportion (12 percent) than British fiction (63 percent), and indeed, was published at almost half the rate of its appearance overall (21 percent). The cultural peripherality implied by this low rate of publication is emphatically reinforced by the likelihood that much of this American fiction probably appeared without payment.

The United States did not sign an international copyright agreement until 1891, when the Chace Act extended limited protection to foreign copyright holders in America, thus gaining some protection for American authors outside that country's borders. A statement by the editors of the *Australian Journal* in 1873 suggests that American writing was widely reprinted without payment. Responding to accusations of plagiarism of American fiction, they wrote that "we see our own original papers—both stories and poetry—so frequently copied by American periodicals, that we never have any hesitation about extracting American productions that are worth copying" (cited in Johnson-Woods, *Index* 7). Multiple other aspects of fiction publication in nineteenth-century Australian newspapers bolster the idea that, having no legal requirement to pay for American stories, editors felt little or no moral obligation to do so.

British fiction—particularly by well-known authors—frequently appeared with explicit claims of copyright in metropolitan newspapers. Some statements regarding the purchase of rights to publication were general: for instance, that the title was "published by special arrangement with the author" or that the "right of publishing . . . has been purchased by the proprietors" of the newspaper. Others were highly specific regarding the extent and nature of copyright: for example, that it was for Australasia as a whole or in a designated colony, exclusive or with the right to reprinting. The presence of such statements resonates with what Sarah Ailwood and Maree Sainsbury describe as the exceptional adherence of Australian colonies, of all British dominions, to copyright law (1).

Similar claims regarding rights to publish were rarely made for American fiction. If the source of American fiction was noted, it was typically the periodical from which a title was taken. Literary journals and monthly magazines (such as the *Argonaut, Harper's Magazine, Lippincott's Monthly Magazine,* and *Scribner's Monthly*) were prominent in this respect. But Australian newspapers also listed major American daily and weekly newspapers and pulp magazines (including the *Argosy, Detroit Free Press, New York Herald,* and *Yankee Blade*) as sources of fiction. Such periodicals were brought to the colonies on ships that passed through American ports on the way to Australia from Britain. It would seem that colonial editors selected and published fiction freely from these copies.

A decline in the proportion of American fiction in metropolitan newspapers after 1891 further supports the idea that, prior to the Chace Act, colonial newspapers reproduced such writing without payment, in that publication was reduced once a legal framework for copyright existed. While American fiction made up 15 percent of known titles in metropolitan newspapers in the late 1880s, by the late 1890s this rate had fallen to 9 percent, with an even more rapid rate of decline in provincial publications.[19] As I discuss in the next chapter, some American authors—including Bret Harte, Julian Hawthorne, Mark Twain, and Hjalmar Hjorth Boyesen—were represented by international syndication agencies operating in the colonies and received payment for at least some publications of their fiction. But these exceptions do not contravene the general lack of payment for American fiction, particularly as these syndicated American authors were published less frequently than British authors represented by the same companies.[20] Given that, for much of the nineteenth century, newspaper editors could acquire American fiction for free, the low rate at which it was published in metropolitan newspapers—especially in comparison to the prevalence of British fiction, which was paid for—indicates the marginal status afforded to the former and the priority given to the latter.

Based only on the nationalities of known authors, provincial newspapers seem also to have privileged British over American fiction, though less markedly than metropolitan papers. Although British fiction was still the single largest national category by known authors in provincial newspapers, it was published at a substantially lower rate (42 percent) in that context than in the metropolitan one (63 percent). Provincial newspapers also published American fiction at more than double—almost triple—the rate of metropolitan newspapers (28 as opposed to 12 percent). Yet the presentation of fiction indicates that, with respect to overseas writing, provincial newspapers maintained the same hierarchy of cultural value as metropolitan ones, greatly preferring British, particularly British men's, writing over American fiction.

The clearest indicator of this distinction in cultural value is the disparity that figure 9 shows in rates of male authorship for British and American fiction. The variable rate of publication of male-authored British fiction in provincial newspapers over time—particularly compared to its stability in metropolitan newspapers—suggests that provincial editors were less consistently able to secure such fiction. But even with this variability, essentially the same proportion of known British titles were by men in provincial as in metropolitan newspapers (62 and 65 percent, respectively). In contrast, American fiction in provincial newspapers had the highest rate of known female authorship of any national category in either context (48 percent). The cultural priority accorded to men's and British fiction in provincial newspapers is sustained by trends in attribution. Although rates of attribution of men and women authors were less divergent than in metropolitan periodicals, in provincial newspapers fiction by both British and American men was more likely to be attributed to them than was fiction by British and American women (this was the case with 61 and 63 percent of titles by men in these respective national categories compared with 49 and 54 percent of titles by women).

The relatively high rate of female authorship of American fiction has much to do with the prevalence of romance fiction among these titles and of female authors of that genre. American women (or "women") romance authors were among the most widely published in provincial newspapers. These include the most featured author in this context, "Bertha M. Clay," as well as the second, fourth, equal sixth, and eighth most published: Mrs. Georgie Sheldon, Harriet Lewis, Emma Garrison Jones, Laura Jean Libbey, and Eliza A. Dupuy, respectively. This growth in American romance fiction contributes substantially to the declining proportion of American fiction by known male authors, from 67 percent of such titles in the late 1860s to 45 percent in the late 1890s.

Due to the scale of fiction in provincial newspapers, this trend in American romance fiction contributes significantly to growth in fiction by women overall, noted in the previous section. There I remarked that gender trends in Australian newspapers moved in the opposite direction to those observed elsewhere—with the presence of women writers growing as the novel's cultural value increased across the nineteenth century. The association of this gender trend with romance fiction resolves that apparent tension and maintains the recognized association of women's authorship with devalued cultural forms. This doubly devalued status of much American writing in provincial newspapers— by women in a cultural context that privileged men's writing and in a genre perceived as inconsequential, then as now—indicates that, despite relatively high rates of publication, American fiction occupied a similarly marginal position in these sites as in metropolitan ones.

The national inscription of fiction convincingly upholds this interpretation, while reinforcing the importance attached to British writing in provincial newspapers. Remarkably, one in every four (25 percent of) titles by known American authors published in this context was inscribed, paratextually or textually, as "British," rising to almost one in every three (31 percent) if only titles inscribed with a national origin are considered. (In contrast, "British" inscription of known American fiction occurs with only one in every ten such titles in metropolitan newspapers, and the reverse is almost never true: only 2 percent of known British fiction was inscribed as "American" in either metropolitan or provincial newspapers.) These trends in national inscription indicate that, when provincial editors published American fiction, they often chose titles that appeared to come from Britain. Such fiction allowed them to represent British culture to their readers at low—if any—cost to the newspapers.

"British" inscription is also common among titles by unknown authors, which comprised rather more of the fiction published in provincial than in metropolitan newspapers (42 as opposed to 34 percent). When nationality was inscribed for such works in provincial newspapers, 57 percent were presented as "British," compared with only 38 percent of titles by unknown authors in the metropolitan context. Whether this unknown fiction was by obscure British writers or by equally obscure writers from other national contexts, as with the "British" fiction by known American authors, these titles offered provincial newspaper editors a presumably cheap way to publish fiction that appeared to come from Britain. Due to the widespread "British" inscription of provincial newspaper fiction, in the cases where nationality was paratextually or textually inscribed, almost the same proportion of titles were "British" in these newspapers (51 percent) as in metropolitan ones (53 percent).

Summarizing an argument made in much recent work on colonial literary and reading culture, Tim Dolin quips that nineteenth-century Australian readers were primarily interested in "bad literature from somewhere else" ("Secret" 130). Certainly, not only American romances but most of the fiction in both metropolitan and provincial newspapers in this period was in popular genres, so if "bad" is a synonym for "popular" I agree with Dolin on this point. With respect to overseas fiction, I would refine his statement in two ways: the "somewhere else" that colonial readers were mainly interested in was Britain; American fiction was accorded an inferior status in both metropolitan and provincial newspapers, despite its high rates of publication in the latter. And the "bad literature" that colonial readers primarily wanted to read was that written by men.

Considering how local fiction was published and presented challenges Dolin's point about readers simply preferring fiction from "somewhere else" more specifically: in both metropolitan and provincial newspapers, Australian fiction was accorded more status than American. In metropolitan newspapers, such relative status is demonstrated by rates of publication. Although local fiction had a marginally lower presence in metropolitan newspapers than overall—23 as opposed to 24 percent of titles by known authors—this still means it was published at almost twice the rate of American fiction (12 percent). Although some authors provided fiction to colonial periodicals for free—presumably for the pleasure or prestige of seeing their writing in print—many were paid, some a substantial amount.[21] The likelihood that metropolitan newspaper editors paid for much of the Australian fiction they published and little of the American, but still published twice the number of titles in the former category, indicates the greater standing of the local product.

The overall equivalence in rates of American and Australian fiction in provincial newspapers—28 and 26 percent of titles by known authors, respectively—belies the generally greater presence of American titles: notwithstanding a significant surge in local fiction in the early 1880s, as figure 9 indicates, in most periods more American than Australian fiction was published. Yet the greater value accorded to local over American writing is arguably even clearer in the provincial context. Such value is apparent in the national inscription of fiction: the inscribed nationality matches the known one for only 47 percent of American titles compared with 76 percent of Australian fiction. In other words, provincial newspaper editors were significantly more likely to highlight the local than the American origins of fiction. More particularly, the shift that occurs in the site of publication of local authors—from metropolitan to provincial newspapers in the late 1870s and early 1880s—indicates the investment, by some quarters of the provincial press at least, in Australian fiction, especially by men.

Figure 8 shows the national and gender trends constituting one side of this shift. While the presence of local fiction in metropolitan newspapers increased from the late 1860s to the late 1870s, after this time it declined: from around 33 percent of titles by known authors in the late 1870s to only 17 percent in the early 1890s (albeit with a slight rise—to 21 percent—in the second half of that decade). Gender trends changed more dramatically. In the late 1860s and 1870s, the male-dominated authorship of Australian fiction matched and often exceeded the general male orientation of fiction in metropolitan newspapers, with a clear majority (76 percent) of such titles by men. That proportion fell suddenly in the early 1880s, to slightly less than half (49 percent) of known Australian fiction published. Even the higher average rate of male authorship of Australian titles across the final two decades of the nineteenth century (58 percent) is considerably lower than for either British or American fiction in metropolitan newspapers.

These shifts in national and gender proportions are concurrent with notable changes in the type of fiction published and its presentation. Prior to the 1880s, metropolitan newspapers emphasized the local origin of the Australian fiction they published. Bush sketches and colonial adventure fiction were prominent, and a clear majority of titles were inscribed as "Australian": many titles referenced Australia or places therein, colonial settings were foregrounded, and fiction was often advertised as "specially written" for that newspaper. In other cases, pseudonyms advertised local authorship: for instance, "Old Boomerang" (the pen name employed by journalist J. R. Houlding) was the most widely published colonial writer in this period. Male authorship of local fiction was also highlighted, not only in the male orientation of the prominent genres but in the representation of gender and nationality. Among titles where both were inscribed, "Australian" fiction was the most likely of all national categories to be attributed to a "male" writer in metropolitan newspapers.[22] Fiction by colonial men was also significantly more likely to be attributed to them than was fiction by colonial women.[23]

With the growing presence, from the early 1880s, of Australian women's fiction in metropolitan newspapers, romances and children's stories became more prominent, and the emphasis on local origins abated (with fewer paratextual or textual references to Australian places). Whereas in earlier decades, the prominent local authors in metropolitan newspapers were men, in the final two decades of the nineteenth century they were women. In the 1880s the first and third most widely published Australian authors were women who have subsequently become part of the Australian literary canon: Ada Cambridge and Catherine Helen Spence. In second position was Onyx, the pseudonym used by Leontine Cooper, a prominent advocate for women's suffrage in Australia at this time. Children's writer Ethel Turner was the most published Australian author in metropolitan newspapers in the 1890s, while journalist and poet Mary Hannay Foott and one of Australia's first internationally renowned authors, Rosa Praed, were fourth and fifth, respectively. There were still fewer Australian women than men contributing fiction to metropolitan newspapers in these final decades: this project has identified fifty-three individual Australian women authors, compared with eighty-seven men. But women were slightly more likely to publish a large number of titles and equally likely to contribute a single one.

In an article from an earlier project, analyzing gender trends in the authorship of Australian novels, I attributed growth in Australian women's writing from the 1880s to demographic and social factors: the increased number of women in colonial populations and the earlier likelihood of women working outside the home in Australia than in Britain or America ("Graphically" 440, 443). Elsewhere, noting the greater likelihood of Australian women achieving book publication in Britain than their more numerous male counterparts, I proposed that the representation of colonial literary culture as male dominated might have been more a defensive response to women's greater cultural success overseas than a description of reality (*Reading* 128). That many of the colonial women writers who published in metropolitan newspapers contributed to, or were responsible for, their families' earnings upholds my point about the social and financial freedoms (and responsibilities) afforded to Australian women.[24] The prevalence of their fiction in metropolitan newspapers might seem, likewise, to add weight to what I described as their greater cultural success: to indicate that colonial women writers were more likely to be published in prestigious locations not only in Britain but in the colonies too.

Yet this latter argument is at odds with aspects of the nature and presentation of Australian women's fiction in metropolitan newspapers in the 1880s and 1890s that suggest the relatively low cultural value accorded to it. Given colonial literary culture's orientation toward men's writing and the male-dominated authorship of British and American fiction in metropolitan newspapers, the high rate of women's authorship of Australian titles and the prominence of female-oriented genres (romance and children's fiction) suggest that it occupied a similar position in metropolitan periodicals as American fiction did in provincial ones: feminized and culturally marginalized. Supporting this view is the relatively low proportion of titles by known Australian women attributed to them in the 1880s and 1890s (60 percent) even as their presence increased. By comparison, 75 percent of fiction by known British women in metropolitan newspapers was attributed to them, as was 83 percent by known British men.

Taken together, these trends in the publication, inscription, and attribution of fiction suggest that greater cultural value was attached to local writing in metropolitan newspapers when male authors predominated, before 1880, than after, when Australian women's fiction had a strong presence. If only metropolitan newspaper fiction is considered—as has largely been the case in Australian literary studies previously—the shift from male to female authorship, and from fiction where "Australian-ness" is frequently emphasized to fiction where it is not, might appear simply to indicate a devaluing of local writing. Perhaps the social and demographic conditions referenced above meant that more Australian women were contributing fiction to newspapers, so this activity was accorded less prestige; perhaps colonial fiction was devalued for some other reason, and the resulting decline in male authors wishing to contribute created opportunities for women. Whatever the cause, given what I have described as the cultural influence of metropolitan newspapers, it seems almost inevitable that these periodicals would direct changes in literary culture in the colonies.

Trends in provincial newspaper fiction cast a different light on the timing and suddenness of these shifts in the publishing practices of metropolitan newspapers. Rather than Australian men's fiction declining from the late 1870s, some parts of the provincial press invested in such writing, emphasizing and promoting its importance and drawing those authors away from metropolitan publication. Prior to the late 1870s, there was little of any fiction—including Australian—in provincial newspapers. This project has discovered only twenty-four titles by known Australian authors in provincial newspapers before 1877, compared with one hundred and six in metropolitan papers. There was little overlap in the authors published, with fiction by only three writers—Marcus Clarke, James Conroy, and N. Walter Swan— appearing in both metropolitan and provincial sites.

However, as figure 9 shows, from the early 1880s provincial publication expanded dramatically, particularly with respect to Australian fiction. In fact, the change began in 1877. For that year and the following two, this project identified more titles (thirty-four) by known Australian authors in provincial newspapers than in all previous years. As the presence of fiction in these newspapers increased rapidly in the early 1880s, Australian authors contributed a larger proportion of known titles (46 percent) than any other national group. Such attention to local fiction was overwhelmingly focused on men's writing: men wrote 83 percent of known Australian titles published in provincial newspapers in these final two decades of the nineteenth century, the highest rate of publication of men's fiction for any period or any national group in either type of newspaper. In the early 1890s, men were responsible for nine in every ten (91 percent of) titles by known Australian authors in provincial newspapers.

This dramatic shift in the publication of Australian men's fiction, from metropolitan to provincial newspapers, was also apparent at the level of individual authors. From the late 1870s, many colonial male authors who had previously published in metropolitan newspapers began appearing in provincial ones, including Grosvenor Bunster, Angus McLean, Atha Westbury, and Robert P. Whitworth. Provincial newspapers also featured fiction by a range of new local male writers, such as Donald Cameron, E. Charles, Henry John Congreve, David Hennessey, Harold M. Mackenzie, Frank Morley, John Silvester Nottage, and Harold W. H. Stephen. Many of these men wrote in genres—especially colonial adventure—that had previously dominated local fiction in the metropolitan context. The valuing of local fiction suggested by this investment in its publication and emphasis on men's writing is reinforced by the attribution of fiction in provincial newspapers, where Australian fiction overall, and by men particularly, was the most likely to be attributed of all categories.[25]

The sudden and dramatic nature of this shift implies new opportunities for publication opening up rather than a more gradual cultural move away from or toward a certain type of writing. The implication that, in the 1880s and 1890s, Australian male authors were drawn to provincial newspapers rather than excluded from metropolitan ones is reinforced by two further publishing trends. First is the capacity of colonial men to publish in both sites. While Ada Cambridge is the only notable example of a local woman writer able to achieve this feat, in the 1880s and 1890s multiple male authors—including Marcus Clarke, James Crozier, David G. Falk, N. Walter Swan, Owen Suffolk, Atha Westbury, and James Joseph Wright—had fiction published in both metropolitan and provincial newspapers. This trend suggests that colonial male authors were able to choose where to publish. Second is the attribution of fiction: even as publication of Australian men's fiction in metropolitan newspapers declined, such titles were more likely to be attributed (72 percent) than Australian fiction by women (as noted above, this was the case with only 60 percent of such titles). To be clear, I am not proposing that metropolitan newspapers aimed above all else to feature Australian men's fiction and were outmaneuvered in this aim by provincial ones. Clearly metropolitan newspapers focused on British writing, particularly by men. However, the weight of evidence suggests that from the late 1870s, provincial newspapers sought to publish Australian, especially men's, fiction, and this made them an attractive option and a focus for such writing.

Even with this qualification, my claim that colonial male authors were drawn toward provincial rather than excluded from metropolitan publication might seem implausible: why would any group of writers elect to publish in a site accorded lower prestige, with a lower readership, and probably less financial resources to pay them? My discussion of provincial newspaper syndication in the next chapter responds to these latter two points. As I show there, the majority of provincial newspaper fiction was supplied by an extensive, and almost entirely unrecognized, array of syndication agencies. Even with the available data, which underrepresents provincial newspapers, some of these syndicates encompassed forty or more newspapers. Such syndicated publication would offer authors readerships as large, if not considerably larger, than that gained by appearance in a single metropolitan newspaper. It is also possible that, even if cultural prestige was lacking, syndication agencies were able to pay authors well enough to make provincial publication attractive. With large numbers of newspapers involved in syndicates, even small amounts of money contributed by individual editors could have enabled considerable payments to local writers.

I also wonder whether this view of provincial publishing as culturally marginal might be ill-founded, relating more to contemporary cultural formations in Australia than to historical ones. As Graham

Law and William Donaldson show for Britain, with book publishing highly centralized in London, nineteenth-century provincial English and Scottish newspapers were the major sites for publishing and promoting local fiction. Colonial Australian book culture was similar to that of provincial England and Scotland: as noted in chapter 3, few local book publishers existed, and those that did often worked in the service of London companies. In Australia, the focus of metropolitan newspapers on British fiction increased the separation of provincial newspapers from the cultural center. Yet this focus also conceivably enabled provincial newspapers to develop cultural prestige by promoting a distinctively local literary culture.

Whatever their cultural prestige relative to metropolitan periodicals, the importance of provincial newspapers in publishing colonial fiction, and the dominance of male authorship in this context, throws new light on a long-standing debate in Australian literary studies regarding gender and the literary tradition. In an important 2008 article, Eggert challenged feminist literary historians' claim of an ideological basis for the male-dominated Australian literary canon ("Australian"). He argued, instead, that works by specific male authors—Rolf Boldrewood, Marcus Clarke, and Henry Kingsley—which began to be referred to as classics in the 1890s, gained this position by virtue of the publishers they chose, the timing of the book editions, and most importantly, the cheapness of those books. These material conditions, not structural sexism, led to male authors eclipsing important colonial women writers, including Ada Cambridge, Catherine Martin, Rosa Praed, and "Tasma" (Jessie Couvreur), in the formation of an Australian literary canon.

While Eggert acknowledges the prior newspaper publication of all these writers, he sees serialization as unrelated to canonization: it implies instant consumption, whereas book publication enables the leisured reading and reflection necessary for accumulating both popular and critical acclaim (138). I agree with Eggert about the importance of book publication to canonization. But where he perceives the earlier book publication of these male authors as a historical coincidence, I would argue that earlier newspaper publication established the basis for it. Colonial readers already privileged men's writing, particularly for local fiction. This background explains why works by Australian men were taken up earlier and offered more cheaply: they had an existing and large colonial market. Where Eggert argues to replace an ideological account of canon formation with a materialist one, I see the material and the ideological working in concert.

The focus on explicitly male-authored Australian fiction in provincial newspapers from the late 1870s also resituates another core argument in Australian literary studies. As chapter 6 discusses in more detail, the Sydney-based *Bulletin* magazine looms large in Australian literary history as the instigator of an "anti-romantic vernacular" style of men's writing that is frequently identified as the basis for an Australian literary tradition. Ken Stewart writes that the reaction to the *Bulletin*'s "opening of the literary floodgates," especially once A. G. Stephens became literary editor in 1896, indicates that "pressure for such outlets had been building for some years" (22–23). Yet the importance of Australian men's writing to the provincial press, and the extensive scale of that publishing, challenges the *Bulletin*'s supposedly originary role. Instead of offering an outlet for unmet demand, it is possible that the *Bulletin*'s literary agenda was an extension, possibly even in imitation, of long-standing provincial practices.

In this respect, it is far from incidental that Stephens, like many other editors, journalists, and authors of the period, previously worked in the provincial press, editing two country newspapers—the *Gympie Miner* and the *Cairns Argus*—before joining the *Bulletin*. As Stewart notes, the movement of people between metropolitan and provincial newspapers means that the "city versus country" dichotomy common in discussions of colonial literary culture is "likely to obscure shared traditions" in the colonial press. Stewart understands these traditions to flow largely from city to country, such that "some country newspapers . . . attained a 'literaryness'" that exposed "country dwellers . . . to some similar influences to those available to the literary minded city dweller" (15). The cultural trends explored in this chapter suggest that the opposite movement, from country to city, may have been just as, if not more, influential for the development of literary culture in Australia.

Writing in the *Melbourne Review* in 1878, James Smith described Australian fiction as eclipsed beneath "the shadow of England's mighty and ever-spreading literature" (cited in McCann 25).[26] While this contemporaneous description resonates with claims by subsequent literary historians, this chapter has shown that literary, publishing, and reading cultures in the colonies were not entirely dominated by British fiction, nor did they slavishly follow British models. As trends in known and inscribed authorship indicate, colonial newspapers were much more oriented to men's writing than was the case in Britain or America.[27] Australian fiction also had a greater local presence than has been recognized—particularly in the decade after Smith's pronouncement—and was published in such a way as to foreground rather than to conceal its origins.

This chapter has also demonstrated clear differences in the fiction published in metropolitan and provincial Australian newspapers in the nineteenth century. Where British fiction clearly dominated in the former—albeit with a prominent colonial inflection in the focus on male-authored fiction—provincial newspapers foregrounded Australian men's writing, especially in the 1880s. Perhaps Smith's comment is simply a coincidence of the place and time in which he was writing: not only in a metropolitan context for a metropolitan audience, but on the very cusp of what would be the embrace and development of Australian fiction by provincial newspapers. Contemporary scholarly accounts of colonial readers rejecting local writing and the absence of an Australian literary tradition do not have this excuse of timing. But they *have* been looking in the wrong place: in the pages of the metropolitan newspapers that have received the vast majority of the critical attention rather than those of the provincial newspapers that published the majority of the fiction.

CHAPTER 5

Fictional Systems

Network Analysis and Syndication Networks

———— ⁓ ————

Nineteenth-century newspapers were part of a strong culture of reprinting content, including fiction.[1] Reflecting this culture, 50 percent of the extended fiction titles in the curated dataset appear more than once. Fiction reprinting has long been studied for the insights it enables into the social and commercial structures underpinning the production and circulation of nineteenth-century fiction.[2] Until recently, researchers have relied on manually searching analog collections and, accordingly, on relatively small and selective samples: the fiction published in particular, typically major metropolitan, periodicals; by specific, predominantly canonical, authors; or as recorded in surviving records of syndication agencies.[3] The expanded access to periodical contents enabled by mass-digitization transforms the possibilities for such research, and prominent projects in digital humanities focus on reprinting.[4] This chapter takes advantage of these opportunities to radically revise existing accounts of the sources of Australian newspaper fiction and of the connections of those newspapers, and of literary culture in Australia, to global practices and systems.

Existing studies of colonial fiction reprinting stress the market dominance of the first and most famous British syndication agency, Tillotson's

Fiction Bureau, and the associated ascendancy of British over local fiction. I demonstrate that Tillotson's was only one participant among many and offer a new account of the nature, timing, and effects of its colonial operations. Previously, Tillotson's has been associated only with major city periodicals. To the contrary, the company primarily engaged with second-tier metropolitan and provincial newspapers and did so earlier, and more systematically, than has been recognized. The consistent presence of local writing in metropolitan newspapers for at least a decade after the arrival of syndicated British fiction shows definitively that the arrival of Tillotson's and other overseas agencies did not end opportunities for colonial authors. Moving beyond the practices of known agencies and agents, I confirm a significant shift in syndication practices in the 1890s, while establishing the role of certain Australian metropolitan newspapers in sourcing and distributing fiction.

For the provincial press, my analysis reveals an entirely new set of activities and actors. As chapter 4 demonstrated, provincial newspapers published significantly more fiction than their metropolitan counterparts, even as they have received almost no critical attention. This chapter shows that reprinting was also far more common in the provincial context and was the source of most of the extended fiction published. Various semiformal editor- and author-led arrangements were implicated in this practice. But most fiction reprinting in provincial newspapers involved an extensive, active, and hitherto essentially unrecognized array of syndication agencies operating within and beyond the colonies. This new account of fiction reprinting and syndication in nineteenth-century Australian newspapers reveals a much more complex, varied, and populated range of processes and structures—local and global—than has been appreciated. It also highlights the extent to which past studies have approached the larger, previously largely intractable, newspaper archive through the lens of smaller, more tractable archives—of particular newspapers, authors, and syndication agencies—and how this strategy has shaped and distorted understandings of colonial literary culture and its connection to the international fiction market. Of course, such partiality is not the exclusive province of analog resources and methods; as the first half of this book emphasized, digital resources and methods institute their own partial view.

I

As mass-digitized collections become core disciplinary infrastructure for literary history, network analysis is increasingly used to explore the extensive datasets derived from them in order to investigate historical connections in literary culture. Network analysis is employed by many of the projects surveyed in chapters 1 and 2 (by Moretti and Jockers, and by scholars who depart from these authors' approach to modeling literary systems). The reason for the method's popularity is clear: its depiction of edges (relationships) between nodes (entities) resonates with a system-based understanding of print and literary culture, common in book history and periodical studies and foregrounded by data-rich literary history. Applied to the extensive datasets harvested from mass-digitized collections, the attractive visualizations enabled by programs such as *Gephi* appear to bring connections and configurations within such systems literally into view (Bastian, Heymann, and Jacomy).

Given my focus in this book, on modeling a literary system, and in this chapter, on newspapers that published the same fiction, network analysis would seem an obvious method to use. However, at least as it is currently employed in data-rich literary history—and arguably, inevitably for research based on mass-digitized collections—network analysis inhibits effective engagement with historical evidence. In particular, a focus on visualization impedes scholars' understanding of the evidence available to construct and interpret network models and creates perhaps insurmountable barriers to recognizing and accommodating the evidence that is absent. These problems with network analysis amplify key issues canvassed in the first three chapters of this book regarding literary history's engagement with what are enormous, but inevitably incomplete, digital collections. Elaborating them is therefore necessary to explain and to justify my (limited) use of the method in this chapter, and to clarify directions in data-rich literary history.

Perhaps encouraged by the routine designation of digital methods as distant reading—maybe necessitated by a lack of statistical literacy—literary scholars tend to present and approach the results of network analysis as visual representations that can be interpreted or "read" to discover the operations of historical systems. Yet network models are contingent on the data available for analysis to an extent that is poorly appreciated in the humanities and inadequately addressed by an approach based on visualization. With the exception of geospatial formats,[5] network analysis arranges nodes entirely according to the proprieties of the available dataset. In a force-directed graph, for instance, algorithms position nodes based on the number of edges they share with others and their strength. As a result, adding new data—an inescapable prospect in a field where only a very small proportion of the documentary record is digitized—will always, and often radically, change the respective positions and strengths of all nodes and edges depicted.

For projects based on mining mass-digitized collections, the considerable gaps in what is available to be modeled mean that network visualizations invariably present fictitious systems: arrangements that are a function of what has been digitized as much as, if not vastly more so than, how a literary system actually cohered and operated. Literary history projects that base their arguments on the structure of network models—for instance, describing the "betweenness" of a work, author, or site of publication—ignore this radical contingency and implicitly maintain that all data, or all data conceivably relevant to understanding a historical literary system, are available.[6] This approach reinforces the false sense of completeness—of coherent and self-contained systems—that network visualizations project.

The apparent completeness of network models obscures another gap in the evidence needed to interpret such structures: the documents explaining the nature and function of the entities and relationships proposed. Although mass digitization is understood in terms of evidentiary excess, it concurrently creates a profound evidentiary imbalance for data-rich literary history, between extensive (though incomplete) information on the contents of books and periodicals and very limited availability of the documents needed to understand the actors and institutions responsible for creating and distributing those contents. For this project, it is not only that the causal factors underpinning different instances of reprinting are multiple, though they are; most of the documents needed to determine what cause applied in what situation no longer exist. Indeed, a key reason Tillotson's has received so much attention in studies of syndication is because its archive, though "scrappy" with multiple gaps, is a comparatively "rich" resource in a context where most of the names of syndication agencies, let alone their activities, are lost to history (Hilliard 655).

A focus on network visualizations also implicitly condones a lack of data publication, as the image of the network model becomes the available "text" for analysis. The most basic way this strategy impedes apprehension of historical evidence is by erasing the decisions and assumptions by which literary data are constituted and arranged. Humanities researchers increasingly recognize data as artifacts rather than facts (Gitelman) and algorithms as arguments that should not be black-boxed (Pasquale).[7] But presenting network models as visual images—without publishing the data underpinning and produced by them—precludes assessment of these underlying procedures and their effects.

When the data underpinning the visualization are unavailable, the default position is to accept network connections as categorically meaningful and equivalent. This approach risks mistaking for historical processes the effects of data construction. That possibility becomes increasingly likely as the scale of data increases and/or when such data are derived from automatic data mining, because both situations limit the capacity to confirm the nature of the individual entities and relationships represented. For analyses of fiction reprinting, for instance, assuming the equivalence of connections created by newspapers publishing the same fiction conflates the multiple possible routes by which a title is obtained: some newspaper editors might have bought the story from the author, others from those purchasing newspapers or from a syndication agency; still others might have "borrowed" it from another newspaper, without payment and with or without acknowledgment. While literary historians seek to understand these underlying processes, the appearance of meaning and equivalence presented by the connections in network models serves to deflect attention from the range, complexity, and conceivable contradiction of historical phenomena.

More generally, network visualizations compound the danger of anachronism associated with metaphoric references to the past in terms of networks. As historians such as Alan Lester have argued, such metaphors risk projecting "contemporary, much faster, networked flows"—most obviously, those of the Internet—onto the historical context (134). Translating metaphor into material form increases the rhetorical impact of this projection. For this project, it was difficult not to allow the sense of immediacy, uniformity, and cohesion presented by the networks I visualized to obscure the variable distances, extended temporalities, and complicated social, economic, and political negotiations involved in publishing nineteenth-century Australian newspaper fiction.

In the embrace of network analysis these issues have not been adequately articulated, and some projects fall prey to the problems they present. The network model that culminates analysis in Jockers's *Macroanalysis* is presented only in visual form (165–66). The data fed into and produced by it are unavailable, and the numerous and extensive ways in which Jockers processes that data—for example, removing all nonchronological expressions of "influence" and connections where the distance between books indicated by the network analysis is greater than the standard deviation—highlights the possibility that data construction, as much as any historically meaningful relationships between works, has produced the connections represented. The resulting, dense network, colored in terms of chronology and gender, projects the sense of immediate and uniform connections that historians have challenged with respect to metaphoric references to historical systems as networks.

In contrast, and keeping with their generally more careful approach to modeling literary data, in applying network analysis other projects in data-rich literary history employ various strategies to forestall misapprehension of the available evidence. When focusing on instances of reprinting rather than large networks arising from the Viral Texts project, Cordell offers nuanced insights into the operations of early American print culture ("Reprinting"). So and Long distinguish between the edges in their network model and connections in modernist literary culture by carefully delineating the assumptions underlying data construction (148). Likewise, in her work on nineteenth-century genre formation, DeWitt avoids mistaking for historical phenomena the patterns arising from data mining by reading each of the "thousands" of articles resulting from searching six databases for seven theological titles (163). Although returning her to the challenge of evidentiary excess that network analysis is intended to overcome, this approach means all 355 articles in her model meet her definition of genre formation: the claim by a reviewer of likeness between two or more titles. While all of these projects rely on visual representations of networks— and while DeWitt's title grounds the value of network analysis in the "Advances in the Visualization of Data" it offers—such strategies avoid key encouragements this method presents to misapprehending available evidence.

They do not counter the more pernicious problem of the representational approach to network analysis: its incapacity to identify and accommodate the effects of evidence not available to be modeled. For many methods employed in data-rich literary history—including those in the previous and subsequent chapters—it is sufficient to establish a broadly representative dataset, or one where areas of partiality are identified and taken into account in subsequent investigations. As discussed in chapter 2, none of the above projects provide such an assessment. But even if they did, this would not constitute a sufficient basis for network analysis because this method dramatically amplifies the challenges of and potential misconstructions arising from working with partial data.

Statistical approaches offer an alternative to representational forms of network analysis, one capable of identifying and accommodating incompleteness in the data available to be modeled and interpreted. The measures I am referring to are not those built into programs such as Gephi: for instance, graph density, modularity, or weighted degree. These characterize the effects of network modeling on the available dataset; they do not accommodate gaps in evidence. Scientific and social scientific applications of network analysis employ alternative statistical approaches to this end. Measures of probability, for instance, assess the likelihood that stated characteristics of a modeled network would remain true if all data were available, while "forest" networks address questions of causality when underlying relationships are unknown but from a finite set.[8] Such approaches recognize that questions relating to system structures and their dynamics are exceptionally sensitive to data completeness. Even with a representative dataset, for the results of network modeling to serve as a justifiable foundation for argument, the likelihood that they are the products of data availability or of random chance needs to be established and shown to be low.

It would be possible to apply these statistical approaches to characterizing and accommodating gaps in data generated from mass-digitized collections, including for this project,[9] and as I noted at the end of chapter 2, some quarters of the digital humanities argue that sophisticated statistical methods should be incorporated into humanities research. But even if literary historians developed the literacies needed to conduct and interpret such measures—and narrowed the form of questions asked of network models accordingly (to consider, for instance, the structural effects of interrupting certain relationships rather than how a system works)—I do not think network analysis, alone, would support an adequate encounter with historical evidence. The probability measures needed to model systems based on highly incomplete datasets are at odds with the centrality of documentary evidence to historical argument. Literary historians focus on what occurred and why, not what might have taken place based on assumptions and probabilities. Perhaps mass digitization will continue to the extent that probability measures relating to collection contents could be employed without too many accommodations (although this situation appears to be a long way in the future, if achievable at all). But even then, the inevitable distinction between these contents and the evidence needed to understand underlying historical events means that network analysis could offer only part of the methodological toolkit for any study.

In light of these issues, I have not based any of this chapter's arguments on the findings of network analysis, nor do I offer any network visualizations. But I do employ the method for practical and exploratory functions. Gephi's "multimodal networks projection" feature enabled me to create a more manageable dataset by converting thousands of connections between fictional titles and newspapers into hundreds of connections between newspapers, associated by the number of common fictional titles. The resulting network models had interesting features: for instance, certain newspapers (such as Melbourne's *Leader*) were highly connected, and metropolitan and provincial newspapers tended to cluster together, with few connections between them. However, I remained acutely conscious of the contingency and partiality of these models: of their status as algorithmic projections of an available dataset, excluding most of the actors and enterprises, local and global, implicated in the system I was investigating. This missing evidence includes not only the three-quarters of nineteenth-century Australian newspapers not digitized by *Trove* but other colonial and overseas periodicals, authors, syndication agencies, literary agents, publishers, and so on involved with fiction reprinting in the colonies. In other words, I treated the connections and patterns proposed by network analysis as potential indicators of reprinting practices, not evidence of them or their meaning.

To construct my arguments, I approached these results with questions that scholars have long asked in literary history and based my answers on forms of evidence the field has traditionally relied upon. If newspapers published multiple titles in common I asked: Who owned these newspapers? What was the physical distance between them? What was the sequence of republication for different titles and did it remain the same over time? I studied digitized newspaper pages to query: Are page layout and typographical features the same in all instances of publication? Are illustrations—and the same illustrations—present? Is the source of fiction acknowledged? I searched critical bibliographies and published records of syndication agencies to find out: Who else published this story? How much was the author paid, who represented her or him, and what other authors did she or he work with? And so on.

The resulting perspective on fiction reprinting in nineteenth-century Australian newspapers, and as those newspapers connected to global systems, is significantly extended by mass digitization and by the exploratory capacities of network analysis. But it is not based exclusively on the contents of a mass-digitized collection and the alignments suggested by a digital method for analyzing them, nor is it a comprehensive view. Rather than delineating a historical literary system, my analysis constructs a narrative out of multiple pieces of evidence, providing important insights but also acknowledging multiple dead ends: places where gaps in the evidence relating to the fiction published and/or to the documents needed to interpret those events limit what I can know.

II

Existing accounts of fiction reprinting in nineteenth-century Australian newspapers identify the mid- to late 1880s as a period of dramatic change, marked by the arrival and immediate dominance of British syndication agencies, principally Tillotson's. Critics agree that prior to this time no established systems existed for sourcing overseas content. According to Johnson-Woods, it is a "mystery" how imported serials came to Australia during this period, but it is likely that pirating was involved, especially where American fiction was concerned (*Index* 6).

Others describe how colonial newspaper editors obtained fiction by contracting with individual British authors (Morrison, "Serial" 311–12; Johnson-Woods, "Mary" 112–13) and through "unauthorized 'borrowings,'" with short fiction more likely to come from local publications and extended fiction from overseas (Law, "Savouring" 81).

Law ascribes Tillotson's dedicated involvement with the colonial market to "financial pressures in their home market" (*Serialising* 80). Whereas the company experienced strong growth in sales to English newspapers from its beginnings in 1873 to the mid-1880s, toward the end of that decade Tillotson's was compelled "to search more energetically for returns elsewhere . . . [through] ventures into America, the Colonies, and Europe" (80). In making this move, Law argues, the agency dealt only with "major city journals" (76). The "standard arrangement for works by well-known writers like [Mary Elizabeth] Braddon" was for Tillotson's "to offer serial rights in a single colony for £75, or entire Australian and New Zealand rights for £100, thus leaving a Colonial editor or agent to sell on copy to other journals" (76). Eggert concurs with Law's assessment of the timing when he argues that overseas "agents . . . saturated the local market with imported serials" from the mid-1880s ("*Robbery*" 129). Others join Law in emphasizing the Tillotson's dominance. Johnson-Woods notes that Tillotson's provided "nearly all of [the] imported stories" in major metropolitan newspapers (*Index* 6). Scholars also generally agree that the entry of overseas syndicates into the Australian market had a deleterious effect on local literary production. Christopher Hilliard argues that fiction was supplied to the Australian colonies so cheaply by overseas syndication agencies, Tillotson's in particular, that local literary production was significantly constrained (662).

This established account would lead us to anticipate relatively haphazard and minor incidents of fiction reprinting in colonial newspapers until the mid- to late 1880s, followed by a sudden and substantial increase and consistency in the practice. The solid gray line in figure 10, indicating the proportion of titles reprinted among metropolitan publications per year,[10] shows the opposite of this trend. High (though uneven) rates of reprinting prior to the mid-1880s are followed by an overall decline. This trend requires qualification, due to a phenomenon I call companion reprinting. From the late 1850s, multiple daily metropolitan newspapers established weekly companions. As might be

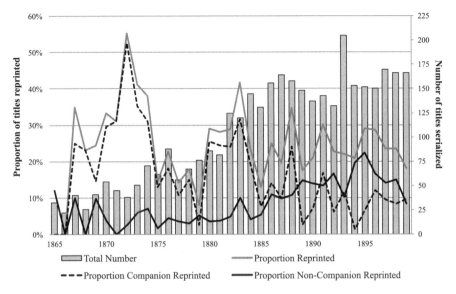

Fig. 10. Number of titles in, and proportion reprinted among, metropolitan newspapers

expected—and as the dotted black line in figure 10 indicates—these jointly owned, often jointly edited, newspapers frequently published the same stories.

Most fiction reprinted between metropolitan newspapers prior to the mid-1880s falls into this category of companion reprinting. The daily *Brisbane Courier* and weekly *Queenslander* were the first to engage in the practice routinely, with an emphasis on American fiction. Perhaps the editors thought the content of these stories would speak to Queensland's frontier society; more likely they felt justified in publishing such fiction for free, due to the lack of American acknowledgement of international copyright in this period, discussed in chapter 4. A number of other daily and weekly companions also frequently published the same stories, including the *Evening Journal* and *Adelaide Observer* in South Australia, the *Telegraph* and *Week* in Queensland, and the *Evening News* and *Australian Town and Country Journal* in New South Wales.[11] Still others, among them the largest and most culturally significant companion newspapers, published significant amounts of fiction individually, but rarely, if ever, together. Such newspapers include the

Argus and *Australasian*, the *Age* and *Leader*, the *Sydney Morning Herald* and *Sydney Mail*, the *West Australian Times* and *Western Mail*, and the *Adelaide Advertiser* and *South Australian Chronicle*.

When companion reprinting is excluded, rates of fiction reprinting among metropolitan newspapers more closely resemble the established narrative. As the solid black line in figure 10 indicates, the proportion of reprinted titles increased across the nineteenth century: it was generally under 10 percent prior to the mid-1880s and between 10 and 20 percent in the following decade, albeit with a sharp decline in the second half of the 1890s. This period of more extensive reprinting corresponds with the time Tillotson's supposedly entered and dominated the colonial market. But it demonstrates nothing of the dramatic and abrupt shift in fiction reprinting that might be expected. Comparing titles syndicated by Tillotson's with fiction in the curated dataset further disrupts the prevailing account of that company's activities. From 1880, almost all the fiction syndicated by Tillotson's appeared either that same or the following year in one or more colonial newspapers (see digital appendix 3).[12]

Such systematic involvement with colonial newspapers suggests that Tillotson's acted offensively rather than defensively in its international expansion. The alignment between the authors published in colonial newspapers prior to 1880 and those syndicated by Tillotson's after this time suggests an explanation for this earlier and alternative mode of engagement. Well before Tillotson's was created, authors subsequently associated with the company were published—and published extensively—in colonial newspapers. In addition to works by Mary Elizabeth Braddon, in the decade prior to 1875, multiple titles by Wilkie Collins, B. L. Farjeon, George Manville Fenn, James Payn, Charles Reade, and F. W. Robinson appeared in metropolitan newspapers, with a number reprinted two or more times. The second half of the 1870s witnessed the publication of more fiction by these and other authors later syndicated by Tillotson's, including Walter Besant and James Rice, William Black, Eliza Lynn Linton, Justin McCarthy, George Macdonald, Margaret Oliphant, and Dora Russell. Again (though less often) many of these works appeared in two or more metropolitan newspapers.

Pirating probably explains earlier, though less extensive, appearances by some of these same high-profile British authors in provincial

Australian newspapers. Works by Wilkie Collins, for instance, were published in multiple provincial newspapers before 1880, as were titles by B. L. Farjeon, Charles Reade, and F. W. Robinson.[13] But as chapter 4 noted, metropolitan newspapers typically published well-known British authors with explicit claims about copyright. Sometimes these claims present a coherent narrative regarding the colonial purchase and resale of rights. For instance, in May 1872 B. L. Farjeon's "London's Heart" was published in the *Sydney Mail* with the statement "the sole right of publishing in this colony Mr Farjeon's new story has been purchased by the proprietors of this journal" (#13977). The *Adelaide Observer* reprinted the story in June 1872 with the notice "the exclusive right of republishing 'London's Heart' in South Australia has been purchased by the Proprietors of the *Adelaide Observer*" (#13976); then, in July 1872, the *Evening Journal*—owned by the same proprietors—began the story with the claim that "the exclusive right of republishing 'London's Heart' in South Australia has been purchased by the Proprietors of this paper" (#19162).

The prominence and prevalence of these assertions—given the Australian colonies' exceptional adherence to imperial copyright law (Ailwood and Sainsbury)—indicate that well-known British authors were published in metropolitan newspapers under contract and with payment. By 1870, then, and throughout that decade, many of the very authors Tillotson's would later seek to court were already negotiating extensively with the Australian press, in person or through agents. Instead of waiting until the mid- to late 1880s, when there was a decline in profits from syndication in Britain, it seems much more likely that authors from the outset urged Tillotson's to engage with the established Australian market, or that the company immediately saw the opportunity to do so.

The type of newspapers Tillotson's dealt with also reconfigures existing perceptions of its relationship to the colonial market and thus explains why its earlier, systematic involvement has been overlooked. Whereas previous studies have stated or assumed that Tillotson's worked only with major metropolitan periodicals, and targeted their analyses accordingly, the company was much more likely to engage with second-tier metropolitan newspapers. The *South Australian Chronicle* was a leading colonial customer of Tillotson's, as were two sets of companion newspapers, the *Adelaide Observer* and *Evening Journal* and the *Telegraph* and *Week* (see digital appendix 3 for details). As the 1880s progressed, and especially in the 1890s, Tillotson's also increasingly contracted with provincial publications, at first the earlier and larger newspapers in this category—such as the *Bendigo Advertiser, Capricornian, Goulburn Herald,* and *Morning Bulletin*—then proceeding to multiple, smaller enterprises, including the *Barrier Miner, Clarence and Richmond Examiner, Elsternwick Leader, Launceston Daily Telegraph, Launceston Examiner,* and *Oakleigh Leader.* The major metropolitan dailies and weeklies typically associated with Tillotson's—the *Age, Australian Town and Country Journal, Illustrated Sydney News, Leader,* and *Sydney Mail*—published, comparatively, very few titles syndicated by that company.

An exception to this latter trend occurs with what Law lists as the "expensive serials" of the 1890s (*Serialising* 89). Tillotson's paid large amounts for these titles by prominent authors, which were not published in its own Bolton newspaper group. Law argues that this fiction was "purchased particularly or exclusively for the American market" (88). But these stories were also acquired by major metropolitan newspapers in Australia, including the *Age, Australian Town and Country Journal, Leader,* and *Sydney Mail* (see digital appendix 3 for details). Although these major newspapers thereby engaged with Tillotson's, the company's primary involvement with second-tier metropolitan and provincial periodicals shows that it moved into the Australian market via the same approach it pursued in Britain: by sourcing fiction for newspapers that lacked the resources to pursue content independently. The focus of earlier studies on major metropolitan periodicals provides the obvious, practical reason why this parallel in Tillotson's activities in Britain and Australia has been overlooked. But this focus, itself, is arguably attributable to the notorious Australian "cultural cringe" encouraging the perception that Tillotson's—as a British company, and despite its provincial position in the home market—would naturally occupy a privileged position in the colonial cultural sphere, dealing only with the most prestigious newspapers.

We might perceive a similar bias in the widespread view that Tillotson's entry into Australia immediately ended opportunities for local authors. The assumption that colonial newspaper editors would invariably select the imported over the local product is challenged by the results in figure 11, indicating the proportion of American, Australian, British, and other national fiction published and reprinted among

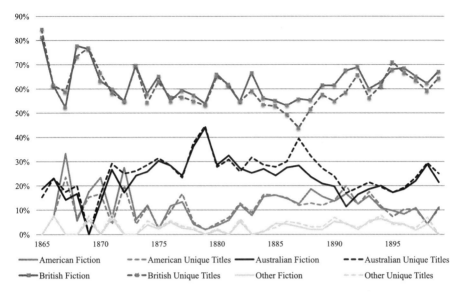

Fig. 11. National proportions of fiction/unique titles in metropolitan newspapers, excluding unknown authors

metropolitan newspapers. The solid lines show yearly proportions overall, including titles reprinted a number of times in a single year, while the dotted lines represent proportions of unique titles, a more accurate means of assessing opportunities for local authors, who were less likely than British writers to have their fiction reprinted in metropolitan newspapers.

As explored in chapter 4, British fiction clearly dominated metropolitan newspapers, and figure 11 shows that it was reprinted more frequently than titles by authors of any other national group. But this graph also indicates generally stable proportions of Australian fiction through the 1870s and 1880s, albeit with a strong surge in its presence in the final years of the 1870s and a gradual decline—coupled with relatively high rates of unique titles—at the end of the 1880s. This surge and decline tallies with my earlier argument that local authors moved to provincial newspapers rather than being excluded from metropolitan ones. Indeed, these results raise the possibility that metropolitan newspapers sought to expand their publication of local fiction at the same time as provincial ones did—in the late 1870s—and to maintain the presence of local fiction—by publishing higher rates of unique titles—as authors moved to provincial newspapers in the 1880s. Whatever the relationship between metropolitan and provincial newspapers in publishing Australian fiction, for at least a decade after Tillotson's entered the market in the late 1870s, and for seven years after the company began systematically to sell fiction to colonial newspapers, Australian authors clearly had sustained opportunities for metropolitan publication.

The trends discussed thus far clearly indicate that Tillotson's was not the predominant actor in colonial fiction publishing that previous histories have claimed. But understanding which companies, individuals, and practices supplied this extensive volume of fiction to colonial newspapers presents a challenge. Based predominantly on indexes of major metropolitan newspapers, advertisements in industry publications, and/or surviving correspondence, Graham Law, Charles Johanningsmeier, Elizabeth Morrison, and others have noted the involvement of various American and British agents and agencies in the Australian market, including the major American enterprises, McClure's Newspaper Syndicate and Bacheller's Newspaper Fiction Syndicate, and British literary agent, A. P. Watt.

This expanded sample suggests that these overseas agencies had a more established presence in the colonies than has been described. For instance, Johanningsmeier establishes McClure's connection with Australia based on author correspondence and the publication of Mark Twain's "The American Claimant" (secured at great expense by McClure in 1892 and appearing in the *Age* that same year) (*Fiction* 76). My analysis shows that Twain's story also appeared in the *Adelaide Observer* and *Evening Journal* in 1892, suggesting that McClure's—like Tillotson's—moved beyond the leading metropolitan papers in engaging with the colonial market. Comparing the titles Watt syndicated in Britain with their appearance in Australian newspapers indicates that this agent's role in colonial fiction publication was likewise more organized and consistent than has been appreciated, with many of the titles in his "belt and braces"—or London and English provincial—syndicates appearing either the same month or the next in colonial newspapers.[14] It is also clear, based on copyright descriptions in metropolitan newspapers, that British book publisher Cassell & Co. was active in supplying fiction to Australian newspapers. However, without more information about these agencies—including the titles they syndicated and the terms under which they were contracted—it is impossible to be precise about the extent of their activities, including in comparison with Tillotson's.

Instead, I have sought to gain a broader perspective on the industry by investigating the presence in metropolitan newspapers of titles by approximately one hundred authors (listed in digital appendix 4), aligned by various sources with well-known syndication agents and agencies: the Authors' Alliance, the Authors' Syndicate, the Northern Newspaper Syndicate, and W. C. Leng as well as Tillotson's, McClure's, Bacheller's, and Watt.[15] Comparing publications by these authors with the rest of the field affirms the established and efficient mechanisms by which newspaper syndication operated, in that their average number of titles in metropolitan newspapers is considerably higher than for other writers. Indeed, all but two of the top twenty most published authors in colonial metropolitan newspapers, and many of the top forty, were aligned with one or more of these organizations.[16]

Yet the perceived dominance of these agents and agencies in the colonial market is simultaneously challenged by the relatively small contribution that these associated authors make to the overall proportion of fiction in metropolitan newspapers, and by the decline in that proportion over time. Figures 12 and 13 compare the proportions of fiction supplied by associated and nonassociated authors: the former charts all writers, the latter focuses on confirmed British authors. The high proportion of fiction by nonassociated authors in figure 12—with the exception of two years (1891 and 1892) always over 60 percent, and typically in excess of 70 percent—is particularly surprising given the high average number of titles that associated authors contributed. Although my list of authors is undoubtedly incomplete, this result emphasizes how much we do not know about the source of fiction in colonial newspapers. What Johnson-Woods describes as a mystery before 1870 remains largely a mystery after 1880. Certainly, figure 12 indicates a situation very distinct from Johnson-Woods's claim that Tillotson's supplied "nearly all" of the fiction imported into the colonies.

To some degree, figure 13 suggests a more recognizable narrative. It shows that a hundred or so authors associated with known syndication agencies and literary agents supplied the majority of British fiction in metropolitan colonial newspapers, including 70 percent of that

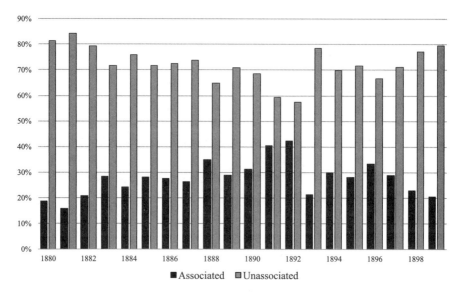

Fig. 12. Proportion of fiction in metropolitan newspapers by associated/unassociated authors

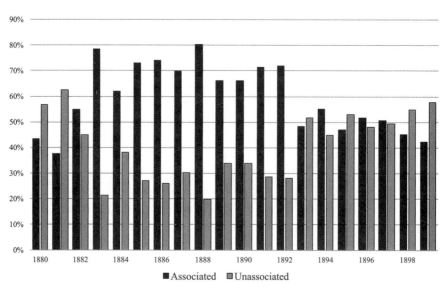

Fig. 13. Proportion of fiction in metropolitan newspapers by associated/unassociated British authors

published between 1882 and 1892. However, the subsequent fall in this proportion, to 50 percent or less, suggests a significant shift in the supply of fiction. Though less obvious, the same trend is present in figure 12, where the overall proportion of fiction by authors associated with these agencies falls from 40 percent in 1892 to 20 percent at the end of that decade.

Further reinforcing the sense of change in the early 1890s is the resonance between these results and two trends from previous graphs. The first is the decline in the proportion of fiction reprinted among metropolitan newspapers in the second half of the 1890s, shown in figure 10. While 22 percent of extended fiction in metropolitan newspapers appeared in two or more (noncompanion) periodicals in 1895, by 1899 that proportion was only 8 percent. The second trend is the decline in Australian fiction in these newspapers. This is not as definitive as would be expected from existing accounts of overseas agencies saturating the local market. But the reduction that figure 11 indicates in Australian writing—from 28 percent of fiction (or 39 percent of unique titles) in 1887 to 22 (or 25) percent by 1899—implies a shift in the source of fiction for metropolitan newspapers. The most probable explanation for these combined trends is competition from new overseas agencies. An increased number of syndication agencies offering overseas fiction at reduced prices would logically produce a decline in the market share of earlier syndicators while increasing the presence of non-Australian fiction. Lower prices would also reduce the need for metropolitan newspapers to join together to purchase stories, thus explaining the lower rate of reprinting among them.

Morrison has proposed this interpretation already, describing the entry of new overseas syndicators and growth in competition as a feature of the colonial fiction market in the 1890s ("Retrieving" 33). But her claim that these new companies were predominantly American is countered by the national origins of the fiction published. As figure 11 shows, while British fiction increased as a proportion of titles in metropolitan newspapers from the late 1880s, American fiction remained stable and even declined. Although American companies are known to have syndicated British fiction, including for Australian newspapers (Johanningsmeier, *Fiction* 75–76), one would expect some growth in the presence of American titles if such companies constituted the majority of competitors in the colonial market. The fact that British authors were responsible for around 60 to 70 percent of fiction in metropolitan newspapers in the 1890s suggests that some, if not most, of this increased competition was supplied by British enterprises.

Although much remains unclear about the involvement of overseas syndication agencies with Australian metropolitan newspapers in the late 1880s and 1890s, the manner in which individual periodicals engaged in fiction reprinting before and during this time offers new insights into the local industry's operations and structure. Melbourne's *Leader* and the *South Australian Chronicle*, and three pairs of companion publications—the *Brisbane Courier* and *Queenslander*, the *Evening Journal* and *Adelaide Observer*, and in the 1890s, the *Telegraph* and *Week*—emerge as being so central to fiction reprinting in colonial metropolitan newspapers that, in the available dataset, few instances of the phenomenon do not involve one or more of these periodicals. The fact that these newspapers also published the most fiction overall affirms the importance of reprinting as a means by which metropolitan newspapers accessed content.[17] More specifically, the nature of reprinting by and among these papers indicates their importance in distributing fiction throughout the colonies.

Table 3 summarizes reprinting by these newspapers and whether they published titles first or subsequently. It shows that the *Leader* routinely published fiction that subsequently appeared in other Australian newspapers, suggesting that its editors sourced and sold titles within the colonies, particularly to those newspapers I have described as second-

Table 3. Instances and sequence of reprinting among Australian metropolitan newspapers, excluding companion reprinting

	1865–79		1880s		1890s	
Newspaper	F	S	F	S	F	S
Leader	12	1	16	4	37	7
South Australian Chronicle	3	6	13	24	30	19
Brisbane Courier and/or *Queenslander*	4	2	12	4	18	19
Evening Journal and/or *Adelaide Observer*	1	6	12	8	28	17
Telegraph and/or *Week*	0	0	6	9	26	37
Total instances of reprinting (all newspapers)	29		78		171	

Note. F = published first, including simultaneously; S = published subsequently tier metropolitan publications. Most of the reprinted fiction initially published in the *Leader* was by authors associated with known syndication agents and agencies. But only a small number of these titles (one in the 1880s, four in the 1890s) can be tied directly to Tillotson's. In this respect, the *Leader*'s position in the colonial culture of reprinting demonstrates the practice Law proposes as standard—for Tillotson's to sell fiction by well-known authors to a single metropolitan publication, leaving it to distribute rights within the colonies (*Serialising* 76)—while emphasizing that Tillotson's was not the only company pursuing this approach. The *Leader* sourced its fiction from international syndication networks rather than relying on that one company.

Although involved in almost as many instances of reprinting as the *Leader*, the *South Australian Chronicle*, until the 1890s, tended to adopt the opposite approach: publishing fiction already published in other colonial newspapers. The *Leader* was its single main source, but the *South Australian Chronicle* reprinted fiction from a range of other newspapers, including major metropolitan publications, such as the *Age, Australasian, Australian Town and Country Journal*, and *Illustrated Sydney News*, as well as smaller metropolitan newspapers, including the *Express and Telegraph, Queenslander, Telegraph, Week*, and *West Australian*. Such interactions refute the view that only major metropolitan periodicals supplied fiction to other colonial publications, while further dismantling claims of Tillotson's dominance in the market. Although one of Tillotson's main colonial customers, the *South Australian Chronicle* accessed fiction from many other sources, including numerous colonial newspapers.

For the three pairs of companion newspapers listed in table 3, the fiction reprinted from other local newspapers was typically by high-profile British authors and often sourced from the *Leader*. In contrast, the fiction these newspapers published first, and then supplied to others, was by lesser-known (or unknown) authors. This latter sequence suggests that the *Brisbane Courier* and *Queenslander*, the *Evening Journal* and *Adelaide Observer*, and in the 1890s, the *Telegraph* and *Week* were colonial conduits for cheaper sources of fiction. In this respect, growth in the number and proportion of titles first published by these companion newspapers corresponds with a structural shift in the sources of colonial fiction in the late 1880s and 1890s. It suggests that these newspapers were signing contracts with newer fiction syndicators, providing a key avenue through which these enterprises gained access to

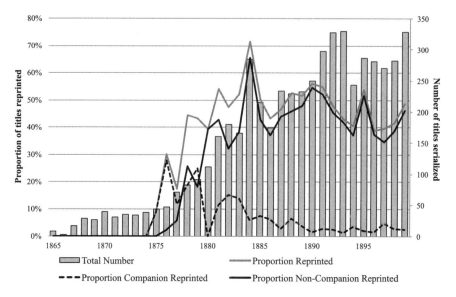

Fig. 14. Number of titles in, and proportion reprinted among, provincial newspapers

the colonial market to compete with, and ultimately substantially to displace, established agencies.

III

The account offered thus far radically expands previous conceptions of colonial fiction reprinting and syndication, indicating a much more populated and dynamic system than has hitherto been recognized. The complexity and interest of that system increases considerably when provincial newspapers are included. The multiple, semiformal and formal systems of fiction distribution discovered in this context—operating for the most part entirely apart from the metropolitan press—indicate new dimensions in the history of the circulation of fiction in the nineteenth century, both globally and within the Australian colonies. As figure 10 did for metropolitan newspapers, figure 14 shows the number of titles published in, and the proportion reprinted among, Australian provincial newspapers, per year, from 1865 to 1899.[18]

The small amount of fiction in these newspapers prior to the mid-

1870s, discussed in chapter 4, is apparent. The fiction reprinting that occurred before this time was from metropolitan, predominantly British but also Australian, periodicals. When fiction reprinting among provincial newspapers became more common, some of this activity was between companion publications, as was the case in the metropolitan context. However, in the provincial press this trend occurred a decade later and involved only one pair of newspapers based in the regional Queensland town of Rockhampton. That town's daily *Morning Bulletin* and weekly *Capricornian* published more fiction in common than any other newspapers in my sample.[19] But even without these companion publications, the solid black line in figure 14 shows a clear correlation from the mid-1870s between growth in extended fiction in provincial newspapers and incidences of reprinting among such publications.

Chapter 4 made the point that provincial newspapers significantly outstripped their metropolitan counterparts in terms of the scale of fiction published. This graph shows that they did the same with respect to reprinting fiction, even though, as with newspaper fiction generally, discussion of this phenomenon has focused almost exclusively on metropolitan periodicals. Virtually as soon as reprinting began, it became a major—in some periods the dominant—source of fiction for provincial newspapers, regularly comprising around 40 to 50 percent, and up to 65 percent, of the titles published. In contrast, among noncompanion metropolitan newspapers this figure only once exceeds 20 percent and is often less than 10 percent.

Some reprinting among provincial newspapers resulted from editor- and author-led endeavors of varying formality. In addition to their shared publications, the *Morning Bulletin* and *Capricornian* published multiple stories in conjunction with other provincial newspapers, including a number each with the *Armidale Express, Bendigo Advertiser, Clarence and Richmond Examiner,* and *South Bourke and Mornington Journal.* These titles were typically acknowledged as having been reprinted from British periodicals (most often *Chambers' Edinburgh Journal*) and the majority appeared first, by a few weeks, in the *Morning Bulletin* and *Capricornian,* although the reverse also occurred. This pattern of reprinting suggests an exchange system, whereby copies of the *Morning Bulletin* and/or its weekly companion were sent to other provincial editors in return for issues of their newspapers. A more formal—though more limited—reprinting arrangement was practiced by the *Goulburn*

Herald, at different times with the *Cootamundra Herald* and *Hay Standard*.[20] The layout and timing of these publications indicates that the *Goulburn Herald* sold partly printed sheets to the other two newspapers, while the unattributed nature of these stories—even those by famous authors such as Wilkie Collins—suggests that the *Goulburn Herald* did not reduce this income stream by paying writers or intermediaries for the rights to publish and reprint.

Another semiformal system of fiction reprinting is associated with local author David Hennessey. Prominent Australian literary and historical scholars have considered the racial and gendered meanings in Hennessey's "lost race" adventure romance "An Australian Bush Track" (Dalziell 51–73; Dixon, *Writing* 91–94; Docker 212–14). But Hennessey's entrepreneurship in syndicating this and other stories throughout the provincial press has not been recognized. In 1895 his "Wynnum White's Wickedness" appeared in at least nine provincial newspapers, including the *Armidale Chronicle, Bathurst Free Press, Gympie Times, Morwell Advertiser, Nepean Times, Port Macquarie News, Richmond River Herald, Traralgon Record*, and *Western Herald*; before the century's end, a further four stories, including "An Australian Bush Track," appeared in various provincial newspapers.[21] The lack of other titles, not by Hennessey, shared between these provincial newspapers implies that the author organized these publications, and Hennessey's position as a journalist, editor, and publisher would have given him the connections to do so. Evidence suggests that Hennessey also sought to syndicate other authors' work. One of a number of publishing enterprises he established, Hennessey and Harper, advertised itself as "Authors' Agents, Press Correspondents, Advertisement Contractors, Publishers, etc. etc.," with services including "Printing and Publishing of Books, Serial Stories, etc., arranged for in England or the Colonies."[22] With one possible exception, I have only discovered examples of Hennessey syndicating his own writing.[23] But even his success in placing his own fiction in the provincial press offers a significantly more substantial example of authorial syndication than the only previously identified colonial example of the practice: James "Skipp" Borlase's abortive attempt to establish a fiction syndication agency in the 1860s (Sussex).

While editor- and author-led endeavors contributed to provincial fiction reprinting, the vast majority of such instances occurred through formal syndicates. In contrast to the metropolitan context, in which

Table 4. Fiction syndicates in provincial newspapers, 1877–99

Syndicate	Years	No. of newspapers	Newspaper colony	Titles	National origin of titles
1	1877–92	39	NSW (14); QLD (6); SA (7); TAS (1); VIC (11); WA (0)	73	Am (17); Aust (39); Brit (8); other (1); unk (8)
2	1883–93	18	NSW (3); QLD (0); SA (3); TAS (1); VIC (11); WA (0)	29	Am (8); Aust (1); Brit (6); other (1); unk (13)
3	1885–90	9	NSW (0); QLD (3); SA (2); TAS (0); VIC (4); WA (0)	15	Am (4); Aust (3); Brit (2); other (1); unk (5)
4	1886–93	28	NSW (2); QLD (1); SA (4); TAS (0); VIC (21); WA (0)	33	Am (8); Aust (0); Brit (22); other (0); unk (3)
5	1887–93	11	NSW (8); QLD (2); SA (1); TAS (0); VIC (0); WA (0)	20	Am (8); Aust (3); Brit (5); other (1); unk (3)
6	1891–99	45	NSW (7); QLD (6); SA (6); TAS (2); VIC (23); WA (1)	50	Am (7); Aust (12); Brit (6); other (4); unk (21)
7	1892–99	13	NSW (4); QLD (0); SA (1); TAS (0); VIC (8); WA (0)	34	Am (11); Aust (3); Brit (13); other (0); unk (7)
8	1892–99	23	NSW (0); QLD (0); SA (2); TAS (0); VIC (21); WA (0)	71	Am (20); Aust (5); Brit (17); other (5); unk (24)
9	1893–99	13	NSW (11); QLD (0); SA (1); TAS (0); VIC (0); WA (1)	28	Am (17); Aust (3); Brit (5); other (0); unk (3)
10	1897–99	21	NSW (18); QLD (0); SA (0); TAS (1); VIC (2); WA (0)	9	Am (1); Aust (3); Brit (1); other (0); unk (4)
11	1897–99	20	NSW (9); QLD (0); SA (2); TAS (1); VIC (7); WA (1)	10	Am (2); Aust (2); Brit (4); other (2); unk (0)

Note. Am = America; Aust = Australia; Brit = Britain; unk = unknown titles were typically reprinted among two or three newspapers, provincial syndicates were extensive, encompassing multiple newspapers and stories. Identifying these syndicates is necessarily a provisional exercise, particularly for the 1890s, when stereotype and reprint columns, rather than ready printed and largely identical supplements, became increasingly common. However, patterns of reprinting in the available sample indicate at least eleven substantial syndicates operating with provincial newspapers. These are summarized in table 4, with digital appendix 5 providing further details of these syndicates, including the titles and authors published and dates of publication.[24]

I have no doubt that the number of newspapers involved in these provincial syndicates, and probably the number of syndicates in operation, was substantially greater than I have been able to discern due to the large number of nineteenth-century Australian newspapers not digitized and the tendency for collection practices to exclude supplements. Indeed, the extent of omission of supplements only became apparent from analyzing reprinting. With multiple periodicals subscribing to the same supplements, fiction frequently appears in a common sequence across multiple provincial newspapers. In analyzing such recurrence, I discovered a number of instances where certain newspapers appeared to publish an irregular number of titles—or only one—in a sequence. Further investigation occasionally confirmed a one-off publication: the newspaper simply happened to have published the same story—often sourced from a popular British or American periodical—around the same time as the syndicate. Much more frequently, a newspaper's apparently singular or irregular publication of the same titles as a syndicate turned out to be an effect of missing supplements. Thus the routine omission of supplements from the collection practices underpinning *Trove*'s newspaper holdings was discoverable only through the inadvertent inclusion of supplements for certain issues.[25]

Even on the available evidence, with newspapers the main source of fiction in the Australian colonies and more fiction appearing in provincial than metropolitan publications, the scale of fiction published by these provincial syndicates makes them the leading local publishers of fiction for nineteenth-century Australian readers. To my knowledge, syndicate 1 in table 4 is the only one that has been described. Morrison identifies this syndicate as having been owned and managed by Donald

Cameron, under the Cameron, Laing and Co. imprint (*Engines* 210–12, 253–56; "Serial" 317–18). To Morrison's excellent account I can add only a little.

Although many early and later titles in the syndicate were from overseas (particularly America), as Morrison notes, Cameron, Laing and Co. focused on Australian fiction. Morrison emphasizes the significance of this investment in colonial writing and its "strongly colonial, but not distinctively Victorian" nature (*Engines* 255). However, I think her claim could be pushed further to identify this local syndicate as one of the most prolific publishers of Australian novels at least in the nineteenth century and probably well into the twentieth. For instance, between 1880 and 1884 Cameron, Laing and Co. published twenty-six extended Australian stories, plus an additional two that were almost certainly Australian. In contrast, the most prolific local book publisher in the nineteenth century, George Robertson, published only nine Australian novels between 1860 and 1889 (Bode, *Reading* 44).

Few of the titles syndicated by Cameron, Laing and Co. were issued as books. Consequently, many are missing from the existing bibliographical record, even though they were written by well-known and popular authors of the period. Comparing the sequence of titles published by this syndicate with those in New Zealand newspapers such as the *Hawera and Normanby Star*, *Tuapeka Times*, and *Waikato Times* (digitized through the National Library of New Zealand's *Papers Past*) suggests that Cameron, Laing and Co. operated beyond the Australian colonies as well as between them.[26] While Morrison proposes that the syndicate ended in 1888 (*Engines* 255), the evidence amassed here suggests that it continued until at least 1892.[27]

While I do not know who owned the other enterprises listed in table 4, their practices help to characterize provincial fiction syndication in various ways. The most notable dynamic is a rupture in the early 1890s, when syndicates 1 through 5 ceased operating and syndicates 6 through 9 began. The syndicates in the first group had the same basic format: two partly printed sheets, usually published as a supplement to the newspaper, which was often only an additional two or four pages in total. Supplements typically started with a poem, followed by an installment of a story and sometimes a short story or two. The remainder was composed of what Morrison describes, in reference to Cameron, Laing and Co., as "a mélange of reprinted material, most of the latter extracted from overseas—chiefly American—magazines and newspapers" ("Serial" 317). Yet within this standard format, the syndicates demonstrated significant variation.

On the available evidence, they differed markedly in scale, with syndicates 3 and 5 noticeably smaller than the others. While most offered a mixture of short, medium-length, and full-length serials, with a preponderance of the latter, syndicate 2 mainly dealt in short stories, completed in two or three issues. These titles were mainly of overseas origin, with the large proportion of unknown authors suggesting unauthorized borrowings from international periodicals. But the local content incorporated elsewhere in its supplements—in the form of poems and illustrations—implies that syndicate 2, like syndicate 1, was Australian.

Syndicate 4 published no local fiction and was exceptional in other ways too. While the other syndicates in this period published one lengthy serial at a time, syndicate 4 offered multiple serials concurrently. For example, George Manville Fenn's "Commodore Junk," W. Clark Russell's "The Frozen Pirate," and a children's serial—"My Plucky Boy Tom" by P. T. Barnum—were published concurrently by this syndicate in 1888. And while a sequence of syndicated titles often appeared months apart in different newspapers, in syndicate 4, publication occurred within a few days across all. This difference in timing suggests that syndicate 4 was highly organized from its beginning, whereas the others grew more organically, with newspapers able to join syndicates at different stages, receiving the full run of partly printed sheets in sequence.

Its selection of authors closely aligns syndicate 4 with the international fiction market of the period. Many of its titles were by the high-profile British writers associated above with known syndication agents and agencies, including Walter Besant, Arthur Conan Doyle, George Manville Fenn, G. A. Henty, Arthur Quiller-Couch, W. Clark Russell, and Robert Louis Stevenson. Two of the titles it published—Mary Elizabeth Braddon's "Like and Unlike" and Hall Caine's "The Bondman"—were syndicated by Tillotson's and actually appeared in provincial newspapers before colonial metropolitan publication. Whether originating from within the colonies or elsewhere, syndicate 4's distinct practices and its supply of fiction from well-known authors quickly won it market share, with multiple newspapers transferring to it from other syndicates, especially Cameron, Laing and Co. Yet even with this apparent success, syndicate 4 shared the fate of the other enterprises in this first group, ceasing operations in the early 1890s.

A new group entered the market at this time, either out-competing earlier syndicates or filling a void left by their demise. Two further syndicates, 10 and 11, began in the final years of the nineteenth century. Other features, besides the period of their operation, differentiate this second group of syndicates from the first. Whereas the first group traded in partly printed sheets, most in the second offered more flexible reprinting formats, allowing editors to incorporate syndicated contents—for instance, three columns' worth for an installment of the serial story—with their own advertising. Earlier syndicates can be clearly differentiated from each other, but this is less true of later enterprises. Although syndicates 6 and 10 regularly featured local fiction, the others published a broader, international mix of titles, including a substantial number by authors of unknown origins. Movement of newspapers between syndicates also occurred more often, suggesting greater competition in the market and the preparedness of provincial editors to take advantage of this.

Of this second group, syndicates 6 and 10 were probably local. As well as featuring a substantial amount of Australian fiction, the former included local advertising on some of its partly printed pages, while the latter incorporated local content among its general-interest materials: for instance, an article on the "Improvement of New South Wales Stock" in a syndicate largely comprised of provincial New South Wales newspapers. Syndicates 8 and 9 were probably American imports. Both, but especially 9, featured American fiction, while syndicate 8 included advertising for American products and services: "Genuine Magic Soap," "Patents" lawyers, "Murray and Lanman's Florida Water." If American, they could be any of the multiple enterprises Johanningsmeier identifies as emerging in the 1890s, for which little, if any, documentary evidence of their operations survives.[28] Based on the contents of the remaining two syndicates, 7 and 11 could be either local or American.[29]

As this discussion shows, the national origins of the fiction published by a syndicate are not coterminous with that syndicate's location. A colonial syndicate might have obtained much of its fiction from readily available overseas sources, just as an overseas syndicate might have included extensive local fiction as a means of accessing a colonial readership that, as chapter 4 showed, had an appetite for Australian fiction. Leaving aside the question of the location of these companies, figures 15, 16, and 17 offer a broader sense of syndication's role in providing fiction for the provincial market and its special significance for American and Australian fiction. These figures represent the total number of titles (the dotted lines) and number of unique titles (the solid lines) published from 1875 to 1899 (again within a calendar year) by British, American, and Australian authors, respectively. In indicating reprinting within national or protonational categories, the distance between the two lines suggests the relative importance of syndication over time.

Figure 15 shows that most British titles in provincial newspapers were unique until the mid-1880s. From that time they were reprinted at a fairly even rate, suggesting that British fiction was consistently syndicated for these newspapers and reinforcing the cultural value accorded to British culture in this context (discussed in chapter 4). Yet while British fiction was the most widely reprinted national category in metropolitan newspapers, the opposite is true for provincial ones: 47 percent of British fiction in provincial colonial newspapers was reprinted, compared with 54 percent of American and 67 percent of Australian fiction. As figures 16 and 17 show, reprinting of fiction in these latter two categories was focused in particular periods. American fiction was most widely reprinted in the late 1880s and 1890s, a period largely coinciding with the second group of syndicates discussed above. While not confirming, this finding lends support to Morrison's proposal that American syndication agencies played a substantial role in the colonial market, though for provincial newspapers specifically. Reprinting and syndication of Australian titles was especially common in the late 1870s and 1880s, representing up to 80 percent of the colonial fiction published. But it remained relatively prevalent in the 1890s, suggesting that Australian fiction was important to both groups of syndicates.

These figures uphold the argument made in the previous chapter: that provincial newspapers were the chief sites for publishing and valuing Australian fiction in the final two decades of the nineteenth century. The relatively low numbers of unique Australian titles published in these two decades—only 257 compared with 681 British and 441 American—suggest that fiction from these other national contexts was more readily available: an unsurprising effect of very different populations. But the much higher rate of syndication of Australian fiction indicates that writers and their agents, provincial newspaper editors, and

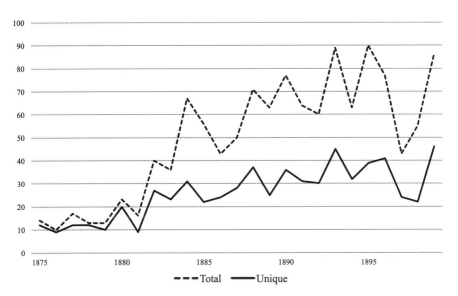

Fig. 15. Number of British titles/unique titles in provincial newspapers

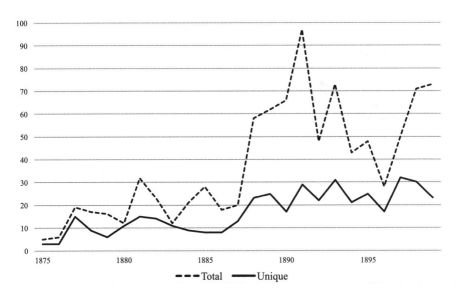

Fig. 16. Number of American titles/unique titles in provincial newspapers

Fig. 17. Number of Australian titles/unique titles in provincial newspapers

the syndication agencies that acted between them sought to extend the small pool of local fiction available to as many readers as possible, and that there was a demand for such writing. Such extensive reprinting of Australian fiction also raises the possibility—though again, in no way proves—that many of the syndication agencies involved in the colonial market at the end of the nineteenth century were locally based. Although fiction was also sourced from overseas, these organizations were clearly connected to colonial authors.

Provincial syndicates present exciting possibilities for future research. Confirming that they were local enterprises would expand the history of Australian publishing and further displace the long-standing view that this activity rarely occurred. Associating these syndicates with American or other overseas companies would add important new transnational dimensions to Australian literary history and to understandings of nineteenth-century literary culture broadly. I hope others might find evidence to support their own arguments in the sequences of titles presented in digital appendix 5, but here we reach the limits of what the extensive sample of fiction used in this study can indicate. While mass digitization and the methods used to analyze the contents of such collections significantly extend the evidence for exploring fiction reprinting and syndication, such evidence is not complete, or sufficient, in and of itself. Though broadly representative, the curated dataset is a partial reflection of fiction in nineteenth-century Australian newspapers, fiction that appeared as a consequence of institutional and social configurations and practices that are often not discernible from periodical contents.

Even with many questions remaining, this chapter profoundly refigures existing conceptions of fiction reprinting as it operated in nineteenth-century Australian newspapers, and as these newspapers connected to a global fiction market. For the metropolitan context, it has shown that Tillotson's Fiction Bureau was not the central and dominant influence that has been proposed but one participant among many in a market in which both local and overseas enterprises played active roles. Although systematically involved in that market earlier than has been recognized, Tillotson's contracted mainly with second-tier—and provincial—newspapers rather than the major metropolitan papers that have been the focus of earlier research. Provincial newspapers were not marginally—and illegally—involved in fiction reprinting but were the major participants in this culture. Along with various editor- and author-led forms of syndication, provincial newspapers were supplied by an extensive group of syndication agencies operating in the colonies and beyond.

Australian fiction had a sustained presence in metropolitan newspapers despite the involvement of international syndication agencies, and it was particularly widely reprinted in the provincial press. When international fiction became more prevalent at the end of the nineteenth century—with British fiction increasing in colonial metropolitan newspapers and American fiction in provincial ones—syndication was already of declining importance as a mechanism for obtaining and distributing fiction in the colonies, as were newspapers as fiction publishers. Much remains to be discovered about the means by which fiction was sourced and circulated in colonial newspapers. But the previous view that British agents and syndication agencies—let alone a single British company, Tillotson's—dominated the Australian market and its supply of fiction cannot offer the framework for future investigations.

CHAPTER 6

"Man people woman life" / "Creek sheep cattle horses"

Influence, Distinction, and Literary Traditions

———— ❧ ————

Debate about the origin of an Australian literary tradition and its distinctive qualities—if any—has in some respects come full circle since the 1930s and 1940s. Then, as David Carter puts it, "Expressions of anxiety about the national culture, its absence, betrayal or unfulfilled promise, were far more common than confident statements of the Australian tradition" (269). That confidence developed in the century's second half, albeit in different forms. Inclusion of Australian literature on university curricula in the 1950s and 1960s was accompanied by the articulation of a nineteenth-century "bush tradition," aligned with the 1890s and the literary "red pages" of the Sydney-based *Bulletin* magazine (Bennett 158–59). The feminist challenge to this origin story in the 1970s and 1980s also focused on the 1890s. But scholars including Marilyn Lake and Susan Sheridan emphasized the importance of women writers and domestic romance to early Australian fiction. The transnational turn has revived the question of whether a distinctive Australian literary tradition existed.

Assuming the predominance of British fiction, most transnational studies concentrate on the marginality of local fiction to colonial literary culture, rather than on the specificity or lack thereof of nineteenth-century Australian writing. Tim Dolin goes this extra step, questioning whether its nineteenth-century origins rendered the "development of a genuinely original Australian literature" impossible ("Secret" 128).[1] According to Dolin, "the fledgling Australian novel . . . had to struggle against the rival universalisms of the great established national literatures" (129) and, more profoundly given the prevalence of popular fiction in the colonies, against the influence of a "trans-national . . . mass consumerism" that emerged in this period and produced "a vast new readership for fiction that was indifferent to the boundaries of the nation state." Due to these cultural and market forces, Dolin suggests that Australian literature never had "enough time on its own to experience that continuous national life" necessary to develop the originality and distinctiveness constitutive of a national literary tradition (128).

The previous two chapters argued that, however powerful the influences from elsewhere, colonial literary culture did not simply follow overseas models: nineteenth-century Australian newspapers were sites of local literary culture in terms of both the contributions of local authors (chapter 4) and the activities of local newspapers and syndication agencies (chapter 5). Yet even a brief survey of the fiction published in this context affirms Dolin's premise: Australians began writing into a market where great international works of literature were present, and where transnational popular genres—romance, sensation, and adventure fiction—were published in prodigious numbers. Although local authors, newspapers, and syndication agencies were significantly more present and active in the colonial market than has been recognized, it is entirely possible that Australian fiction largely resembled—that is, imitated—popular genres imported from elsewhere. Of course, given the scale of fiction involved, this relationship is not one that can be ascertained simply by reading. Working at the rate of a story a day, reading all of the extended fiction harvested in this project would take more than sixteen years; in this light, selecting a sample and systematizing analysis of the contents without computational assistance would present an insurmountable challenge.

This chapter therefore approaches the question of whether Australian writing demonstrates features distinct from imported fiction in the first instance by using an integrated application of two machine-learning methods: topic modeling and decision trees. Topic modeling has been used extensively in digital literary studies, albeit often in the gray literature attached to the field: in blogs, conference presentations, and shared code. Its results create what Lisa Rhody calls a "model of language" capable of distinguishing word patterns, or "topics," within documents and across a corpus (np). But the focus on corpus-wide "topics," largely separate from the literary works these patterns arise from, undermines the method's usefulness for literary history. Decision trees provide a means of tying the results of topic modeling to literary works and, more particularly, of associating word patterns with historical categories of documents. I use this integrated approach to explore whether, and if so what, characteristics distinguished the American, Australian, and British fiction in colonial newspapers.[2] Because nineteenth-century fiction is widely recognized as highly gendered,[3] the capacity of this integrated method to predict authorial gender offers a valuable test case. I show that juvenile fiction and romance writing exemplify the word patterns that best distinguish women's and men's fiction. These findings reinforce the gendering of popular fiction in the nineteenth century, while the different political implications of titles aligned by this method with women's fiction warn against simplistically ascribing historical and literary meaning to word patterns.

We might expect gendered tendencies in fiction to be more apparent than national (or protonational) ones. But word patterns emerge as more strongly indicative of whether an author is American, Australian, or British than male or female. The language shown by this method to be characteristic of Australian fiction is the most distinctive and arises from prominent descriptions of nonmetropolitan colonial settings, characters, and activities. Such stories resonate in certain ways with accounts from the 1950s and 1960s of an Australian bush tradition, as well as with subsequent feminist critiques of that tradition's masculinism. Yet a focus on the bush is evident in Australian fiction prior to the supposedly foundational decade of the 1890s. And these stories depart from conceptions of a bush tradition in other ways, especially in prominently depicting Aboriginal characters. Tendencies in word usage identified in British and American fiction are subtler and suggest contrasting attitudes toward history and time, and to the capacity of individuals to effect change. Some Australian fiction also displays the ambivalent, even pessimistic view of history and time that tends to characterize British writing. But colonial fiction is more likely to demonstrate the optimism and belief in the individual also found in American stories. Correlations between these attitudes toward history and time in Australian fiction and major trends in authorship and publication situate an orientation to the "new" and "old" worlds as an important cultural distinction within colonial literary culture.

I

Topic modeling—especially latent dirichlet allocation (LDA) using Mallet software (McCallum)—has attained a similar degree of prominence in digital literary studies that network analysis has for book and periodical historians. As multiple articles and blogs elaborate, topic modeling is an unsupervised statistical classification method for identifying patterns in the use of words within documents and across a corpus.[4] The researcher allocates the number of topics that the program will create, and a machine-learning algorithm sorts all words in a corpus (barring the excluded or "stop words" specified by the researcher) into that number of groups based on the probability of their co-occurrence. Words that occur in the same document more often than would be expected based on their presence across the corpus are designated as "topics."

Mallet presents this information in various ways. Words are depicted in terms of their rate of occurrence across the corpus and within a topic; topics are represented with respect to their presence in the corpus and in each document. Each topic is also characterized by a list or "key" of its most prominent words. The representation of words in context, in these keys and in the thousands of additional words that compose a topic, enables the same word to have different connotations depending on the other words likely to occur in the same documents. For instance, *blood* is prominent in two topics in the one-hundred-topic model explored in this chapter (the keywords for which are listed in digital appendix 6). The other keywords in these topics associate the word, respectively, with lineage (topic 56—"king lord people priest god queen court church men country ancient *blood* true called royal religion war prince catholic") and battle (topic 98—"man men hand *blood* fight fellow blow life head knife pistol ground danger party time body brave enemy killed").

Beyond the statistical and semantic richness of its outputs, I was drawn to topic modeling for conceptual as well as practical reasons. The method's exploration of word patterns within documents and across a corpus resonates with the book's organizing framework of the historical literary system. Applied to text files in the curated dataset—and by association, to literary works that were published, circulated, and read at a particular time and place—topic modeling returns word patterns that relate a semantic context to a historical and material one. While topic modeling cannot replicate the experience of reading these stories in the nineteenth century, it indicates conceivable or potential word associations informing the meanings produced by readers in the past. In practical terms, the method was designed to work with the type of textual data that *Trove* provides: unstructured text (that is, without machine-readable annotations) of similar, relatively short length (as occurs with newspaper fiction installments).

Topic modeling also deals effectively with a major challenge of the textual data in *Trove*'s historical newspaper collection: its OCR errors. As chapter 3 discussed, title information is manually corrected to a high degree of accuracy. But this is not the case with the body of articles, and for this textual data, OCR quality is highly variable. Despite *Trove*'s success in crowd-sourced text correction, very few of the text files harvested for this project have been amended in this way, and their number makes manual correction unfeasible. However, because certain OCR errors tend to recur (for instance, "tbc" for "the"), and to occur with greater frequency in particular documents (those with bad OCR), topic modeling is able to produce topics comprised largely or entirely of OCR errors and to indicate the presence of such topics in each document. These topics can be excluded from analysis, as I do with the one-hundred-topic model used here. Unless a document's text is very badly corrupted, its remaining—legible—words can still be categorized and investigated with respect to word patterns across the corpus.

The one-hundred-topic model investigated in this chapter is based on text files representing 75 percent of the extended fiction in the curated dataset and 81 percent of unique titles. Sampled stories have at least three text files, which was the number analyzed for each so as not to create topics dominated by lengthy works or to exceed available computing power. This subset also provides a representative sample of fiction in terms of the date of publication, authors' gender and nationality, and newspapers' locations. Digital appendix 7 describes the parameters by which this one-hundred-topic model was created, including a summary of the sample's relationship to the curated dataset; digital appendix 8 presents the topic model's results and inputs, including my stop-words list. In addition to Mallet's standard inclusions, my stop words incorporate those created by Jockers for *Macroanalysis* ("Expanded") as well as an extensive list of people and place names produced by analyzing the text files using Stanford's Named Entity Recognizer (Finkel, Grenager, and Manning).[5] Although this chapter seeks to explore the relationship between the contents of stories and their national or protonational associations, I did not want the extensive references to particular places (or character names) in this fiction to overdetermine the composition of topics.

Despite its considerable strengths, topic modeling's uncertain epistemological standing presents a challenge for employing the method in literary studies (Liu, "Meaning" 414). Various proposals have been made as to how a topic should be conceived, including as a "fiction" that alludes to works that might have been created but were not (Buurma); as a lens for viewing a corpus where there is no correct magnification, just more "appropriate" lenses "depending on the analyst's substantive focus" (DiMaggio, Nag, and Blei 582); or as a "discourse or a kind of poetic rhetoric" rather than words linked by a single referent or concept (Underwood, "Topic" np). Andrew Goldstone and Ted Underwood describe topics as "interestingly slippery objects that require interpretation" ("Quiet" 363). Emphasizing their varied potential meanings—topics might "reflect rhetoric frames, cognitive schemata, or specialized idioms . . . [or] even indicate a discourse in Foucault's sense" (361)—they also note the capacity of topics to exceed interpretive boundaries. Goldstone and Underwood's articles and associated datasets and visualizations also exemplify many of the strategies digital literary scholars employ to create a robust foundation for interpreting topics beyond the allusions of the prominent keywords, which in no way exhaust a topic's meaning (Schmidt). These include analyzing all words in a topic, tracing the occurrence of words in different topics, examining the documents where a topic is most prominent, graphing a topic's presence in the corpus generally or over time, and considering relationships between topics based on those most likely to occur prominently in the same documents (Goldstone and Underwood, "Quiet"; Goldstone and Underwood, "What").

While these approaches are useful for exploring word associations across a corpus, they are not appropriate to the historical question I want to ask: were certain word patterns more likely to occur in or to characterize writing by men or women, or by American, Australian, or British authors? Existing approaches view the corpus in terms of topics and largely remain within the heuristic parameters of those (ambiguously defined) entities. A topic is selected for analysis because of some feature *it* demonstrates: for instance, its keywords are interesting to the researcher, or the topic is statistically prevalent. Typically, documents are considered only when they contain the highest proportions of words in a selected topic. My question, in contrast, begins with literary works and their historical features and seeks to explore word patterns that are most likely to characterize certain categories of documents. While the existing approach uses documents to exemplify topics that are intuitively or statistically interesting, I want to see if certain topics exemplify fiction by particular (gendered or national) categories of author.

In their introduction to a special issue on the method for the *Journal of Digital Humanities*, Elijah Meeks and Scott Weingart treat this focus on topics and words rather than documents as an inevitable effect of topic modeling, describing it as "distant reading in the most pure sense: focused on corpora and not individual texts" (np). But topic modeling does signify a relationship where the document is the principal or organizing entity. Each document is characterized by varied proportions of all topics, such that document *x* has, for instance, 5 percent of its words in topic 0, 2 percent in topic 1, 20 percent in topic 2, 0.1 percent in topic 3, and so on up to the number of topics modeled and 100 percent of the words analyzed. The terminology currently used to describe the method in digital literary studies contradicts and obscures this presence of all topics in each document, in that only the dominant topics in a document can conceivably be understood as fictions, frames, poetic registers, semantic fields, or discourses.[6] However, these varied proportions of topics can be used to describe or characterize documents: that is, they can function as rich documentary metadata.

This chapter reconnects topics—conceived simply as patterns of words—to the historical documents from which they arise by interpreting this documentary metadata using another unsupervised statistical classification approach: decision trees.[7] The goal of this analytical tool—to identify the most "important" variables in complex datasets—has been applied to questions in fields ranging from ecology to economics and sociology. "Importance" is defined by explanatory power: the capacity of a variable, based on where it is split along a spectrum, to explain a feature of a dataset. I used this method to identify the proportions of particular topics (the variables) that align most strongly with (explain or predict) whether a story is by a man or woman, or an American, Australian, or British author (the features of the dataset I am interested in understanding). Decision trees thus allowed me to treat the rich metadata provided by the presence of every topic in each document as multidimensional descriptors of word patterns in nineteenth-century Australian newspaper fiction, connected to historical and material features of those documents.

As with topic modeling, decision trees are a probabilistic method, though they operate via an explicit mechanism of training and prediction. The researcher specifies the maximum number of "splits"—or nodes with two branches determined by the degree of a variable—that the decision tree is allowed to use to create pathways that are most likely to sort the dataset into designated categories. For instance, the decision tree in figure 18 is the result of a trial where I specified a maximum of two splits to predict whether authors were male or female. This model specifies that a document is likely to be written by a woman if it has more than 1.58 percent of topic 9 (where the keywords are "mother dear girl sister child children papa poor father home girls lady pretty tea room house daughter school brother"). For those documents with less than this amount, the presence of topic 16 ("boy head time round long half work hand give bit poor fellow night dog called hands won morning boys") at 1.65 percent is predicted to distinguish titles by male authors above that threshold and by female authors below it. (Digital appendix 9 contains the code and results of all trials for decision trees discussed in this chapter.)[8]

To produce these decision pathways the algorithm trains with a random sample where it "knows" both the different degrees of topics in a document and the category of authorship it seeks to explain.[9] Following training, decision trees apply what they have "learned" from the

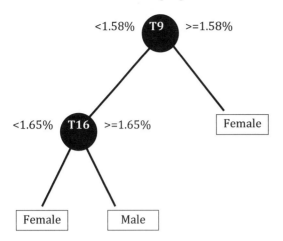

Fig. 18. Decision tree for gender: maximum two splits (trial 2)

"known" data (for example, that titles by women tend to have more than 1.58 percent of topic 9) to the remainder to determine how well these predictions generalize, a procedure known as cross-validation. Because each trial of training and testing occurs with a random sample, no two decision trees are identical. For this chapter I conducted ten trials for gender and nationality, for a range of maximum splits, to identify the decision trees that made the most accurate predictions and to discover consistencies in the topics specified. The most accurate trees highlight cases where decisions about the training set—the relationships proposed between the presence of topics and historical features of documents—are most generalizable to the remaining data; the consistent appearance of particular topics and hierarchies of topics across multiple trees indicates decisions that are robust rather than effects of the sample used.

The primary or root node in figure 18—topic 9—was consistent across all trials for gender with two splits (and with four and six splits also), meaning that its relative presence or absence was highly significant and robust in differentiating men's and women's fiction. The tree in figure 18 was the most accurate for predicting authorial gender with two splits. Its 72 percent overall accuracy was made up of 74 percent success in predicting female authorship and 71 percent for male authorship. (In other words, the specified pathways misallocate slightly more male than female authors.) Relative success rates for the different categories, like overall accuracy, differ with each trial and relate to the trade-offs involved in seeking the highest accuracy for individual categories, as well as the highest overall or average accuracy for all categories.[10]

A decision tree can involve any number of splits, and increased accuracy in predicting gender and nationality with multiple pathways suggests other applications for this integrated method.[11] But as in figure 18, this chapter focuses on the initial two layers of nodes. These indicate the topics and thresholds that successfully categorize the largest number of titles by authorial gender or nationality. In this respect it is significant that, after the first two splits, accuracy increased only gradually in the decision tree trials I conducted: for instance, a two-split decision tree predicted authorial gender in 72 percent of cases, compared with 75 percent accuracy with six splits and 85 percent with one hundred splits. This trend shows that the gender and nationality of most authors is predictable by a small number of topics and, hence, a limited range of word associations.

Although the calculations are complex,[12] this integrated method enables an approach to topic modeling that resonates with a widespread understanding, in literary studies, of how fiction and social formations relate: namely, that certain literary tendencies align with authors' belonging to particular social groups. Showing that certain word associations are likely to characterize women's fiction, for instance, does not mean that all women writers use those words, or that they occur with the same frequency in all women's fiction that displays this characteristic. In indicating tendencies or inclinations in the type of literary language used by groups of authors, this integrated method employs quantitative measures without reducing literary meaning to them. It also offers an intelligible foundation for moving between the literary system and the individual literary work. Analyzing the topics identified as "important" by decision trees generates an investigation of the language that most characterizes a category of author (rather than of a discourse, framework, or rhetoric appearing across an entire corpus). And investigating the titles where these "important" topics are most prominent supports analysis not of the topics themselves— as would be the case if topics were chosen by virtue of their heuristic interest or prevalence—but of literary tendencies in the relevant category of authorship.

To return to figure 18, given the keywords comprising them, the capacity of topics 9 and 16 to predict authorial gender suggests a tendency for women's fiction in nineteenth-century Australian newspapers to focus on family relationships, especially between women and children, and on the sentimental and emotional narratives these relationships imply, and for fiction by men to avoid such references while foregrounding boys, their bodies, and activities. The titles that feature topics 9 and 16 most prominently—and thus exemplify the word associations that tend to occur in fiction by women and men, respectively—are children's fiction, aimed at girls and boys. While much of this fiction is by unknown or obscure authors, titles by well-known Australian writers—Ethel Turner's "A Dreadful Pickle" (#1545) and Catherine Helen Spence's "The New Mamma" (#21693)—are first and fifth, respectively, in terms of the presence of topic 9, while Mark Twain's "The Adventures of Tom Sawyer" (#20651) has the sixth-highest level of topic 16.[13] For children's fiction to exemplify or foreground gendered tendencies in authorship implies that it laid the foundations for later gendered patterns of reading and writing with respect to the language and ideas of fiction that men and women would become accustomed to.

Although topics 9 and 16 combined to produce the most accurate two-split decision tree for gender, the secondary node most consistently present across multiple trials was 91. Its keywords ("eyes face girl looked hand voice head man dark turned stood hands lips moment smile half long woman low") suggest a concern with female characters, their appearance, and relationships with men. Figure 19 presents a two-split decision tree featuring these topics (again with 72 percent accuracy, in this case made up of 67 percent success in identifying fiction by women and 77 percent for fiction by men). According to this decision tree, documents with relatively high proportions of topics 9 or 91 are likely to be by women; documents are even more likely to be by men if proportions of both topics are relatively low. Among the titles where topic 91 is highly represented, children's fiction for girls again features: the children's story "Miss Baby" (#7855) has the second-highest proportions of both topics 9 and 91. But this time romance fiction is also prominent. Titles by well-known authors where topic 91 is prominent include the children's story "Miss Elizabeth" (#3631), by Australian author Lilian Turner, in fifth place, and romance titles by British author (and Australian expatriate) Effie Adelaide Rowlands, including "At Great Cost" (#12839) and "Pretty Penelope" (#12840),

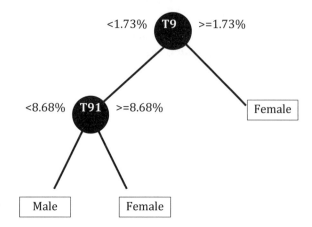

Fig. 19. Decision tree for gender: maximum two splits (trial 8)

in fifteenth and seventeenth place, respectively.

At face value, the word patterns aligned with women's writing reinforce the association of nineteenth-century popular fiction with gender norms. Not only do words prominent in fiction for girls tend to occur in writing by and for women generally—suggesting an infantilizing of women characters and readers—but the co-occurrence of word patterns common in girls' and romance fiction implies the early introduction of girl readers to women's primary aim in the normative gender order: securing a man. This reading is only made more depressing by the implication that these ideas about women and girls were most forcefully expressed in women's fiction. Many of the titles where topics 9 and/or 91 are prominent uphold this interpretation: for instance, Turner's "Miss Elizabeth" introduces its titular character by describing the gaze of the gardener, Jem Watson, lingering on her beautiful young figure (#3631/I); "A Dreadful Pickle" features eleven-year-old Miss Laurayne, pampered and "almost worship[ped]" by her father and three older brothers (#1545/I), who is disciplined to remain in her proper, domestic place when she leaves home without permission and her fine clothes and money are stolen by "an old Jewish-looking man" who threatens to hang her (#1545/IV).

However, at least with topic 9, the focus on female characters indicated by its keywords can have progressive political meanings. For instance, the sentimentality in "The New Mamma" regarding love between mothers and children reinforces the idea that motherhood fulfils women's natural role. Yet in keeping with the reputation of its author, Spence—a prominent colonial feminist and suffragist—the main female characters are decisive and have complex inner lives and relationships with each other. The main male character, the father, is also progressive: paying close attention to his daughter's schooling and complementing his "tender care, his thoughtfulness" for his wife with "his actual sharing of the fatigues of the nursery" (#21693/IV). All of these stories are characterized by women writing about women and girls and thus reinforce the notion that nineteenth-century popular fiction was highly gendered. But the contrasting effects of that focus—to reinforce traditional gender roles or to imagine alternative ones—warn against simplistically interpreting the meanings of word patterns. It foregrounds the necessity of reading the stories—not just the topics—highlighted by this integrated method.

II

One might expect that these gendered tendencies in fiction, in indicating transnational patterns in language, would reduce the likelihood of discerning fiction based on authorial nationality. In fact, this integrated method is better at predicting whether an author is American, Australian, or British than a man or a woman. Challenging the idea that Australian fiction failed to develop original characteristics, it emerges as the most distinctive category due to representations of nonmetropolitan colonial life.[14] These representations conform to long-standing conceptions of the bush tradition in colonial fiction in some ways, while departing in significant others. The American and British fiction in nineteenth-century Australian newspapers can also be predicted based on word patterns. Although more ambiguous in their implications, these tendencies in word usage suggest contrasting attitudes toward time and differing beliefs about the capacity of individuals to change history.

Decision trees can predict author nationality for this corpus with 59 percent success with two and four splits, increasing only marginally to 61 and 62 percent with six and eight splits, respectively. While the overall percentages are lower than for gender, the improvement on expected accuracy is almost double. Because three categories (Ameri-

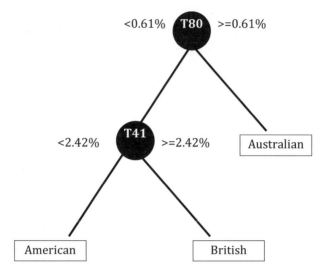

Fig. 20. Decision tree for nationality: maximum two splits (trial 5)

can, Australian, and British) are involved rather than two (male and female) the expected accuracy for predicting nationality is approximately 33 percent, versus 50 percent for gender. With two splits, the capacity of decision trees to predict nationality with 59 percent success is an improvement on expected accuracy of 79 percent, compared with 44 percent for gender.

The model in figure 20 depicts the basic structure of all decision trees for nationality and has a 59 percent overall success rate, composed of 55 percent success in predicting American authorship, 45 percent for Australian, and 77 percent for British. Topic 80 ("creek sheep cattle horses men verandah hut country man horse track township blacks tree river squatter tea gum night") is consistently situated as the root node in all trees, regardless of the number of splits allowed. A title is predicted to be Australian based on the presence, above a very low threshold (here, 0.61 percent), of the words associated with topic 80, and to be either American or British based on the relative absence of these words.[15]

While that trial accurately predicts Australian titles in only 45 percent of cases, other decision trees achieve greater success, also using only the presence of topic 80 to distinguish Australian from British and American fiction. For instance, the decision tree in figure 21 suc-

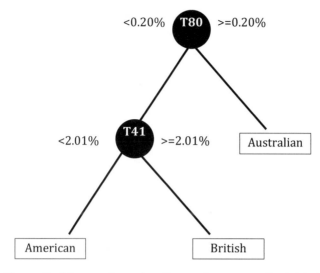

Fig. 21. Decision tree for nationality: maximum two splits (trial 3)

cessfully identifies 59 percent of Australian titles above a threshold of 0.2 percent of topic 80. It has an overall accuracy of 58 percent, with 42 percent success in predicting American authorship and 74 percent for British. And while both of these examples are worse at identifying American than British fiction, with the same hierarchy and slightly different tipping points other decision trees show higher rates of accuracy for American authorship (up to 74 percent) with correspondingly lower rates for the others. Although the most accurate predictions for Australian fiction are lower than for either British or American—an outcome I will return to—the important point here is that the hierarchy of topics remains the same, even as training and testing produces varied outcomes with respect to topic thresholds and rates of prediction of the different categories.

Although place names were excluded prior to topic modeling, topic 80's keywords clearly suggest nonmetropolitan Australian settings, known as "the bush." This setting differs from what chapter 4 described as the marked presence of Australian locations in the Australian fiction in colonial newspapers—and likewise, of British locations in British writing and, to a lesser extent, of American locations in American fiction. In that chapter, where titles were characterized in terms of an inscribed nationality based on textual references, most mentioned a major city in their opening paragraphs: especially London, or perhaps Liverpool or Birmingham, for British fiction; New York or Boston for American; and Sydney or Melbourne for Australian. In contrast, as topic 80's keywords imply, the titles identified here as Australian reference bush landscapes ("creek country track tree river gum"), rural dwellings ("verandah hut townships"), and station life ("sheep cattle horses horse squatter"). (In Australia, stations refer to very large landholdings for raising livestock. Before midcentury, *squatter* was a term for free settlers who had moved beyond legal boundaries to appropriate land; after this time, it described someone who leased large tracts of land from colonial governments to raise stock.)

To say that the titles in which topic 80 is most prominent are mainly by Australian authors might seem an obvious outcome of a method that seeks to predict fiction by nationality. But for other categories—gender above, and American and British fiction below—when titles are ranked in order of the prominence of a predictive topic, even those at the top of that list are often not as prescribed: this is a probabilistic method, after all. In contrast, where authorship is known, almost all titles in which topic 80 features highly are Australian, including 91 percent of the first one hundred and 89 percent of the first two hundred. The first title by a non-Australian author to appear in this list is Anthony Trollope's "Harry Heathcote of Gangoil: A Tale of Australian Bush Life" (#15472), and this comes in twentieth place. The dominance of colonial authors among titles with high proportions of topic 80 reinforces the distinctively Australian character of these bush references.

Some of the Australian fiction in which topic 80 is prominent is by well-known authors. Mary Hannay Foott, best known as a poet but also a staff writer for the *Brisbane Courier* from the late 1880s, was responsible for the titles ranked first and second in this list: "A Whim of the Mistress" (#4686) and "The Black Dingo of Weeri Yeela" (#4562), published in 1894 and 1892, respectively. Rolf Boldrewood's "Robbery Under Arms" (#13336), published in 1882, is ranked forty-fifth in terms of the prominence of topic 80, and Rosa Praed's "Outlaw and Lawmaker" (#19959) and "Mrs. Tregaskiss" (#19574), published in 1893 and 1895, are fifty-fourth and fifty-sixth, respectively. But these are the exception rather than the rule. Most Australian authors of titles with high proportions of topic 80 are little known to literary historians—if known at all—and the rate of unknown authorship is also high in comparison with ordered lists for other predictive topics: 44 percent of the first one hundred titles ranked in terms of the prevalence of topic 80 are by unknown authors, as are 47 percent of the first two hundred.

In many of these instances of unknown authorship, pseudonyms and titles insinuate an Australian—and in most cases, a bush—origin for the fiction. Among the titles where authorship is unknown and topic 80 is prominent pseudonyms include "Old Bushman," "Bulloo," "Bush Naturalist," and "An Old Settler," and rural Australian locations and fauna feature prominently in titles such as "Kooralgin: Pioneering in the Never Never" (#4708), "Coomina, the Golden Valley" (#4723), "Blue Gum among Debbil-Debbil" (#7885), "Bonshaw: A Moreton Bay King" (#12964), and "Our Bush Parson, and the Great Flood of the Darling River" (#4647). The likelihood that many of these unknown authors were Australian—based on the presence of topic 80 and implications of these pseudonyms and titles—reinforces my argument, in chapter 4, that local fiction was considerably more prevalent in colonial newspapers than this project has established definitively. The substantial presence of unknown authors might also suggest the low quality of this fiction. In the stories I have read this is sometimes the case. But for the most part the quality of these works does not seem worse than writing by well-known nineteenth-century Australian (or other) authors. What is true is that most of this fiction was never published in book form and consequently has received little attention from literary or cultural historians.

Bringing these works into the conversation shows that fiction in Australian newspapers routinely depicted rural colonial spaces, activities, and characters. While metropolitan and provincial newspapers are equally represented across the spectrum of titles characterized by the relative presence of topic 80, those that feature this topic most prominently appeared in metropolitan publications. This is the case with nine of the first ten titles ranked in order of the presence of topic 80 (seven of which were published in a single newspaper, the Brisbane-based *Queenslander*) and seventeen of the top twenty. If we understand this focus on the bush as the imagining of the nation that Benedict Anderson aligns with both the novel and the newspaper in the nineteenth century, this trend indicates that such recourse to rural places occurred most explicitly in city newspapers. While the tradition of bush writing is aligned with the Sydney-based *Bulletin*, its broader prominence in metropolitan newspapers suggests that magazine might have foregrounded, but did not create, the tradition. More particularly, the *Queenslander's* prominence in this trend raises the possibility that the literary tradition usually attributed to the *Bulletin* might have been more pronounced in other metropolitan periodicals.

Before elaborating on the relationship between topic 80 and the bush tradition, it is useful to consider the nature of stories where that topic is present just above the predictive threshold for Australian authorship. Such fiction is connected to this tradition in having rural settings and describing the bush and its effects on characters' lives. Many demonstrate the contrasting perspectives on the bush—as either beautiful or brutal—associated, respectively, with the works of the two major authors of the Australian bush tradition, "Banjo" Paterson and Henry Lawson. But where the bush tradition features characters within the landscape, these threshold stories are more likely to present characters viewing the bush from a slightly separate place.

The type of references to the bush in these threshold stories, and this slightly separate perspective, is indicated by two examples selected at random from titles in which topic 80's words composed 0.2 percent of those analyzed. Janet Carroll's "By the River's Side," published in 1882, begins by describing "Langonga Station on one of the branches of the Murray" in romantic terms: it has "all the advantage of river grassy plains, shady gullies and round topped hills that jealously guard [the station] with their earthly bulk" (#13540/I). Though referencing a similar environment, Mary Gaunt's "The Other Man," published in 1894, contrastingly depicts "a stock route, bounded on either hand by ugly wire fences, which stretched away in parallel lines across the stony plain far as the eye could see. A lonely, dreary prospect—the stony plain and the ugly fences." While Carroll's hills guard the station, Gaunt's "dim hills bounded the horizon" and "watery sunshine . . . gleamed hopelessly in the shallow pools on the roadway" (#470/I). These threshold stories for topic 80 view the bush from the station and its immediate surrounds, while others adopt alternative vantage points: for instance, describing the bush as a traveler enters or leaves a township or passes by the Australian coast on a sailing ship.

The engagement with the bush in these passages supports my claim that topic 80, even at relatively low levels, describes a distinctive aspect of nineteenth-century Australian fiction. (And I can easily imagine a project that extends conceptions of the bush tradition with reference to the different perspectives on the bush—including gendered ones—presented by these threshold stories.) However, it is important to recognize that references to the bush vary across the spectrum of titles encompassed by the relative presence of topic 80, even as the fiction discussed below—where that topic is most prominent—exemplify features present in this bush fiction generally.

While setting their narratives more firmly within the landscape, titles in which topic 80 is most prominent display the same, contrasting attitude to the bush demonstrated above. As in Paterson's and Lawson's work, whether the bush is a place of beauty or brutality, it presents dangers, often in the form of bushfires or native wildlife. Also resonating with accounts of the bush tradition, specifically with feminist critiques of it, is the male orientation of stories with the highest proportions of topic 80. Notwithstanding Foott's authorship of the first and second titles in this respect, most are by men. Where authorship is known, women wrote 35 percent of the fiction analyzed for this chapter but only 16 percent of the first one hundred, and 21 percent of the first two hundred, ranked by the prominence of topic 80. This male dominance resonates with both the general orientation of colonial literary culture to men's writing, also discussed in chapter 4, and specific references in topic 80's keywords to "men . . . man . . . squatter" and to the male-dominated arenas of sheep and cattle raising.

Yet these stories simultaneously challenge core conceptions of the bush tradition, and of nineteenth-century Australian literature broadly. The most obvious difference is in timing. While the bush tradition is identified with the 1890s, stories published earlier in the century—in the 1880s, and even more so prior to this decade—are more likely to be identified as Australian by the presence of topic 80 than those published in the century's final decade. This trend is somewhat qualified by the slight overrepresentation of titles from the 1890s among those with the highest proportions of topic 80. Although Australian fiction from this decade was slightly less likely to feature the bush than in earlier periods, when the bush was referenced it was more likely to be foregrounded. This trend implies increasingly self-conscious representations of the bush. But such portrayals were a consistent feature of colonial fiction, rather than something that emerged only late in the nineteenth century, in concert with the political movement to federation.[16]

Another difference between these titles and existing accounts of the bush tradition is the prominence of rural communities. Where that tradition stands in opposition to domesticity, these stories are more likely to feature families in the bush than the archetypal, solitary "noble frontiersman" and to be driven by emotional bonds between men, women, and children rather than by intense male friendship or "mateship" (Nile 2–3). The focus on families occurs not just in threshold titles for topic 80 but in those where that topic is most prominent. One title in this latter category does show a man spending time alone in the bush: F. E. Lockwood's "The Genii of the Vanguard" (#8476), first published in 1899 and ranked seventh in terms of the prevalence of topic 80. But in this case, the protagonist, Jack Jones, is forced due to circumstances to work as a fencer on the boundaries of a remote station and evokes the domestic realm often: thinking of his wife and children, writing them letters, and working explicitly for them. He also has as many interactions with the wives of other men—the shepherd, the station manager—as with the men themselves. And when he joins up with another man to fence the boundary, they develop a friendship based on their common, and hidden, high birth, and the sensibilities this endows them with, thus also complicating the fierce egalitarianism supposedly underpinning Australia's bush tradition.

In terms of existing scholarship on the bush tradition and colonial fiction generally, the most surprising aspect of these stories is their consistent and prominent portrayal of Aboriginal characters, and the complexity of those representations. A central argument in Australian postcolonial literary studies is that, beginning in the nineteenth century, fiction replicated the legal lie of *terra nullius* by not depicting Australia's original inhabitants. The repression required of such concealment is understood to give Australian literature a peculiarly Gothic character, wherein the "haunted" or "occulted bush" is "full of unseen 'presences,'" and the successful occupation of the land is "replaced by *preoccupation*, by a bothersome sense of something that is already there" (Gelder 119).[17] Such haunting is aligned with ambivalent representations of the bush, in the sense that either its beauty or its brutality conceals "something deeply unknowable and terrifying in the Australian landscape" (Trigg xvii). Such a sense of danger displaces fear and suspicion of Aboriginal people onto the bush.

In considering the stories where topic 80 is most prominent, I did find this racialized displacement in one. The fearsome dingo in Foott's "The Black Dingo of Weeri Yeela" that the young protagonist Will Hanson is sent out to hunt is black (dingoes are most often red or tan) and described as "a big black fellow" that kills sheep. More pointedly, Will discovers the dingo stalking a young, vulnerable white girl who has wandered away from her parents into the bush (#4562/IV). The lost child is another key component of the Australian Gothic, including in the nineteenth century, and is interpreted as standing "in part for the apprehensions of [Anglo-European] adults about having sought to settle in a place where they might never be at peace" (Pierce xii).

Much more frequently, the unsettled colonial condition is evoked by depicting, not repressing, the Aboriginal presence. Aboriginal characters widely populate the fiction in which topic 80 is most prominent. These characters are generally presented in friendly and harmonious, though inequitable, relationships with colonists: for instance, teaching them about bush foods, guiding them through the bush, looking after stock, or simply spending time around the station. Such Aboriginal characters are roughly drawn sketches or stereotypes—the childlike native, the lazy black, the harmless primitive—and their purpose in these narratives is to assist, and thereby to justify, the colonial mission.

Other titles in which topic 80 is prominent directly signify the fear underlying the colonial mission, describing attacks by Aborigines, and bloodshed. For instance, the title in which topic 80 is most present, Foott's "A Whim of the Mistress," opens with "treacherous blacks [who] had made a plan to kill the white women and children on one of the stations while the men were out on the run looking after the cattle" (#4686/I). Likewise, in "The Genii of the Vanguard," Jack Jones returns to his remote camp to find the visiting station "manager faint from loss of blood, with a spear through his thigh. The horses were speared, his faithful [dog] dead, and the hut looted of all food and clothing" (#8476/I). Members of this Aboriginal group are also described as cannibals. In both stories Aboriginal people come out of the bush and attack small, vulnerable outposts, thus conflating bloodthirsty tribes with the country's natural hazards. But the presence of Aboriginal people is not denied or repressed.

And even in these stories that begin with frontier violence, colonization is affirmed and justified through Aboriginal presence: specifically by the actions of "good" Aboriginal characters who save white people from "bad" ones. Thus, in "A Whim of the Mistress," the "treacherous blacks" are defeated by the actions not of colonists but of a "brave Warrego black," "Kombo, who was not one of the Cornoo blacks but . . . heard the others talking" and warned the intended victims at great expense to himself. He arrives at the homestead

> without any clothing, dripping wet and shining in the rising sun like a new-blacked boot, and streaming with blood from a gash in the right arm, where a greenstone tomahawk, caught in the muscle, dangled betwixt elbow and shoulder. He uttered his warning, and the women and children were saved.

The place where this noble savage ("without any clothing," "shining," "new") crossed the river while under attack "was forever after known as 'Kombo's Crossing'" (#4686/I). There the story is set, with that strange layering of Aboriginal connection, European colonization, and Aboriginal naming that often occurs in Australia. Another noble savage figure saves Jack Jones in "The Genii of the Vanguard." Jack is not attacked with the station manager because an Aboriginal spirit comes to him, first in a dream, then in the form of a monster, then as "a fine looking native youth" who introduces himself to Jack as "Muldarbie" (#8476/I), a Ngarrindjeri word for a spirit or sorcerer (Clarke 68). Muldarbie tells Jack,

> I am young forever. I am the ruler of many tribes. . . . I can change myself into many forms. All this land is mine. These men who fled down the hill are bad men; they would have killed and eaten you, if I had not frightened them. They have eaten all their fat, and now they will rob your camp and spear your dog. But I have saved your life. (#8476/I)

In both stories, then, white people are "saved" by noble savage figures whose innate human goodness, free from the corrupting influence of civilization, provides an imprimatur to the colonial enterprise.

Although the presence—not the absence—of Aboriginal characters is used to justify colonization, these stories are still structured by a pattern of repression and emergence. In some, juxtaposed stereotypes, by ascribing a duality or unknowability to Aboriginal characters, hint at colonization's potential instability. For instance, in "Kooralgin" (1898), by "Old Bushman," "Jerry . . . my blackboy" is the innocent and reliable companion who warns the narrator about a coming bush-fire and then wanders happily along bringing up the horses while his master rushes off to fight the fire. But released from his duties, "Jerry" becomes something barely human as he joins "a flock of native com-panions . . . celebrating the close of day by indulging in the most gro-tesque capers, hopping on one leg, flapping their wings, and bowing their red-capped heads and long necks in graceful salutation to one another" (#4708/I). The colonized companion is revealed to be only a surface for the uncolonized other, both "grotesque" and "graceful."

Where "good" Aboriginal characters defeat "bad" ones, the repres-sion required of colonization is even more unsettling, to the extent that certain features of "A Whim of the Mistress" and "The Genii of the Vanguard" appear to question the premise of the enterprise itself. One might assume that naming Kombo's Crossing after an Aboriginal char-acter from the narrative past would set the stage to remove Aboriginal characters from the narrative present. In fact, "A Whim of the Mistress" goes on to present multiple Aboriginal characters, binding them to yet another story of a child lost in the bush. Here, however, a white woman steals the child—in place of her dead child, whose body she places in a cave in the bush—and takes that child, Bobby, to the city. The child's return and recognition by his true mother is presaged by Bobby, now a man, trying to kill one of his Aboriginal "friend[s]," "Spider," at the place he was originally taken from. Unable to see the scene, the station manager hears "a gasping entreaty for mercy, a heavy plunge, and the noise as of a deadly struggle in the water," before breaking through "the scrub" and coming to the aid of another Aboriginal character, "Cubbie, who was trying in vain to wrench Spider from Bobby's hold" (#4686/IV). The description, shortly after this murderous scene, of Bobby, Cubbie, and Spider sitting companionably together, "the morn-ing's quarrel apparently quite forgotten," throws into relief the vio-lence underpinning all the other seeming friendships between Aborig-inal and European characters in these stories (#4686/VII).

Alternatively, in "The Genii of the Vanguard," one might imagine Muldarbie's claim to own all the land would stand as a figurative state-ment by a spectral figure, enabling rather than precluding white pos-session of the country. Instead, as Jack is taking the injured manager back to the homestead, the shepherd responds to news of the attack in a way that perceives Aboriginal people as savage but also as following a clear and continuing law that situates Europeans as trespassers on their land: "I'd never have brought my family here if I'd not known how strict the tribal laws are. The natives would kill and eat their own children rather than hunt on ground not their own" (#8476/I). Thus, the cannibalism of these "bad" Aboriginal characters is surreally refigured as an action compelled by a legal and moral framework that forbids transgressions in relation to land.

Beyond the appearance of "blacks" as a keyword for topic 80, other of the top one hundred words in this topic—including "track mob party tracks"—reinforce the prominence of Aboriginal characters in nineteenth-century Australian fiction. These narratives of Aboriginal complicity in colonization, and of Aboriginal and European violence, suggest significant new understandings of how colonization was imagined and enacted in Australia. More particularly, the omission of these stories from Australian literary history implies the role of literary criticism, rather than colonial ideology, in the exclusion of Aboriginal characters from the Australian literary canon. Rather than a racist conspiracy by literary critics, I think the representational framework in identity politics produces and sustains this belief in Aboriginal invisibility in literature.

Reading this fiction, it is immediately obvious that Aboriginal characters must have featured in colonial bush fiction. Stations and other rural industries in Australia in this period could not have functioned without the slave labor that Aboriginal people provided, so stories that depicted the bush without Aboriginal characters would have seemed false. In identity politics in literary criticism, however, oppression and emancipation are equated with nonrepresentation and representation, respectively; the claim that Aboriginal characters were excluded from colonial fiction expresses this political framework to the occlusion of the fiction published. As analysis of mass-digitized collections enables scholars to identify and challenge previous curations of the literary-historical record, I expect similar disjunctions between the contemporary canon and the fiction of past periods will come to light.

In contrast to Australian fiction, decision trees do not align the American and British writing in colonial newspapers with topics indicative of distinctively American and British places or experiences. As figures 20 and 21 show, these national categories are predicted based on the relative lack (for American fiction) or presence (for British) of topic 41 ("man people woman life things time girl knew men talk poor place house women suppose money looked sort years"). The implications of topic 41 are far from obvious based on its keywords, which combine different categories of people ("man people woman girl men women"), references to finances ("poor money"), time ("time years"), forms of thought and communication ("knew talk suppose looked"), and general types or states of being ("life things place house sort").

Reading the three (all British) titles in which topic 41 is most prominent, I initially wondered whether these word associations indicated melancholy or even tragic themes. Justin McCarthy's "Camiola: A Girl with a Fortune" (1885) begins in a graveyard, with the narrator meditating on the meaning of life and death (#4988/I); Mrs. Robert Jocelyn's "Only a Flirt" (1897) opens with the difficulties a young, motherless girl faces due to her father's unwise generosity (#19888/I); another of McCarthy's titles, "The Riddle Ring" (1897), features Jim Conrad "alone and lonely" in Paris, rejected by the woman he loves (#4673/I). However, this latter story's tone is lighthearted: Jim is soon distracted by the discovery of a heavy gold ring and the possibilities that the mystery of its ownership presents for his literary ambitions and future fortunes. Reading further—in these and other titles—and doing so by highlighting the first one hundred most prominent words in order to identify passages most indicative of the presence of topic 41, I came to associate its relative presence—and, accordingly, British fiction—with a focus on the passage of time and its effects, and more particularly with a pessimism, or at least an ambivalence, about the capacity of individuals and their actions to shape events.

Titles in which topic 41 is prominent foreground reflection, by narrators and characters, in thought and in conversation, on the implications of the past for the present and the future. (In this respect, the emphasis on thought, communication, and time in the most prominent twenty words resonates with references in the top one hundred to "talking understanding thinking heard looked reason true," as well as "times life long ago.") These meditations have a highly universal aspect: everyone—"man woman girl people men women person"—

is subject to time and its passing, and even a great "family" (another prominent word) can be forgotten. For instance, McCarthy introduces a house central to "Camiola" by noting that

> such historic associations as the place had were bound up with the family history of the great man whose tomb was made in the church by the water. All manner of odd endowments and foundations bore the name of some member of that gifted and eccentric house whose fame reached its loudest with this one great man, and then was no further renewed. The family had become extinct, its title appeared no more on the roll of English peers. (#4988/I)

Although clearly describing the English aristocracy, the broad nature of these references—for instance, to "such historic associations," to "the family of the great man," "the name of some member," "the church by the water"—universalizes the events described: evoking the idea of a great family's fall as much as the fall of a specific great family. The passage also foregrounds the interrelationship of the past, present, and future in references to future endowments and foundations produced by a great, now forgotten, name or the reverberating sound of "fame" through history, until its echo is exhausted.

Often in titles in which topic 41 is prominent, the consequences of time passing are associated with money and marriage. Money as well as reputation can be won and lost, and the possibility of change in financial circumstances is associated with "hope," but mostly dread ("trouble worse afraid doubt"). Marriage was the main way for nineteenth-century women (and indeed, some men) to secure their financial futures and is a prominent theme in these stories. However, marriages that privilege money over love have negative outcomes. The protagonist of "Camiola" marries a rich old man she does not care for and suffers terrible guilt about her feelings after his death; the girl suffers in "Only a Flirt" because a mean-spirited aunt, left widowed with "only" six hundred pounds a year, is invited to live with the family; and Jim Conrad's sweetheart in "The Riddle Ring" chooses to marry a rich old man instead of him.

As long as the poverty is genteel rather than absolute, marrying for love can bring a sort of happiness, as shown in the housekeeper's description of Mrs. Clangarthe and her husband—the Major—in Frances Hodgson Burnett's "The Tide on the Moaning Bar" (1892), ranked fifth in terms of the presence of topic 41:

> Mrs. Clangarthe had been a great beauty in her day, and came of a very fine, very poor, Irish family; and on the strength of this she used to lie on the sofa, and sit in an easy chair all day, joking with the Major, and letting the children run wild. They had made away with plenty of money in their time, shabby as things seemed now; and they were as carelessly happy, good-tempered a set as ever I saw in my life. (#13469/I)

In the reflective mode characteristic of this topic—here of one character contemplating the life of another—having married for love, Mrs. Clangarthe and the Major are "easy . . . joking . . . happy, good-tempered." Likewise, the widowed father's passionate love for his wife in "Only a Flirt" is contrasted approvingly with his sister's greater concern for money than for her husband's death. Yet there is no certainty in marrying for love. Loved ones die (with great frequency in these stories), and even Mrs. Clangarthe and the Major's relationship and apparent disregard for money have a wildness and carelessness that is irresponsible (here, in its consequences for the children) as well as appealing.

In contrast to these reflections on the relationship between past, present, and future, titles in which topic 41 is relatively absent— identified by decision trees as a tendency in American fiction— foreground the narrative present. Such fiction focuses on specific things, people, and events in the present moment. A sense of this difference can be gleaned by comparing the first two sentences of two stories, both describing bodies of water: the first with the highest proportion of topic 41, the second with among the lowest. McCarthy's "Camiola" opens with:

> A church and churchyard stand on the edge of a river. The waters of the stream wash the outer churchyard when the tide is full, or even half full; and sometimes in the stormy days of winter and spring the waves toss themselves far over the wall, and sport and splash among the quiet tombs and hillocks of the dead. (#4988/I)

This scene is universal—the church, churchyard, and river could be almost anywhere—and both timeless and timely in its focus on tides and seasons. In contrast, "Atholbane: A Romance of Kenmore Castle" (1870), by American author Sylvanus Cobb, opens on:

> June 20, A. D. 1096. Towards the close of the day a man stood upon the shore of Loch Tay, one of the most beautiful and picturesque sheets of water in Scotland, gazing at times over the towering summit of Ben Lawers, where the clouds were rolling up in great black masses, and anon upon a small boat that was struggling with the rising wind near the middle of the lake. (#85/I)

Such references to a specific date open many stories with the lowest proportions of topic 41. The subsequent reference to the time of day and the activities of a particular man contrast the temporal interconnectedness in McCarthy's story. Likewise, the objects of the man's observance—the summit of a specific mountain and the progress of a particular, small boat—are very different from the reflection by a disembodied narrator on extended time in "Camiola." The comparison is extensible: McCarthy's story goes on to reflect on the inevitability of "death and man's sad, transitory career" (#4988/I), while Cobb's offers a detailed description of the man's age, hair, eyes, clothes, and character (#85/I).

Contrary to my initial assumption, the emotional tenor of fiction in which topic 41 appears in very low proportions can be as melancholy as in those stories in which topic 41 is prominent. But even when representing the pains of romantic love or grief, these stories are characterized by direct description and a focus on the narrative present. For instance, American author Caroline Lee Hentz's "The Blind Girl's Story" (1872) opens on a specific moment in which

> all is still and solitary—the light burns on the table, with wasting splendour. The writing desk is open before me, with the last letter unfolded—the letter I have cherished so fondly, though every word seems an arrow to my conscience. (#20763/I)

As well as orienting the story to a particular character and place (the lover at the writing table with a specific and meaningful letter), this passage emphasizes the immediate present, for instance in the stillness of the moment, the precise hue of the light as it burns, or the experience of guilt as an arrow.

As with all topics, 41 is present along a spectrum, so the relationship to time in most of the fiction identified as British or American based on its relative presence or absence is not as extreme as in these examples. Even so, the predictive capacity of this topic suggests that, among the titles published in nineteenth-century Australian newspapers, British fiction tends to be more concerned with the span of time and the implications of its passage for general states of being, as well as for the challenges of attaining and retaining money and reputation. In contrast, the American fiction is generally more direct, focused on the present time and on the actions of individuals in it. While topic 41 does not determine the emotional tenor of these stories, this attitude toward time in British fiction cannot be separated from a preoccupation with—and uncertainty and ambivalence about—the future and one's ability to improve on the present. While this perspective might be termed pessimism, the tendency in American fiction to focus on the present and individual characters implies a relatively confident or optimistic view of the individual's capacity to alter her or his circumstances.

These meanings I have attributed to the relative presence and absence of topic 41 resonate with prevailing ideas about differences in British and American national characters. However, it is important to recognize that these decision trees are not working with British and American fiction, per se, but with those stories published in colonial newspapers. As chapters 4 and 5 have explored, much of the American fiction in this context was highly popular in nature, often extracted from dime novels and by authors who might have been contracted to write a story each month, or even more frequently. In contrast, much of the British fiction was by authors more invested in the literary qualities of their writing and involved in staged publications—typically, syndication followed by different forms of book publication—that allowed more time for writing and revising. This context makes it possible that the association of British and American fiction with the relative presence and absence of topic 41, respectively, relates to differences between literary and popular genres. Literary fiction often emphasizes characters' interiority, focuses on the human condition, and explores the complexities of social, political, or ethical situations; popular fiction frequently foregrounds the narrative present and direct description of settings and characters.

Some trends in the fiction divided by topic 41's relative presence or absence appear to support this argument. The one hundred titles in which topic 41 is most present (conceivably literary fiction) have fewer than half the number of unknown authors than do the one hundred titles where this topic is lowest (conceivably popular fiction): the totals are 41 and 87, respectively. Reinforcing the association of low levels of topic 41 with popular writing is the considerable presence among such fiction of American dime and romance novelists, including "Nick Carter," "Bertha M. Clay," and Mrs. E. D. E. N. Southworth. In contrast, a number of stories in which topic 41 is highest are by canonical literary authors. Oscar Wilde's "The Picture of Dorian Gray" (#15603), which famously deals with concealing the consequences of transgression through time, is thirty-ninth in this respect, while Anthony Trollope's "He Knew He Was Right" (#15473), describing the failure of a marriage due to unreasonable jealousy, is eighty-second.

Yet many stories in which topic 41 is prominent are by British authors of popular genres—including multiple titles by Charlotte Brame, Margaret Oliphant, and Dora Russell (writers of romance, occult, and sensation fiction, respectively). And some of the fiction with among the lowest levels of this topic is by canonical authors. These include, in forty-sixth place, Victor Hugo's "Ninety-Three" (#14334), describing the unfolding horrors of the French Revolution, and in ninety-ninth place, Charles Dickens's "Pickwick Papers" (#177), recounting the adventures of the Pickwick Club as they travel through the English countryside. The adventurous or satirical nature of these works, as opposed to the philosophical or moral seriousness of those by Wilde and Trollope, reinforces the association of high levels of topic 41 with reflection and ambivalence and of low levels with direct description and the narrative present. But the presence of popular and literary fiction on both sides of the threshold for topic 41 suggests that its capacity to identify British and American fiction in colonial newspapers has not simply to do with the former having greater literary qualities. It would seem, rather, that a relationship exists between the attitudes toward history of these different cultures and the fiction they produced.

III

So far I have argued that representations of nonmetropolitan colonial spaces make Australian fiction the most distinctive national or proto-national category in nineteenth-century Australian newspapers. However, I have also noted that rates of prediction for American and British authorship are generally better than for Australian. Table 5 reinforces this point, showing that, with two, four, six, and eight splits, the average success rate for predicting British and American fiction is better than for Australian fiction—and with the exception of eight splits, markedly so. Understanding why these outcomes do not contradict each other, and exploring other tendencies in these stories, requires further consideration of the workings of decision trees and how they use topics to predict nationality.

The first relevant issue is the number of decisions used in the above trees to categorize the different national literatures. Consistently with two splits, in most cases with four, and for some decision trees with six splits as well, Australian fiction is predicted based on one decision only: the relative presence of topic 80. In contrast, American and British fiction are identified based on at least two decisions: the relative absence of topic 80 *and* relative degrees of topic 41 (with four, six, and eight splits, often many more than two decisions are involved). While British and American stories are first separated from Australian ones and then from each other, Australian fiction is allocated a single route, which involves being distinguished from American and British fiction from the start. Greater accuracy in predicting British and American than Australian authorship relates, in part, to the greater number of decisions allocated to the task.

Table 5. Average success rate (%) for predicting author nationality from ten decision trees, including and excluding topic 80

Number of splits	2		4		6		8	
Topic 80 included	Y	N	Y	N	Y	N	Y	N
American	58	59	66	51	64	55	61	60
Australian	49	34	49	41	49	46	57	51
British	65	55	56	58	64	56	60	48
Overall	57	49	57	50	59	53	59	53

Decision trees consistently adopt this structure because they are designed to make the logically optimal choice at each node: the one that successfully allocates the greatest number of titles into the necessary two "buckets." The association between Australian fiction and topic 80 is sufficiently strong that, for every decision tree trialed, the largest two buckets these models can create involves Australian fiction (characterized by the relative presence of topic 80) on one side, and all other fiction (characterized by the relative absence of that topic) on the other. But the optimal decision at each node does not always produce equally accurate predictions for all categories. Indeed, the strength of topic 80's association with nineteenth-century Australian fiction—what we might call its overdetermination—limits the capacity for decision trees to predict Australian authorship.

Such overdetermination is also the reason why, when permitted additional splits, decision trees often employ topic 80 at multiple nodes. The example in figure 22, for instance, uses topic 80 on three occasions: at the apex of the tree and to distinguish American from Australian fiction, and British from Australian fiction, at two of the final three nodes. So consistently is Australian authorship aligned with the relative presence of topic 80 that the algorithm finds gradations of that topic to be the optimal way of dividing titles on multiple occasions. The view that topic 80 overdetermines the prediction of Australian authorship is reinforced by the improvement in outcomes for this category between six and eight splits. As table 5 shows, the average success rate for predicting Australian fiction increases from 49 percent with six splits to 57 percent with eight, whereas for American and British fiction it declines (from 64 percent in both cases to 60 and 61 percent, respectively). Having reached the point at which increasingly refined thresholds for topic 80 are no longer optimal for distinguishing Australian fiction, a more nuanced characterization of this category is possible, with a decline in predictive outcomes for the other national literatures being the trade-off.

The strength of topic 80's association with Australian authorship shows that stories depicting nonmetropolitan colonial sites and lives were not only characteristically Australian, they were the most distinctive feature of this literary system broadly. Even so, the algorithm's reliance on this topic limits what we can learn about colonial writing. One response would be to look at multilevel decision trees to see how

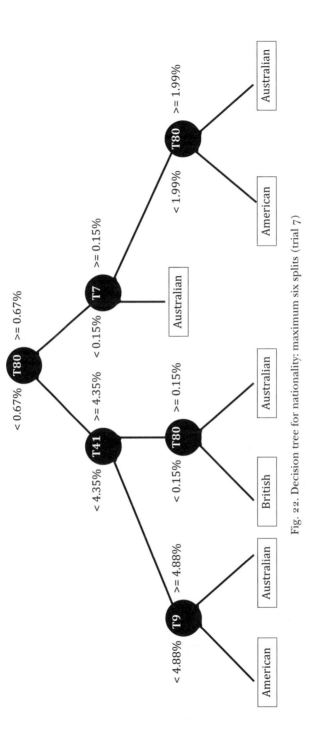

Fig. 22. Decision tree for nationality: maximum six splits (trial 7)

such fiction is identified beyond topic 80. But the complexity of those models—in the number of decisions involved, but more particularly, in their nested structure—makes this avenue problematic.

I elected instead to remove topic 80 from the data offered to the decision trees. Table 5 compares average success rates of predictions with this modified data to overall results for two, four, six, and eight splits. As would be expected given topic 80's importance in differentiating Australian from American and British fiction, this strategy reduces the accuracy of the decision trees overall, with all splits, and for each category. However, the average overall decline is less dramatic than might be expected—between 6 and 8 percent—indicating that decision trees were able to find other topics with predictive capacity. And with the exception of two splits (for reasons I elaborate below), prediction of Australian fiction is less generally impacted than for American and British writing.[18] This outcome suggests that topic 80's absence was just as important—if not more so—in predicting British and American fiction as its presence was for identifying Australian writing.

Figure 23 shows the most successful decision tree for nationality with four splits excluding topic 80. Its 53 percent overall accuracy is made up of 58 percent success in determining American authorship, 48 percent for Australian, and 54 percent for British. The robustness of the hierarchy and range of topics depicted—namely, topic 41 as the primary node, with topics 91 and 11 as secondary—is reinforced by their recurrence in multiple trials with four splits. With the addition of an extra topic, this hierarchy and range also occur in multiple decision trees with six splits, including in the most successful trial at that level, shown in figure 24. In that case, the 56 percent overall success rate—with 62 percent success for American authorship, 52 percent for Australian, and 54 percent for British—is achieved with slightly different tipping points than those in figure 23, and by differentiating American from British fiction in one of the final nodes via the relative presence or absence of a topic clearly suggestive of American slang (71—"goin afore reckon jest aint thar wot wasn folks gal wos feller bout kin tucker mighty won guess agin").

Topic 41's primary position in all decision trees that exclude topic 80 reinforces its importance in predicting British and American fiction. As in the decision trees discussed above, across the various trials conducted without topic 80, British fiction is always associated with

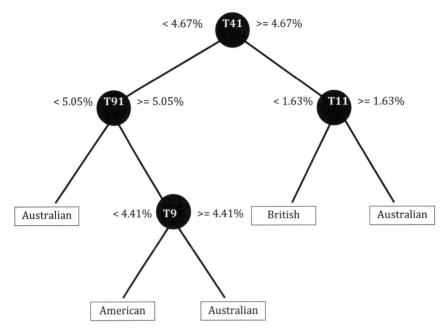

Fig. 23. Decision tree for nationality, excluding topic 80: maximum four splits (trial 1)

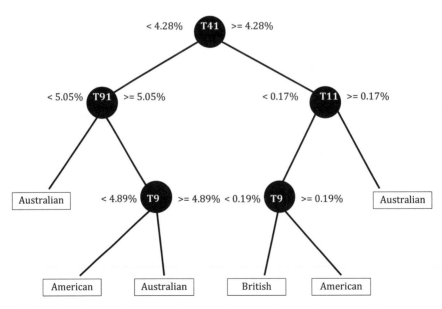

Fig. 24. Decision tree for nationality, excluding topic 80: maximum six splits (trial 4)

the relative presence of topic 41, and American fiction with its relative absence. With increased splits, American fiction occurs more often on the positive as well as the negative side of the threshold for topic 41: in one of ten trials with four splits, six of ten with six splits, and eight of ten with eight splits. But the opposite is much less true for British fiction, which is not predicted in association with the relative absence of topic 41 in any of ten trials with four splits, and is predicted in only two of ten with six splits and one of ten with eight splits. These results indicate that American fiction in colonial newspapers was more likely to demonstrate the attitude toward time and history that more typically characterizes British fiction than vice versa. This finding resonates with the "British" inscription of known American fiction discussed in chapter 4 and is also suggestive of the influence of this more established literary tradition on American authors. Given the large amount of popular British fiction in colonial newspapers, the rare association of British authorship with low levels of topic 41 further challenges the idea that this topic's opposite extremes distinguish popular and literary modes of writing.

Excluding topic 80 makes it possible to explore the relationship of Australian fiction to topic 41. As figures 23 and 24 show, Australian authorship is predicted on both sides of the threshold for this topic. But it is more often associated with topic 41's relative absence. This association occurs in ten of ten trials with two, four, six, and eight splits. In contrast, Australian authorship is aligned with the relative presence of topic 41 in zero of ten trials with two splits, three of ten with four splits, eight of ten with six splits, and ten of ten with eight splits. Australian fiction's appearance on both sides of the threshold for topic 41 explains why the predictive success for local fiction is so low for two splits with topic 80 removed (see table 5). Such models are forced to place Australian fiction on one side of the threshold for topic 41, whereas it is more likely than American or British fiction to occur on both. This finding suggests that, in a substantial amount of colonial fiction, the attitude toward history and the individual's place in it resembled that in British writing. But in the larger proportion of such fiction, the treatment of time was closer to that characteristic of American stories.

This is a result that many Australian literary historians will be inclined to disregard: the field has long assumed that, if nineteenth-century Australian authors followed any overseas literary tradition, it would be Britain's.[19] But perhaps what we are dealing with here has less to do with following a literary tradition than with the cultural or even psychic effects of living in a newly emerged or emergent nation as opposed to a place represented or understood as the "old country." Literary language that is focused on the present and optimistic about the future might well be more likely in societies in which occupation is predicted on denying the prior ownership of indigenous peoples, and where fortunes can be made and social positions changed rapidly with work and luck rather than inheritance. The idea that nineteenth-century Australian fiction displays two different attitudes toward history and time—one of the old world, the other of the new—is bolstered by significant correlations between the relative presence and absence of topic 41 and trends in the authorship and publication of Australian fiction.

Among the local newspaper fiction where topic 41 is highest, canonical Australian authors clearly dominate. Catherine Helen Spence is first and third, with "Afloat or Ashore" (#15271) and "Substantive or Adjective" (#15273), while Rolf Boldrewood's "Robbery Under Arms" (#13336) is second. Multiple titles by Ada Cambridge appear in the top ten—"In the Dead of Night" (#6662), "A Woman's Friendship" (#17169), "Mrs. Carlisle's Enemy" (#12899), and "A Mere Chance" (#12894) (her "A Successful Experiment" [#12895] is eleventh)—and other fiction by Spence and Boldrewood, as well as by Rosa Praed, features topic 41 prominently. Given the large number of Australian titles uncovered by this project, the concentration of canonical Australian writers among those where topic 41 is highest is remarkable and reinforces the topic's association with serious or moral themes. Spence, Boldrewood, Cambridge, and Praed were all published in Britain and are often described as having a British orientation in their writing. The same is true of other authors whose fiction is characterized by the relative presence of topic 41, including Francis Adams, Mary Gaunt, and Louise Mack.

Authors of Australian fiction with the lowest proportions of topic 41 are less prominent in Australian literary history, if they are known at all. Horace Earle, John Rae, Harold Brees, Foster Osborne, Gustaf Dillbert: as far as I know, these authors' reputations have not survived the nineteenth century. Among the authors in this group are those—

mostly men, and for the most part not well known in Australian literary history—who were widely published in provincial newspapers, particularly in the 1880s: E. J. Bowling, Grosvenor Bunster, William Aubrey Burnage, Donald Cameron, Henry John Congreve, Angus McLean, Harold W. H. Stephen, Atha Westbury, Robert P. Whitworth, and James Joseph Wright. In chapter 4 I associated these authors with the growth in provincial newspaper publishing from the late 1870s, and in chapter 5, with the provincial newspaper syndicates that supplied much of that fiction. Well-known authors of titles with low levels of topic 41 tend to be thought of as writing a more distinctively Australian style of fiction, and include Bertha Southey Adams, a prominent nineteenth-century Tasmanian poet and author, as well as Guy Boothby, Marcus Clarke, Charles De Boos, Ethel and Lilian Turner, and Eliza Winstanley.

The correlations I am describing are not absolute. For instance, while titles by Boldrewood have among the highest proportions of topic 41 of the Australian fiction analyzed, some of his works show relatively low levels of this topic, and while the provincial male writers just mentioned are mainly aligned with low levels of topic 41, some of them (Bunster, Cameron, Stephen, and Whitworth) published certain titles with relatively high levels of this topic. A number of other Australian authors, including well-known ones, do not show a clear tendency either way in terms of the relative presence or absence of this topic, including Louisa Atkinson, John Arthur Barry, Mary Hannay Foott, Catherine Martin, John Silvester Nottage, and "Tasma" (Jessie Couvreur).

Notwithstanding these exceptions, the idea that topic 41 indicates some sort of distinction in colonial literary culture gains further support from correlations between its relative presence and absence and publishing trends. Australian stories with relatively high and low levels of this topic were more likely to be published in metropolitan and provincial newspapers, respectively: while metropolitan periodicals published 62 percent of unique Australian fiction analyzed for this chapter, this is the case for 70 percent of the fifty titles where topic 41 is highest, but only 48 percent of the fifty titles where that topic is lowest. A more pronounced gendered difference in authorship exists, with women writing 35 percent of the Australian fiction investigated in this chapter but 64 percent of the fifty titles in which topic 41 is most prominent, compared with only 24 percent of the fifty where it is lowest. Such trends are consistent for the top and bottom one hundred titles and more broadly.[20]

These correlations—between Australian fiction with relatively high rates of topic 41, canonical Australian authors, metropolitan newspaper publication, women's writing, and a more British style of fiction; and of relatively low rates of this topic with generally lesser known authors, provincial publication, men's fiction, and what has been seen as more distinctly Australian writing—align with findings in the previous two chapters. The idea that metropolitan newspapers might have focused on fiction with a more "Old World" conception of history resonates with their much higher rates of publication of British authors and of women writers, and with the prevalence of British syndication agencies in this context. Likewise, the notion that fiction in provincial newspapers might have demonstrated a more "New World" conception of history tallies with their higher rates of publication of Australian and American fiction and of local male authors, and with the importance of local and American syndication agencies in supplying such stories.

If a generally "New World" and "Old World" approach characterized the Australian fiction in metropolitan and provincial newspapers, respectively, the models in figures 23 and 24 suggest some other ways in which local writing tended to differ from American and British stories. In decision trees where Australian and American fiction are associated by the relative absence of topic 41, they are differentiated by topics associated, in section 1, with gendered tendencies in fiction. Reinforcing the male orientation of colonial fiction, Australian stories are less likely than American ones to reference female characters and their appearance (topic 91). Local stories that contain such references are more likely than American fiction to do so in the context of familial relationships (topic 9).

In decision trees where Australian and British fiction are aligned by the presence of topic 41, they are distinguished based on topic 11 ("gold tent mate mining miners miner diggings diggers shaft digger store creek mates gully luck reef mines quartz golden"). Reflecting the historical importance of successive gold rushes to colonial history and patterns of migration, topic 11's keywords again emphasize the masculine and rural focus of nineteenth-century Australian fiction, with male actors ("mate miner digger mates") conducting a male activity (mining) in a recognizably nonmetropolitan colonial setting ("creek gully reef"). Certain colonial mining adventures in the curated dataset—Rolf Boldrewood's "The Miner's Right" (#7731) and David Hennessey's "An Australian Bush Track" (#6071)—have received significant attention in Australian literary history, described as both exposing the dangerous fluidity of colonial society and securing colonization (Dalziell 51; Dixon, *Writing* 24). The vast body of colonial mining fiction indicated by this integrated method expands the literary context for interpreting these canonical works and suggests new avenues for exploring colonial notions of the land broadly.

So much remains to be learned about the fiction in nineteenth-century Australian newspapers, perhaps especially the local writing. In this respect, themes such as the representation of Aboriginal people, gender distinctions in juvenile fiction, and the depiction of miners and mining cry out for further investigation. Certainly, it cannot be said of colonial fiction, as Dolin proposes, that it lacked original or distinctive features. I have argued that it differentiated itself in ways that resemble the bush tradition described by mid-twentieth-century Australian literary scholars. But these stories were more communal and domestic than such accounts allow, even if they were just as male oriented—in authorship and in the activities they describe—as feminist literary critics argued in the 1970s and 1980s. The bush was also prominent in local fiction throughout the nineteenth century, instead of emerging as a theme in the 1890s, and far from excluding Aboriginal characters, these narratives asserted colonial ownership by prominently and consistently depicting them, sometimes in highly unsettling ways.

Perhaps because their national cultures were at a stage where local surroundings were taken more for granted, American and British writers, at least as they were published in Australian newspapers, do not appear to have shown the same interest in describing characteristically American or British settings. Instead, these literary traditions were characterized by divergent attitudes toward history and time. The propensity for American fiction to focus on the narrative present, and on individual specificity and agency, suggests an optimistic view of the future and of the capacity for present actions to shape it. British fiction tends, instead, to emphasize the interconnectedness of past, present, and future and the difficulty for individuals to intervene in and alter this relationship. That Australian fiction demonstrates both attitudes toward history and time, while diverging from American and British literature in other ways, speaks to the complexity of cultural distinction in a transnational fiction market and points to a world of future research opportunities.

Conclusion

Whither Worlds and Data Futures

———— ⌘ ————

When I originally conceived the title for this book, my reference to a "world of fiction" had three meanings, and these have continued to underpin and shape my thinking throughout. The most straightforward concerns the global origins of fiction in nineteenth-century Australian newspapers. While British, Australian, and American works dominate, and have been my focus, these newspapers include fiction from many other places: Austria, Canada, France, Germany, Holland, Hungary, Italy, New Zealand, Russia, South Africa, Sweden, and more. An even wider range of geographical locations are evoked in the inscription of stories, which are presented as coming from the above countries and far beyond: Belgium, Burma, Chile, China, Cuba, Egypt, the list goes on. This sheer multitude of origins, real and inscribed—and the frequency of global voyages in these stories—indicates a pronounced geographical focus in the creation, publication, and reception of colonial newspaper fiction. Given that many of the original readers for these stories would have recently arrived in the colonies from elsewhere, this global consciousness suggests the role that newspaper fiction played in connecting new, Australian spaces and lives to preexisting conceptions of the world and readers' place in it.

This multitude of fictional origins offers a framework for intervening in, uniting, and advancing key features of the so-called transnational turn in literary scholarship. As noted in the introduction, like many other national literary fields in the last decade or so, Australian literary studies has reassessed the effectiveness of the nation as the foundational framework for analysis. Scholars have sought, in Dixon's words, to "explore and elaborate the many ways in which the national literature has always been connected to the world" ("Australian" 20). Such research has pursued three broad paths: first, considering the ways in which Australian authors and works relate to local and international cultures, intellectual formations, languages, and systems of cultural value and acclaim; second, exploring relationships between Australian writing and international publishing and media systems, including their implications for Australian literature as a cultural formation in the past, present, and future; and third, examining how readers in Australia, now and in the past, experience literature that arises from and establishes connections to other local, national, and international contexts.

The "world of fiction" in nineteenth-century Australian newspapers enables me to unite these dominant trajectories of the "transnational turn." It permits me to investigate how literary culture in the colonies emerged in dialogue with a range of cultural and intellectual traditions and was connected to a publishing industry that was both global and thoroughly local. By analyzing fiction that was experienced at particular times and places, by specific communities, I integrate discussion of the transnational conditions of authorship and publishing with a focus on reception to explore the frameworks of meaning and value through which early Australians engaged with stories that came from around the world as well as from within the colonies. Underlying these arguments is an intention to extend a transnational consciousness to data-rich literary history. With notable exceptions, there is a tendency in that field to treat large corpuses of American and British literature as a universal literary record. In exploring—and offering for exploration by others—a digitized body of works from around the world, published in the Australian colonies, I hope to disrupt the implicit national biases and globalizing impulses present in data-rich literary history.

Analyzing this fiction exposed new transnational formations and influences on colonial literary culture. Treating literary anonymity as a distinctive presence rather than an absence, and exploring the phenomenon at scale, chapter 4 highlights its operation along a spectrum. I use the extensive information about authorship contained in the paratext of stories to investigate the cultural meanings attributed to fiction, and thus to contrast the value conferred on British fiction in the colonial context with the cultural marginality of American writing. Chapter 5 presents a new account of the operations in Australia of the major British fiction syndicator, Tillotson's Fiction Bureau, while uncovering previously unrecognized connections between international syndication networks of the period and second-tier metropolitan as well as major provincial newspapers. Chapter 6 demonstrates distinct tendencies in writing by men and women that traversed the American, Australian, and British fiction in colonial newspapers, as well as contrasting attitudes toward history and time in this American and British writing. Where the British fiction published in nineteenth-century Australian newspapers tends to focus on the complex interrelationship of past, present, and future, and to be pessimistic about the capacity of individual actions to alter history, American stories tend to be oriented to the present and to emphasize individual agency.

Although nineteenth-century Australian newspapers were strongly connected to global cultures and markets, what became increasingly apparent were the previously unrecognized and distinctive features, as well as the incredible dynamism and richness, of colonial writing, publishing, and reading. Most remarkably, this book shows an entirely new structure and organization for nineteenth-century Australian literary culture, one in which the metropolitan periodicals that have received almost all the critical attention emerge as less prolific, and less interconnected, in their publication of fiction than their neglected provincial counterparts. I establish that provincial newspapers published the majority of fiction in the Australian colonies, sourced from an extensive, active, and hitherto unrecognized group of syndication agencies, local and international. Among these companies were the major publishers of Australian fiction, certainly in the nineteenth century and probably up until the 1970s. To put the case bluntly, this book shows that Australian literary, book, and periodical scholars have been investigating colonial writing, publishing, and reading through a framework that obscures the major parts of it.

Within this profoundly revised framework, many other features of colonial literary culture come into view. Local fiction had a greater presence in nineteenth-century Australian newspapers than has been appreciated and was almost certainly significantly more prevalent than this project has determined. Contrasting the female-dominated authorship of British and American periodical fiction, the dominance of male authors in nineteenth-century Australian newspapers, and the preference of editors and readers for writing by men shows that colonial literary culture did not develop along British lines but forged its own distinctive forms. There is also a major shift in the publication of local fiction from the late 1870s. What had been interpreted as a withdrawal of newspapers from such publishing, and a feminization of what Australian literature did appear, emerges as a transition from metropolitan to provincial newspapers as the locus for colonial men's fiction. In terms of fiction reprinting and syndication, the view that British agencies and syndicated British fiction overwhelmed local publishing and writing from the mid-1880s is unfounded. I also determine the role of individual metropolitan newspapers in sourcing and distributing fiction in the colonies and the presence of numerous author- and editor-led forms of syndication in the provincial press.

Such distinctiveness in publishing and reception likewise characterizes the contents of the local fiction in Australian newspapers. Resonating with mid-twentieth-century accounts—and subsequent, feminist critiques—of an Australian bush tradition is the focus in many of these stories on nonmetropolitan colonial settings, as well as their male-dominated authorship and concern with male characters and traditionally masculine activities. But these features of colonial writing are present throughout the century rather than emerging in the 1890s, and such stories concentrate more on rural families and communities than on the individual bushman and intense male friendships seen as definitive of the bush tradition. Most challenging to existing understandings of the Australian literary tradition is the prominence of Aboriginal characters in these stories. Rather than attempting to justify colonization through silence about the Aboriginal presence in Australia, these works did so by foregrounding the coexistence of Aboriginal and European people in the bush and by describing both harmonious and violent interactions. Alongside this bush tradition, Australian fiction demonstrates the contrasting attitudes toward history and time that tend to characterize British and American fiction in this context. Correlations between these contrasting attitudes and publishing trends raise the possibility that the common perception of colonial writing as an extension of a predominantly British tradition is an artifact of the metropolitan newspapers and authors that have been the focus of scholarship.

The second, original meaning of my title was as a tongue-in-cheek reference to the view that mass digitization offers "a world of fiction": unmediated access to every work from every time. This is the complacent attitude that chapter 1 criticizes in the two paradigms in data-rich literary history that dominate external perceptions of the field: Moretti's distant reading and Jockers's macroanalysis. These authors proclaim their opposition to close reading, even as they assume, in common with that midcentury critical mode, that literary works are stable and singular objects, reducible to "the text." I attribute this equivalence between close and distant reading to a common disregard for the critical nature of the disciplinary infrastructure (analog and digital) that enables the study of literature, and for the historical insights such infrastructure presents. In distant reading and macroanalysis, the idea that mass-digitized collections and the literary data derived from them provide direct access to the facts of literary history yields models of literary systems, and arguments made on their basis, that are abstract, limited, and often ahistorical.

Chapter 2 offers an alternative framework for data-rich literary history: one that supports the modeling of literary systems while acknowledging and representing the constructed, contingent, and transactional nature of literary data and mass-digitized collections. I use the scholarly edition as a theoretical and technical framework for meeting this challenge. The scholarly edition has for centuries been used to model literary works: its curated text proposes an argument about the imagined whole (the ideal), while its critical apparatus explains and justifies that argument with reference to the available parts (the documentary manifestations that can be accessed). It performs this latter task by presenting the history through which those parts have been transmitted to and understood in the present and, hence, by which the whole can be known. The argument about the whole is thereby presented as an effect of inquiry at the same time as it stands as a scholarly object for analysis.

I adapt the scholarly edition to the modeling of literary systems, offering in chapter 3 a historical introduction to a curated dataset of over 9,200 works of extended fiction in nineteenth-century Australian newspapers. That chapter elaborates the history of transmission constitutive of that data, explaining as much as possible the remediations, transformations, and omissions involved in the transition from the nineteenth-century newspapers that were published, circulated, and read in the Australian colonies, to their collection and curation, ultimately as digital objects in *Trove*, to the discovery and representation of the fiction they published. Available alongside this book as a downloadable dataset from the University of Michigan Press, and as a searchable, browsable, and wholly or partially exportable database through the Australian National University's Centre for Digital Humanities Research, this curated dataset embodies an argument about how literary works existed and interrelated in the past. With additional critical apparatus detailing specific data constructions, it offers a rigorous and reliable basis for the discoveries and arguments I present. It has this capacity not because it is comprehensive or true but because its incompleteness and conditionality have been acknowledged and investigated.

This scholarly edition of a literary system is also, vitally, a rigorous and reliable foundation for future investigation and research. And this brings me to the third intended meaning of my title: as a reference to the "world" of possibilities for the study of fiction that this scholarly edition makes possible. It extends the insights gained from analyzing the relevant disciplinary infrastructure—in this case, the major mass-digitized historical newspaper collection in *Trove*—to all literary historians. And in writing this book, I have become increasingly conscious that the arguments I offer barely scratch the surface of what it is possible to do with the extensive, historicized, and curated collection of textual and bibliographical data that this scholarly edition presents.

A recent discovery I made using the curated dataset—without the aid of computational methods but in conversation with a colleague—is illustrative of these possibilities. Considering the curated dataset, my colleague in French literature, Glenn Roe, remarked on the inclusion of Eugène Sue's "The Mysteries of Paris," noting that it was one of the first and most famous serialized French novels. I mentioned that the curated dataset also included two Australian city mysteries. Publication of the earliest of these, "The Mysteries of Sydney," began in *Bell's Life in Sydney* in 1850, eight years after Sue's original work. "Mysteries of Melbourne," attributed to "Kelp," was published twenty years later in the *Emerald Hill Record*, a South Melbourne newspaper.

Research showed us that multiple international adaptations of this popular, nineteenth-century genre had been identified. *Wikipedia* lists titles for Amsterdam, Berlin, Boston, Hamburg, Lisbon, Lyon, Marseille, and more. And alongside city mysteries for London, Philadelphia, and New York, Stephen Knight considers *The Mysteries of Melbourne Life*, published in 1873 by Donald Cameron (whom we know from this book as one of the colonial male authors widely published in the provincial press and as owner of the major local syndicate, Cameron, Laing and Co.). But Glenn and I found no record of either of these earlier Sydney or Melbourne city mysteries.[1] These two stories offer a research project, in and of themselves. Their appearance and the defiant attribution of the earlier, Sydney, one—as "Not by the Author of 'The Mysteries of Paris' or 'The Mysteries of London' but by One of Ourselves"—signals yet another way in which local fiction in nineteenth-century Australian newspapers connected to and emerged out of a transnational fiction market, while emphasizing local authorship and distinctively colonial forms of expression.

The scale of the fiction encompassed by this scholarly edition and its international breadth make me confident that almost any historian of nineteenth-century literature will find something to extend their knowledge and enrich their research in this representation of a literary system. To take as an example just one of the thousands of authors in this scholarly edition, a researcher interested in Ivan Turgenev might ask which of his works appeared in nineteenth-century Australian newspapers, how they were presented, and on that basis, how his form of Russian Realism was represented and received on the other side of the globe. That scholar might choose to investigate the other Russian authors whose work was published in colonial newspapers, whether such publications were widespread or limited to certain newspapers, and, in that respect, what social or political motivations attended the publication of such fiction. Alternatively, she might consider what translations were used and the insights this provides into the source(s) of Russian fiction for the colonies. As noted in chapter 2, as well as supporting users to search and browse fiction by title, author, and newspaper, the database enables full-text searching. While *Trove* makes that same text searchable, it returns results for all articles; the curated dataset focuses on fiction. What new collections of literary works—colonial, national, or transnational—and possibilities for future research might arise from returns of searches of the curated dataset for *murder* or *ghost* or *native*?²

This scholarly edition of a literary system could be used to extend lines of investigation initiated in this book, whether through in-depth reading or computational analysis. Chapter 6 identifies multiple new features of colonial fiction for exploration. What new understandings of nineteenth-century depictions of Aboriginal people might arise from reading more widely in the literary works that feature such characters prominently? What are the implications—for understanding colonization, or historical forms of Australian masculinity, or environmental history—of the multiple mining stories chapter 6 also indicates? More broadly, the chapters in the book's second part variously argue that provincial newspaper fiction was different from that published in metropolitan newspapers: in how it was presented and sourced and in its contents. What new perspectives on colonial literary culture would result from analyzing works of the major local provincial authors identified?

For those interested in applying computational methods to the curated dataset the scope for future research is just as broad. One could investigate what I have proposed as a geographical consciousness in this literary system by adapting the text-mining and geospatial methods that Matthew Wilkens uses to investigate the "geographic imagination" of nineteenth-century American literature. Alternatively, one could explore the male orientation of nineteenth-century Australian newspaper fiction using methods developed by David Bamman, Ted Underwood, and Noah Smith to investigate the relationship between characterization, gender, and dialogue in a large collection of eighteenth- and nineteenth-century English novels. Or one could gain new perspectives on modes of influence within this literary system—of canonical works on others, or of different national literary traditions on each other—by applying Andrew Piper and Mark Algee-Hewitt's topological models of lexical relationality.

These are simply some of the questions and approaches that I can think of. Equally important, if not far more so, to the future use of this scholarly edition are those questions and approaches I have not conceived. Such future research is possible because the meanings that this scholarly edition makes possible are not inherent in the curated dataset but emerge from interactions with it. Like a mass-digitized collection—or a scholarly edition of a literary work—the meanings of a scholarly edition of a literary system are produced transactionally. Those transactions are supported by the historical details Carol and I have accumulated regarding literary works and their documentary manifestations and are shaped by the organization of that information into uniform fields and hierarchical structures in accordance with both database form and my arguments about the nature and meaning of the literary system. But the outcomes of those inquiries are not predetermined: they exceed the detail and the form; they are unpredictable because they arise from a documentary record that is formed and reformed in the investigation of it. The above example of "The Mysteries of Sydney" is emblematic in this respect. I had seen that story in the database and registered the signature's reference to other city mysteries. But the implications of those details coalesced into historical meaning only when my colleague brought his knowledge and understanding to the transaction. Like any scholarly edition, this one is created to enable future outcomes that I—as its editor—did not perceive in its construction.

All three original meanings of a "world of fiction" were foundational to the title's invocation of the "future of literary history." Thus, this future refers to the new directions in nineteenth-century Australian and transnational literary history the book inaugurates; to the potential applications of this particular scholarly edition of a literary system for other researchers; *and* to the scholarly edition's capacity more broadly as a framework for realizing the potential of mass-digitized knowledge infrastructure for literary history. Yet in writing this book, the "world" and "future" of my title gained another, less positive, though equally important, meaning: one that has become fundamental to my focus on a structure for literary history in the digital age. That meaning relates to the impact of the so-called real world—of funding, government, institutional politics, and the perpetual crisis in humanities—on the study of fiction and the future of literary history.

I complete this book in the context of uncertainty in future government funding for *Trove*'s newspaper digitization program (Wynne).[3] This situation carries distinct déjà vu. My last book, *Reading by Numbers*, offered a new history of the Australian novel by analyzing *AustLit*, the most extensive, online bibliography of a national literature then available. That book was finalized in the shadow of looming—later enacted—cuts to *AustLit*, and now I find myself in a similar position with *Trove*. This is despite the fact that *Trove*, as well as offering the largest collection of mass-digitized historical newspapers internationally, is vitally important to researchers and the Australian community and is recognized as world leading in how it presents and supports engagement with its holdings. It would seem that Australia has an unfortunate habit of creating world-leading digital humanities resources and then defunding them. Of course, this is not a uniquely Australian problem. As I write we face the possibility, for instance, that America's National Endowment for the Humanities, and the multiple digital-knowledge infrastructure projects it supports, will be defunded. While I have sought to make the point that all collections—analog or digital—are selections, such funding cuts are depressingly pointed examples of why mass digitization is no magic solution to previous constraints on access to the documentary record.

I raise the issue of funding not simply to protest present circumstances but to note their continuity with the past and to highlight the actions they require of literary historians for the future. While the prevailing discourse of crisis encourages a perception of the present as different from and worse than past times, the humanities have always been subject to the "real" world. Financial and other constraints have inevitably limited, and will always limit, which of an essentially infinite array of cultural objects can be collected, preserved, and transmitted. Rather than a reason to despair, this situation emphasizes the continuing importance of long-standing editorial and curatorial practices for the present and future of the humanities.

Far from an esoteric preoccupation, textual scholarship has always been a response to real-world conditions and constraints: to the need to identify, understand, and manage gaps in the documentary record so as to provide an effective and explicit foundation for current and future interpretations and insights. Notwithstanding the influence of researchers such as Moretti and Jockers on academic and public perceptions of digital humanities, this space of mediation, collection, translation, and curation—of understanding and managing the constraints presented by the real world—is where much of the field actually sits. I offer the scholarly edition of a literary system as a contribution to this ongoing work: as a framework for enacting curatorial practices in the context of data-rich literary history and emerging digital, particularly mass-digitized, knowledge infrastructure and for extending insights gained through such practices to the broader discipline. In providing a rigorous and publicly accessible representation of how past literary works existed and interacted with one another—and with publishers, readers, and the world—and in offering arguments on that basis, I have sought to build on historical practices to enable and demonstrate the future of literary history. I have sought, in other words, to encounter the constraints of the real world, and to pursue knowledge not only despite, but with them.

Notes

Introduction

1. I compare major mass-digitized historical newspaper collections in chapter 3.

2. Dickens's "Little Dorritt" in Melbourne's *Leader* in 1856 is the first title by an established international author listed in Johnson-Woods's *Index*. Earlier works by Dickens in daily and weekly Australian newspapers include "Pickwick Papers" (*Sydney Gazette*, 1838), "Master Humphrey's Clock" (*Australasian Chronicle*, 1840), "Barnaby Rudge" (*Australasian Chronicle*, 1841), "American Notes for General Circulation" (*Southern Australian* and *Sydney Morning Herald*, 1843), "Martin Chuzzlewit" (*Launceston Examiner*, 1845), and "Hard Times" (*Argus*, 1854). Record IDs for these works in the curated dataset are: #177; #856; #860; #498 and #499; #2259; and #460.

3. Johnson-Woods describes Braddon as "queen of the colonies" due to the scale of her fiction ("Mary"), but this project has discovered more titles by local author James Joseph Wright than Braddon (eighty-nine versus eighty-six).

4. As I discuss in chapter 1, Moretti proposed this concept in "Conjectures on World Literature" and developed it in two subsequent books: *Graphs, Maps, Trees* and *Distant Reading*.

5. For articles and blogs that use distant reading in this way, see Alexander et al.; Erlin and Tatlock; Liddle; Goldstone, "Distant"; and Underwood, "Dataset".

6. See Dinsman; Lohr; Piepenbring; Rothman; Schultz; and Sunyer.

7. Book history often employs a systemic conception of print culture—

most famously in Darnton's notion of the "communication circuit"—as well as quantitative methods. On parallels between distant reading and book history and the advantages of the latter framework over the former, see Bode, *Reading* 7–25.

8. Stories of more than sixty thousand words include Walter Besant's "They Were Married!" in the *Sydney Mail* in 1887 (#13291) and Rolf Boldrewood's "The Final Choice" in the *Australasian* in 1885 (#13337).

9. The database is accessible at http://cdhrdatasys.anu.edu.au/tobecontinued

10. For instance, the essays in a recent special issue of *Australian Literary Studies* explore "the ways in which Victorian literary texts and ideas were transformed by their arrival and reception in the Australasian colonies and then re-transmitted around the trade lines of Empire" (Martin and Mirmohamadi np).

Chapter 1

1. For example, the final chapter of Moretti's *Distant Reading* (211–40) uses network analysis to analyze Shakespeare's *Hamlet*.

2. Media discussion of Jockers's analysis of plot includes Cockroft; and Piepenbring. Eileen Clancy summarizes academic criticism of the Syuzhet package Jockers uses for this analysis in two *Storify* posts ("A Fabula of Syuzhet," storify.com/clancynewyork/contretemps-a-syuzhet; "A Fabula of Syuzhet II," storify.com/clancynewyork/a-fabula-of-syuzhet-ii). More recently, Jockers and Kirilloff have collaborated to explore the relationship of gender and characterization.

3. On the limitations of bibliographical records for quantitative analysis, see Elliot.

4. Folsom's essay on database as a new genre also associates digital technologies with comprehensive and direct access to the literary-historical record, even as the resource he refers to—*The Walt Whitman Archive* (whitmanarchive.org/)—enacts a carefully historicized approach to the documentary record. Responses to this essay, including by Freedman and by McGann ("Database"), represent early rejections of this paradigm of transparency in digital humanities.

5. Moretti is a coauthor on the pamphlet but, unlike the other authors, no specific role or insight is ascribed to him.

6. An exception to this lack of data publication occurs in a pamphlet that Moretti and Jockers authored collaboratively with others (Allison et al.).

7. In a copublished article, Jockers confirms the hints he gives in *Macroanalysis*: that his data are unpublished because they are derived from proprietary collections (Jockers and Mimno 752). But this does not explain why he cannot name the authors and titles studied or provide textual data at the level of word frequencies.

8. Jockers's copublished article with Kirilloff includes a bibliography of the 3,329 works in their corpus, as well as a note about the various sources they are derived from.

9. For foundational work in this area, see McKenzie; and McGann, *Textual*.

10. The technique misclassifies 33 percent of works in terms of nationality, 14 percent of works in terms of gender, and an unspecified proportion of works in terms of chronology (Jockers, *Macroanalysis* 153).

11. Reinforcing Moretti's disinterest in his underlying datasets, although he describes an increase to fifty novels per year for all national contexts, the graph shows British novels increasing to thirty titles, Japanese and Spanish novels to a little over forty, Italian novels to thirty-five, and Nigerian novels to only twenty-five titles per year (*Graphs*, 6).

12. Oft cited is Moretti's claim that "between interpretation (that tends to make a close reading of a single text) and explanation (that works with abstract models on a large groups [*sic*] of texts) I see an antithesis. Not just difference, but an either/or choice" ("Moretti" 74).

Chapter 2

1. Shillingsburg offers an accessible account of the shift in scholarly editing from an archetypal to a historical and material approach (167–68) and of the distinctions between the implied, represented, and interpreted work (170–81).

2. Algee-Hewitt and McGurl model a literary system using ranked lists of books judged to be important by various organizations. Literary systems could also be constructed based on data employed in book history, such as number of print runs, sales records, or library holding and borrowing data.

3. Humanities scholars have long recognized archives as manifesting structures of authority rather than as neutral containers; see Manoff for a concise summary of this extensive debate.

4. Because typically created from existing analog collections, digital ones can grow at the faster rate of digitization than manual collection. Database and interface features can be renovated more quickly than physical infrastructure; even if development is lengthy, when changes are implemented, for the end user they take effect instantaneously. Crowd-sourced corrections—a celebrated feature of *Trove*'s newspaper collection—mean that searchable text can change even when the number of digitized documents remains constant.

5. Research that discusses this relationship includes Mussell, *Nineteenth*; Solberg.

6. For these projects see McGann, "Complete"; Brown, Clements, and Grundy; McGregor et al.

7. For instance, humanitiesdata.com seeks to identify publicly available

data of interest to humanities research so as to support verification and collaboration; the *Journal of Cultural Analytics*, launched in 2016, has a platform for data publication and reviews, and its first "debate" explored the requirements of data reuse (Allison; Goldstone, "From").

8. More recently, McGann describes the scholarly edition as "a model, a theoretical instantiation, of the vast and distributed . . . network in which we have come to embody our knowledge" (*New* 26).

9. Underwood and Sellers make this point in the online working paper ("How" 31) that accompanies their article ("*Longue*") and published datasets and code ("Code"). The number of publications required for their argument emphasizes the necessity of a dedicated format to support data-rich literary history.

10. All of the fields I created are available for export—wholesale or selective—from the database. But due to spatial limitations not all fields are available for searching and browsing through its interface. As with the creation of future formats for data publication that combine sustainability and accessibility, an interface that enables users to select displayed fields would be preferable to the format I provide.

11. Full publication details for any of the authors, titles, or newspapers cited in this book can be accessed by searching the database. Where I refer to a specific publication event—including in chapter 6, for which specific text files were subjected to topic modeling—I provide the title ID (and, where quoting the text, the chapter number).

Chapter 3

1. Changes in printing technologies include the inventions of the cylinder and rotary presses, both of which significantly increased printing rates. Scholarship on political and cultural developments in nineteenth-century British and American literary culture is extensive and includes Brantlinger on literacy; McGill ("Copyright") on copyright; Hewitt on taxation; Easley (*Literary*) on celebrity authorship.

2. Examples of relevant work include Brake, *Print*; Donaldson; Hack; Johanningsmeier, "Determining"; Law and Morita; McGill, *American*; Rubery.

3. While noting an "absence of local evidence of specific prices charged by booksellers," Johanson contends that there was essentially no market in the Australian colonies for expensive multivolume novels and that readers were "not interested in buying . . . 6s editions" either (231, 213). Askew and Hubber comment that colonial lending libraries "probably reached only about 3%" of the population (122).

4. Editor, "Australian Serial Literature," *South Australian Register*, July 23, 1867, 2, nla.gov.au/nla.news-article39194214

5. Editor, "'Marjory's Mistake': Another Original Story for the 'Miner,'" *Barrier Miner*, April 22, 1895, 3, nla.gov.au/nla.news-article44167084

6. For instance, "Another Admirer" writes, "SIR,–The story of 'Andrew Fairfax' was novel, interesting, and powerful, and the same may be said of 'Ishmael,' even though in many points he is very like 'Andrew.'" "To the Editor," *Euroa Advertiser*, February 23, 1894, 2, nla.gov.au/nla.news-article65534559

7. H. Williams Mitchell, "The Serial Story (To the Editor)," *Naracoorte Herald*, August 7, 1877, 4, nla.gov.au/nla.news-article146440320

8. Editor, "Harold Netherly; or, The Game of Life," *Bowral Free Press*, May 24, 1884, 2, nla.gov.au/nla.news-article112455201

9. Editor, "'Cecily's Ring': 'The Miner's' New Serial," *Barrier Miner*, March 11, 1893, 2, nla.gov.au/nla.news-article44126776

10. Editor, "The Mystery of Sea-Cliff Towers," *Murrurundi Times and Liverpool Plains Gazette*, April 16, 1898, 4, nla.gov.au/nla.news-article130525099

11. Editor, "A Novel without a Name," *Newcastle Chronicle*, June 17, 1876, 3, nla.gov.au/nla.news-article110990578

12. Some of these projects have been published (Crittenden; Johnson-Woods, *Index*; Morrison, "Contribution"; Webby, *Early*) while others are available only on-site, as card indexes, or are unavailable.

13. On these developments, see Eggert, "*Robbery*" 68, 129; Law, *Serialising* 80; Morrison, "Retrieving" 28; Morrison, "Serial" 319.

14. For more information on these projects and recent steps by *AustLit* to index international newspaper fiction, see Bode and Hetherington (nn 2, 4, 5).

15. For those unfamiliar with the Australian context, Victoria was one of six colonies, along with New South Wales, Queensland, South Australia, Tasmania, and Western Australia.

16. Analysis of *Trove* uncovered five titles—including Dickens's "A Tale of Two Cities" (#13814)—published in the *Age* prior to 1872.

17. NLA, "Australian Newspaper Plan," nla.gov.au/australian-newspaper-plan

18. NLA, "Australian Newspaper Digitization Program Selection Policy," nla.gov.au/content/australian-newspaper-digitization-program-selection-policy. For discussion of *Trove* and copyright, see Sherratt, "Asking."

19. NLA, "Australian Newspaper Plan." Funding cuts to *Trove*, discussed in the conclusion, will likely change processes for selecting, and responsibilities for digitizing, historical newspapers.

20. NLA, "About Digitised Newspapers and More," trove.nla.gov.au/ndp/del/about

21. For instance, to the (supplied) question "What does the collection cover?" the *British Newspaper Archive* answers, "The British Library's newspa-

per collections are among the finest in the world, containing most of the runs of newspapers published in the UK since 1800" (findmypast, "About the British Newspaper Archive," britishnewspaperarchive.co.uk/help/about). Conflating the cultural institution's analog holdings with the commercial organization's digital ones, this reply obscures the nature and scope of the digital collection while denying the existence of gaps between historical and digital records.

22. NLA, "Australian Newspaper Digitization Program Selection Policy."

23. NLA, "What Is a Newspaper?," nla.gov.au/content/what-is-a-newspaper

24. NLA, "Australian Newspaper Plan: Key Indicators for Measuring Progress," nla.gov.au/content/key-indicators-for-measuring-progress.

25. NLA, "Workflow Process Overview," nla.gov.au/content/workflow-process-overview

26. NLA, "OCR Overview," nla.gov.au/content/ocr-overview; NLA, "Technical Details," help.nla.gov.au/trove/digitised-newspapers/technical-details; NLA, "Workflow Process Overview."

27. NLA, "Australian Newspaper Digitization Program Selection Policy."

28. For each state's and territory's missing newspapers, see NLA, "Wanted: Australia's Missing Newspapers," nla.gov.au/australian-newspaper-plan/about/collect. On gaps in Australia's analog newspaper holdings, see Morrison, "Archaeology."

29. I have found no basis or explanation for this estimate, which occurs a number of times in *Trove*'s documentation and associated publications (see Berthon and Wan Wong; NLA, "Australian Newspaper Digitization Program Selection Policy"; NLA, "Trove Help Centre: New Titles: Why Isn't My Newspaper Title Digitised?" help.nla.gov.au/trove/using-trove/digitised-newspapers/new-titles).

30. These Gordon & Gotch figures, and hence my assessment of the proportion of nineteenth-century Australian newspapers digitized in the relevant years, differ from those presented in an article in *Victorian Periodicals Review* (and corrected in the following issue of that journal). Working from digitized copies of the directories, I did not realize that some tables extended over opposing pages while others were on a single page, and my counting was therefore inaccurate. I appreciate—in the sense of perceiving, not so much of enjoying—the irony of discussing errors arising from digitization in a project that seeks to articulate a humanities approach to such documents.

31. For provincial newspapers in all three colonies, rates of digitization for those operating in 1890 based on Kirkpatrick's figures (*Country* 47) are very similar to those operating in 1892 based on that Gordon & Gotch directory.

32. While some limit paratext to textual documentary features, McGann

(*Textual*) and McKenzie extend the concept to other material and social elements, ranging from cover art, font, binding, and illustrations to markings on individual copies.

33. Supplements are often perceived as peripheral or irrelevant to newspapers' "real" contents (see Brake, "Lost").

34. Such stories' length makes them easier to overlook when zoning pages, and a zoning error is more likely to affect their discovery: short fiction is often composed of one article, meaning a single zoning error renders that title effectively invisible to my paratextual method. In contrast, extended fiction typically involves multiple installments with the same or similar paratext.

35. Extensive crowd-sourced manual correction of *Trove*'s OCR-rendered newspaper text has significantly improved its quality but is mostly directed at genealogical information and has not greatly improved the textual data collected in this project.

36. NLA, "API Technical Guide," help.nla.gov.au/trove/building-with-trove/api-technical-guide. *Chronicling America* and *Europeana Newspapers* also provide APIs, but these are less useful for targeted searching and exporting of content due to the lack (in the case of *Chronicling America*) or only partial implementation (in the case of *Europeana Newspapers*) of article segmentation.

37. All appendices to this book are published alongside the digital version on the University of Michigan Press website.

Chapter 4

1. Other useful studies of literary anonymity include Brake, *Print*; Easley, *First-Person*; Griffin; Mullan.

2. Anonymous, "Captain Lacie: A Celebrated Australian Novelist," January, 8, 1897, 4, trove.nla.gov.au/ndp/del/article/97578456

3. Captain Lacie (James J. Wright), "The Outlaws of Cradle Mountain. A Story of Van Diemen's Land. Founded on Fact," *Mercury and Weekly Courier*, August 1, 1902, 3, trove.nla.gov.au/newspaper/article/58580976

4. In most cases neither gender nor nationality has been determined, but in a small number either a gender or a nationality has been identified. For instance, the widespread use of "Bertha M. Clay" as a pseudonym for fiction in American newspapers presents a convincing argument that these titles were American in origin. But the gender of the individual or individuals behind the pseudonym is unknown.

5. *Story* appears 1,068 times in the titles of fiction in the curated dataset, followed by *tale*, 457 times, and *Australia(n)*, 432 times; *romance* and *life*, with 371 and 343 appearances, respectively, are the next two most common terms.

6. This title appeared in multiple provincial newspapers in 1892; it had been published in the colonies fourteen years earlier in the *Australian Journal* as "Found Guilty; or, The Hidden Crime" and was featured in the *New York Ledger* the year before that, in 1877, under the title "The Lord of Strathmore; or, The Hidden Crime."

7. Determining if the opening paragraphs of hundreds of works indicate a national origin was clearly time consuming. Stanford's *Named Entity Recognizer* (Finkel, Grenager, and Manning), employed to develop the stopwords list for chapter 6, might have offered an automated solution to this problem but would not have helped—and would, in fact, have created inaccurate inscriptions—for stories that cite locations but where contextual features indicate the narrative perspective is foreign to that place. Deciding which references should be considered indicative of a story's origins was also complicated. For instance, should stories prominently set in a manor house, or referencing lords and ladies, be inscribed as British? In these and other instances I decided such references were not unambiguously indicative of national origin.

8. For an interesting discussion of original and changing textual meanings, see Frow, "Reading."

9. See, for example, Boyd 5–6; Brake, "Writing" 64; Casey n8; Hughes and Lund, "Textual/Sexual" 144; Hughes and Lund, *Victorian* 103; Lund 26.

10. Such studies include Brake, "Writing" 61; Brantlinger 32; Mays 178; Lovell 9–10; Pearson 196.

11. Feminist literary historians have extensively debated whether men or women were more likely to use opposite sex pseudonyms. Some argue that women were more likely to use male pen names to avoid either the shame associated with middle- and upper-class women earning a living by writing fiction and/or the nineteenth-century perception of "women novelists . . . as inferior to male writers" (Casey n6; see also Sutherland 156, 159–60). Others propose that men were more likely to use female pseudonyms due to the nineteenth-century view of fiction authorship as feminized (Judd 82; Tuchman with Fortin 53). Among the colonial newspaper fiction identified in this project, titles by known male authors were inscribed as "female" only seven times, compared with eighty-one cases where the opposite occurs.

12. Interestingly, these non-British titles—"The Life and Adventures of Toby Frundle," by Australian author Timothy Short, published in 1839 in the *Southern Australian*; and the earliest title discovered by this project, "Travels and Adventures in Southern Africa," by South African author George Thompson (Esq.), published in 1828 in the *Sydney Monitor*—are the only ones attributed to a named author prior to 1843, when Dickens's "American Notes for General Circulation" was published with attribution in the *Sydney Morning Herald* and *Southern Australian*.

13. In 1841 the United Kingdom had a population of 26.7 million (Mitchell with Deane 8–9), compared with 17 million in the United States (U.S. Bureau of Statistics 249) and only 220,968 in the colonies (Australian Bureau of Statistics). These same reference sources are used for the later population statistics.

14. Of the fiction where nationality is "inscribed," 29 percent of titles are "Australian"; where nationality is "known," 24 percent are by an Australian author.

15. Average proportions of both British and women's writing were notably higher in Western Australian newspapers. Perhaps the high rate of immigration in this colony—the discovery of gold transformed Western Australia's population from under 30,000 in 1880 to over 170,000 in 1899—explains this difference, in that newly arrived readers, accustomed to female-authored periodical fiction, were in the majority. But with only fourteen Western Australian newspapers included in this study, averages for this colony have little effect on overall results.

16. Fiction by known authors of other nationalities made up 3 and 5 percent of titles in metropolitan and provincial newspapers, respectively. While this other national fiction deserves further investigation, because of the relative scales of publishing, I focus on American, Australian, and British fiction.

17. The curated dataset contains 3,792 titles from metropolitan newspapers and 5,249 from provincial ones. An additional 206 titles were published in three suburban newspapers: the *Elsternwick Leader, Oakleigh Leader,* and *Port Adelaide News* (defined as periodicals located at least ten but not more than thirty kilometers from the center of the colony's capital).

18. In fact, fiction by other national authors was the most male-dominated category in metropolitan newspapers (81 percent), but the small number of titles involved (73) compared with the number by British authors (1,514) makes the proportional result less significant.

19. While eighty titles by known American authors appeared in provincial newspapers in 1891, in 1892 this fell to forty-four, declining to only twenty-one titles in 1896.

20. For instance, in the 1880s and 1890s, Harte was the most widely published American author identified by this project in metropolitan newspapers. But he was responsible for only nineteen titles, compared to forty-five by Braddon in these same decades.

21. The *Australian Journal* (a magazine rather than a newspaper) generally did not pay for fiction (Campbell 56). But both Ada Cambridge and Marcus Clarke "gained more from Australian serial rights than from English publication" (Stewart 23), with the *Age* paying Cambridge "the extremely large amount" of £197 for Australian serial rights to "A Black Sheep" (Morrison, Introduction xxvi).

22. In metropolitan newspapers between 1865 and 1879, where both gender and nationality were inscribed, 88 percent of "Australian" fiction was "male" authored, compared with 75 percent of "British" fiction and 84 percent of "American."

23. The prevalence of pseudonymous publication of local authors in metropolitan newspapers complicates the interpretation of attribution and its relationship to cultural value. A considerably lower proportion of Australian than either American or British fiction is classified as "attributed," both before and after 1880 (the proportions are, for Australian fiction, 46 percent before 1880 and 67 percent after; for American, 58 and 73 percent; and for British, 60 and 80 percent). However, much of this local writing was published under pseudonyms that clearly identified writers and aligned them with oeuvres. Indeed, some of the most well-known colonial authors used pseudonyms, including "Rolf Boldrewood" and "Maud Jeanne Franc." When pseudonyms are included, Australian fiction in metropolitan newspapers was significantly more likely to be attached to an author name than other national categories, before and after 1880 (this is the case with 84 and 96 percent of Australian titles, compared with 67 and 79 percent of American and 64 and 90 percent of British titles).

24. Well-known examples include Ada Cambridge, Maud Jeanne Franc, and Mary Hannay Foott.

25. Of titles by known authors in provincial newspapers, 70 percent of Australian fiction was attributed, compared with 57 percent of British and 59 percent of American. Fiction by Australian men was attributed in 73 percent of cases compared with 56 percent for Australian women. For British and American fiction the gender division for men and women was 62 and 49 percent and 63 and 54 percent, respectively.

26. Other nineteenth-century commentators contradicted Smith. As Docker notes, A. G. Stephens's 1899 introduction to his *Bookfellow* magazine highlighted colonial readers' interest in local writing and challenged Henry Lawson's complaints regarding opportunities for Australian authors (239).

27. Unless researchers are mistaken about dynamics relating to gender and nationality in British and American periodicals, for conceptions of such phenomena are largely based on the same approaches that produced a view of Australian newspaper fiction as predominantly British: studies of specific—usually canonical—authors; contemporaneous anecdote; and sampling of particular (often "small" or literary) magazines.

Chapter 5

1. Identifying and reprinting relevant or interesting content was a central part of the nineteenth-century newspaper editor's job. Although "scissor-and-paste" journalism was discussed in a pejorative sense, there was no "clear

professional consensus . . . about how much copying was too much, or how soon was too soon to reprint another paper's material" (Nicholson, "You" 275). On reprinting in colonial Australian newspapers, see Kirkpatrick, *Sworn* 8–9.

2. Key scholarship includes, for America, Johanningsmeier, *Fiction*, and McGill, *American*; for Britain, Donaldson, and Law, *Serialising*; and for Australia, Hilliard, and Morrison, "Serial."

3. On the inadequacy of most critical bibliographies for studying fiction reprinting, see Johanningsmeier, "Frank" 285.

4. Nicholson used keyword searches to identify reprinted American jokes and slang in British newspapers ("Looming"). As noted in chapter 2, the Viral Texts project employs a text reuse discovery algorithm to identify reprinted passages in multiple genres (Cordell and Smith; see also Cordell, "Reprinting"; Smith, Cordell, and Dillon; Smith, Cordell, and Mullen).

5. Although in geospatial models the position of nodes is determined cartographically, their size and the connections between them are an effect of data availability.

6. For instance, Cordell draws conclusions from the finding that "*Brown-low's Knoxville Whig* has the highest betweenness centrality in this network" ("Reprinting" 432). His more recent work—outlined in a blog post ("Two")—steps away from this approach in seeking alternative ways of rendering network models so as to "discern the links that truly seem indicative of historical connections rather than data artifacts" (np). The historical constraints he imposes—according additional weight to examples of reprinting with temporal or geographical proximity—are promising in terms of the capacity to use network models for exploratory purposes but do not overcome the broader problem, also noted by Cordell, of constructing networks based on the highly partial datasets derived from mining mass-digitized collections.

7. More recent scholarship has challenged transparency as an ideal for understanding and governing algorithmic operations (Ananny and Crawford).

8. This method constructs millions of networks, containing all possible combinations of causes, to explore and contrast the range of possible dynamics.

9. For instance, statistical measures of probability could be used to extrapolate from observed republications to calculate the probability that the 50 percent of titles appearing only once in the curated dataset would be republished if the approximately 80 percent of colonial newspapers not digitized by *Trove* were included; a "forest" network could be devised to explore the system dynamics that result when all possible causes of reprinting in nineteenth-century newspapers are considered.

10. Measuring the number of unique and reprinted titles within a calen-

dar year aims to limit inclusion of instances where two newspapers published the same story from different sources (this happened but was much less likely to occur in the same year). However, this approach understates reprinting in the curated dataset because it excludes the limited number that occurred in consecutive years (for example, when one newspaper began publishing a story in December of one year and another in January of the next).

11. I have discovered 69 titles shared by the *Brisbane Courier* and *Queenslander*, 102 by the *Evening Journal* and *Adelaide Observer*, 77 by the *Telegraph* and *Week*, and 31 by the *Evening News* and *Australian Town and Country Journal*. Strictly speaking, the daily *Evening Journal* and weekly *Adelaide Observer* were not companions: the latter was paired with the daily *South Australian Register*. However, the same proprietors published all three, meaning the same structure and rationale as companion reprinting underpins the stories shared by companion newspapers. Thanks to Elizabeth Morrison for noting this distinction.

12. The list of titles in digital appendix 3 is undoubtedly incomplete. As noted already, I have not identified all fiction in nineteenth-century Australian newspapers, and Law mentions authors in connection with Tillotson's—including F. W. Robinson, George MacDonald, and Henry Lucy—without listing syndicated titles (Law, *Serialising* 77).

13. Provincial newspapers that published fiction by these authors prior to the 1880s include the *Benalla Ensign, Capricornian, Fremantle Herald, Goulburn Herald, Newcastle Morning Herald,* and *Northern Star*.

14. Titles syndicated by Watt in Britain and published the same month in Australian newspapers include James Payn's "The Heir of the Ages," Walter Besant's "The World Went Very Well Then," William Black's "Wolfenburg," and S. R. Crockett's "The Grey Man." Titles that appeared in Australian newspapers a month after their British appearance include Black's "Sunrise," Besant's "All Sorts and Conditions of Men," and Robert Buchanan's "Master of the Mine." See Law, *Serialising* 106–7 for a list of Watt's "belt and braces" publications.

15. The sources linking these authors to syndication agencies or agents are Colby; Jones; Johanningsmeier, *Fiction*; Law, *Serialising*; Turner. While Colby, Jones, and Turner focus on Tillotson's, Johanningsmeier considers American syndication broadly, and Law explores a number of Tillotson's competitors, including individual agents and companies.

16. The top twenty most published authors in metropolitan newspapers between 1865 and 1899, including the number of publications, were M. E. Braddon (64); Dora Russell (44); James Payn (33); Adeline Sergeant (31); B. L. Farjeon (29); Wilkie Collins (28); William Black (27); Ada Cambridge and George Manville Fenn (25); Margaret Oliphant and W. Clark Russell (24); Walter Besant (23); J. Monk Foster, Bret Harte, and W. E. Norris (22); Henrietta Eliza Vaughan Stannard (writing as "John Winter Strange") (20);

F. W. Robinson, G. A. Henty, and Henry Herman (18); and David Christie Murray (17). Cambridge, an Australian writer, and Herman, a British author, are the two exceptions in this list: highly published authors not associated with well-known syndicators in the sources I have consulted. In Herman's case, this is probably an omission of the sources, given his long-standing collaboration with Murray, who was syndicated by Tillotson's and represented by A. P. Watt. Herman and Murray wrote several novels together, including three published in colonial newspapers. Also associated with these well-known agencies and among the top forty most published authors in colonial newspapers are Hawley Smart (16); S. Baring-Gould and Joseph Hatton (15); H. Rider Haggard, William Le Queux, and Eliza Lynn Linton (14); Robert Buchanan and John K. Leys (13); Hall Caine and Thomas Hardy (12); and Margaret Hungerford (11).

17. Of the eight newspapers centrally involved in reprinting fiction within the colonies, five are the most prolific metropolitan publishers of fiction in this study: the *Queenslander* (322 titles), *Leader* (302), *Adelaide Observer* (274), *Evening News* (265), and *South Australian Chronicle* (251). The other newspapers I have identified as heavily involved in reprinting—the *Evening Journal, Telegraph, Week,* and *Brisbane Courier*—are in ninth, tenth, eleventh, and thirteenth place, respectively.

18. As in figure 10, I assessed rates of reprinting among provincial newspapers based on the number and proportion of nonunique titles per year. While essential for comparison, this approach particularly understates provincial reprinting, which was more likely to occur in consecutive years than metropolitan reprinting was.

19. This project uncovered 124 titles published by both newspapers.

20. The *Goulburn Herald* published fourteen titles in common with the *Cootamundra Herald* and twenty-five with the *Hay Standard.*

21. "An Australian Bush Track" was syndicated in 1896 (*Bathurst Free Press, Gympie Times, Telegraph, Week, Western Grazier*); "The Dis-Honourable: A Mystery of the Brisbane Floods" in 1895 and 1896 (*Barrier Miner, Bathurst Free Press, Morwell Advertiser, Richmond River Herald, Traralgon Record*); "The Mystery of Sea-Cliff Towers" in 1897 and 1899 (*Bendigo Independent, Goulburn Herald, Murrurundi Times, North Queensland Register*); and "The Bells of Sydney" in 1899 and 1900 (*Clarence and Richmond Examiner, Ulladulla and Milton Times*). Sampson Low, London, published the first three stories as books in 1896.

22. Advertising. *Dungog Chronicle,* May 7 1895, 4, nla.gov.au/nla.news-article134307271

23. Price Warung's "An Endorsement in Red" appeared alongside Hennessey's "The Mystery of Sea-Cliff Towers" in Hennessey and Harper's 1898 Christmas annual and was subsequently republished in the *Western Grazier* in 1898.

24. The broader database also contains multiple short stories (completed in a single issue) published by these provincial newspaper syndicates.

25. Other features of the analog collection sometimes responsible for this same patchy publication of a sequence of syndicated titles include minimal availability of issues of a newspaper and poor microfilm quality, leading to digital pages so illegible that manual title correction was impossible.

26. Titles that in the 1880s were published by Cameron, Laing and Co. and appeared in New Zealand newspapers include "Denis Devine," "In the Folds of the Serpent," "The Mystery of Major Molineux," "Marc Grecli," "Dora Dunbar," and "Days of Crime and Years of Suffering." These publications precede the involvement of the Australian syndication agency S. & D. Reid, with New Zealand newspapers in the 1890s (Harvey). Such reprinting suggests the value of a future, comparative study of nineteenth-century Australian and New Zealand newspaper fiction.

27. I have decided, on the balance of evidence, that syndicate 1 ceased operating in 1892, but it is also possible it continued, publishing fiction I have allocated to syndicate 6. Supporting the first interpretation are the different newspapers involved (more than half of those associated with Cameron, Laing and Co., up to and including 1892, no longer published the same fiction after 1893); the different locations of these newspapers (syndicate 6 worked mostly with Victorian rather than New South Wales publications); and the different type of fiction published (syndicate 6 contained a large number of titles by unknown authors). Supporting the second interpretation are the involvement, in both syndicates, of many of the same authors (including Kenneth Hamilton, Harold M. MacKenzie, Atha Westbury, and James Joseph Wright) and many of the same newspapers (almost half of those associated with syndicate 1 appear in syndicate 6, although two-thirds of the newspapers in syndicate 6 did not feature in syndicate 1). A change in ownership might explain such dramatic shifts in publishing and business practices. But Cameron, Laing and Co. was acquired by S. & D. Reid in 1888 (Harvey 84), so the timing seems to discount this explanation.

28. While Johanningsmeier provides a long list of these companies (*Fiction* 96), he notes the difficulty of investigating even the major American syndicates—Bacheller's and McClure's—due to "the paucity of available manuscript and secondary materials" (71).

29. Syndicate 7's serialization of four stories by American periodical author "Bertha M. Clay" could indicate an American company or an Australian agency that acquired fiction from American sources; alternatively, its inclusion of advertisements for colonial companies in its partly printed pages—for instance, for "Australian Explosives" and a Melbourne dentist—could indicate a locally based agency or an overseas syndicate producing partly printed pages especially for the colonial market. Intriguingly, a number of stories published by this syndicate appeared previously in either the

Evening Journal and/or the *Adelaide Observer*, raising the possibility that these metropolitan companions syndicated fiction for provincial newspapers. For syndicate 11, the mixture of international fiction and inclusion of miscellaneous American materials could suggest an overseas syndicate operating in the colonies or a local company extracting content from international newspapers.

Chapter 6

1. Dolin later adapted this argument to focus on nineteenth-century Australian readers rather than fiction ("Fiction").

2. I consider only these three national categories because the samples available for other national literatures are too small for the integrated method used in this chapter.

3. The claim that nineteenth-century men and women wrote distinct types of fiction is foundational to much twentieth-century feminist literary scholarship (for example, S. Gilbert and Gubar; P. Gilbert). Numerous stylometry projects focus on distinguishing male and female authors based on word frequencies (for example, Olsen; Rybicki).

4. Examples abound, within and beyond digital humanities, and include Blei; DiMaggio, Nag, and Blei; Underwood, "Topic."

5. The stop-words list also includes some common OCR errors, although ultimately, I elected to deal with this issue by excluding topics comprised primary of such words.

6. Other strategies for relating topics and documents—for instance, considering documents in terms of the major topics they contain or deeming a topic present when it constitutes a certain percentage of words in a document—acknowledge the presence of all topics in each document. But the thresholds they implement (such as three main topics or 5 percent of words) introduce random and universal divisions into a spectrum and omit possible implications of the relationship between topics and documents: for instance, that the degree of presence of a topic—or all topics—is important for characterizing documents or that the threshold for significance for a topic is different depending on its prevalence in the corpus or its word associations.

7. I use regression trees, which express decisions as numerical choices; classification trees are also decision trees and offer true or false choices.

8. The code is written in MATLAB. Although proprietary, the software is commonly employed in academic research and was used in this case because it contains the necessary libraries for creating classification trees. Equivalent methods are offered in open-source numerical software such as Python, but the MATLAB implementation was superior.

9. Random samples were composed of equal numbers of titles from the

relevant categories, equivalent in size to 80 percent of titles in the smallest category: so, for exploring gender the method trained with random samples of men's and women's fiction, where both were equivalent in size to 80 percent of the available titles by women, and for exploring nationality it trained with random samples of American, Australian, and British fiction, where all were equivalent in size to 80 percent of the available titles by American authors.

10. To take an extreme example, predicting that titles with more than 0.001 percent of topic x are by male authors might well be accurate in 99.99 percent of cases. But this high rate of predictive success would almost certainly come at the expense of very low accuracy in identifying female authors: the predictive success would simply indicate that most documents contained more than that very low level of topic x.

11. For instance, this integrated method could aid in categorizing fiction by unknown authors or, trained on an appropriate sample, in predicting fictional genres.

12. Variables can be nonlinear, so the calculations involved in producing decision trees are more complex than those for finding the topic with the highest—or lowest—levels in a particular category. For example, almost all of topic x could be in titles by women. But this might mean that titles by American and Australian women tend to contain large proportions of words associated with topic x, while in titles by British women, these same words are barely present. In that case, the majority of topic x's words would appear in women's fiction, without the presence of that topic characterizing the majority of women's fiction in the corpus. Rather, the root node signifies the topic that, above or below a set proportion in documents, most effectively categorizes—to continue the above example—the largest number of titles by women on one side of the threshold and by men on the other. The calculations underpinning secondary and subsequent nodes are more complex still, in that they involve identifying the topics and thresholds that most successfully predict a category *after* titles have been initially divided by the decision specified in the primary node.

13. Topic 16 is also prominent in fiction by the well-known British author of juvenile fiction George Manville Fenn: in order of its presence, his "Aboard the Sea-Mew" (#1570), "Iron Trials" (#6183), and "In Marine Armour" (#14014) are seventh, eighth, and tenth, respectively.

14. By contrast, the method had very low rates of success in predicting fiction—overall or Australian—published in the various colonies, suggesting that, for newspaper fiction and at the level of word patterns at least, the similarities between colonial literary cultures were significantly more pronounced than their differences.

15. In models with more splits, American and British stories are sometimes aligned with relatively high levels of topic 80. In such cases, they are

distinguished from Australian writing by the relative presence of military allusions (topics 96 and 7). This outcome suggests that, when representing rural colonial settings, British and American authors tended to do so in terms of military pursuits rather than agricultural or social ones.

16. While 14 percent of titles analyzed for this chapter were published prior to 1880, 21 percent of those categorized as Australian by the presence of topic 80 appeared before this time. In contrast, fiction first published in the 1890s comprises 51 percent of the titles analyzed and 44 percent of those identified as Australian by the presence of topic 80 (for the 1880s, the respective percentages are basically equivalent—34 and 35 percent). These results are the average proportion of titles categorized as Australian by the presence of topic 80 based on the thresholds in figures 6.3 and 6.4 (0.61 and 0.20 percent, respectively).

17. Other expressions of this argument include P. Carter; Gelder and Jacobs; Steele; and Trigg. Although dominant, the view that Aboriginal characters were absent from colonial fiction is not total. For exceptions, see Hadgraft 10–14; and Allen.

18. When topic 80 is removed, the accumulated average reduction in accuracy at four, six, and eight splits is 17 percentage points for Australian, compared with 22 for British and 25 for American fiction.

19. But there are suggestive precedents in Australian literary history for this view. For instance, Judith Wright's 1965 *Preoccupations in Australian Poetry* ascribed nineteenth-century writing a "double aspect" or split "inner reality; first, and persistently, the reality of exile; second, though perhaps we now tend to forget this, the reality of newness and freedom" (xi). Thanks to Leigh Dale for alerting me to this association.

20. Of the one hundred titles ranked highest and lowest, respectively, in terms of the presence of topic 41, 69 and 47 percent were published in metropolitan newspapers and 59 and 25 percent were by women. The same trends occur when considering all Australian titles above the higher (4.67 percent) and below the lower (4.28 percent) thresholds for topic 41 defined in figures 6.6 and 6.7. In this case, 70 and 52 percent of titles, respectively, were published in metropolitan newspapers and 50 and 26 percent were by women.

Conclusion

1. As already noted, James "Skipp" Borlase's proposed syndication of the title never eventuated (Sussex 105).

2. As noted in the introduction, beyond the curated dataset, the database also publishes all of the fiction discovered in analyzing *Trove*, including over twelve thousand titles not discussed in this book: a rich and virtually unexplored resource for future research. The database also allows users to

interact with *Trove*'s digitized newspaper collection to identify and index new fictional titles and installments and to edit the bibliographical fields of records not included in the curated dataset, and all of the text files. If used, this facility for text correction means that the text files in the database (though not those held by the University of Michigan Press) will become different from those analyzed for this project. I consider that the poor quality of the OCR-rendered textual data, and the opportunity to improve it, makes the ambiguity introduced by potential changes to this aspect of the curated dataset worthwhile in the interests of providing a better resource for future research.

3. While finalizing the book I discovered that, following extensive protests regarding cuts to *Trove*, its funding has been secured for another four years. This news is very welcome, but the point still stands that mass digitization does not solve all problems of access to the documentary record.

Bibliography

Ailwood, Sarah, and Maree Sainsbury. "Copyright Law, Readers and Authors in Colonial Australia." *Journal for the Association of the Study of Australian Literature* 14, no. 3 (2014): http://www.nla.gov.au/openpublish/index.php/jasal/article/view/3271/4094.

Alexander, Marc, Fraser Dallachy, Scott Piao, Alistair Baron, and Paul Rayson. "Metaphor, Popular Science, and Semantic Tagging: Distant Reading with the *Historical Thesaurus of English.*" *Digital Scholarship in the Humanities* 30 (December 2015): http://dsh.oxfordjournals.org/content/30/suppl_1/i16.full

Algee-Hewitt, Mark, and Mark McGurl. "Between Canon and Corpus: Six Perspectives on 20th-century Novels." *Stanford Literary Lab Pamphlet* 8 (2015): https://litlab.stanford.edu/LiteraryLabPamphlet8.pdf

Algee-Hewitt, Mark, Sarah Allison, Marissa Gemma, Ryan Heuser, Franco Moretti, and Hannah Walser. "Canon/Archive. Large-Scale Dynamics in the Literary Field." *Stanford Literary Lab Pamphlet* 11 (2016). https://litlab.stanford.edu/LiteraryLabPamphlet11.pdf

Allen, Margaret. "Three South Australian Women Novelists: Catherine Spence, Matilda Evans and Catherine Martin." PhD diss., Flinders University, 1991.

Allison, Sarah. "Other People's Data: Humanities Edition." *Journal of Cultural Analytics*, December 8, 2016: http://culturalanalytics.org/2016/12/other-peoples-data-humanities-edition/.

Allison, Sarah, Ryan Heuser, Matthew Jockers, Franco Moretti, and Michael Witmore. "Quantitative Formalism: An Experiment." *Stanford Literary Lab Pamphlet* 1 (2014). http://litlab.stanford.edu/LiteraryLabPamphlet1.pdf

Ananny, Mike, and Kate Crawford. "Seeing without Knowing: Limitations of the Transparency Ideal and its Application to Algorithmic Accountability." *New Media and Society* 15, no. 7 (2016): 1–17.

Anderson, Benedict. *Imagined Communities: Reflections on the Origin and Spread of Nationalism.* London: Verso, 1983.

Askew, M., and B. Hubber. "The Colonial Reader Observed: Reading in Its Cultural Context." In *The Book in Australia: Towards a Cultural and Social History*, edited by D. H. Borchardt and W. Kirsop, 110–38. Melbourne: Australian Reference Publications in association with the Centre for Bibliographical and Textual Studies, Monash University, 1988.

Atkinson, Alan. *The Europeans in Australia.* Vol. 3, *Nation*. Sydney: NewSouth Publishing 2014.

Australian Bureau of Statistics. "3105.0.65.001: Australian Historical Population Statistics, 2014." http://www.abs.gov.au/ausstats/abs@.nsf/mf/3105.0.65.001

Bamman, David, Ted Underwood, and Noah Smith. "A Bayesian Mixed Effects Model of Literary Character." *Proceedings of the 52nd Annual Meeting of the Association for Computational Linguistics.* June 23–25, 2014, Baltimore, Maryland: alc2014.org/acl2014/P14-1/pdf/P14-1035.pdf

Bastian, Mathieu, Sebastien Heymann, and Mathieu Jacomy. "Gephi: An Open Source Software for Exploring and Manipulating Networks." *International AAAI Conference on Weblogs and Social Media.* 2009.

Bennett, Bruce. "The Short Story, 1890s to 1950." In *The Cambridge History of Australian Literature*, edited by Peter Pierce, 156–79. Cambridge: Cambridge University Press, 2009.

Berthon, Hilary, and Wan Wong. "Facing the Future of Australian Newspapers." 79th *IFLA World Library and Information Congress*, 2013, Singapore. http://library.ifla.org/234/1/153-berthon-en.pdf

Blei, David M. "Topic Modeling and Digital Humanities." *Journal of Digital Humanities* 2, no. 1 (Winter 2012). http://journalofdigitalhumanities. org/2-1/topic-modeling-and-digital-humanities-by-david-m-blei/

Bode, Katherine. "Graphically Gendered: A Quantitative Study of the Relationships between Australian Novels and Gender from the 1830s to the 1930s." *Australian Feminist Studies* 23, no. 58 (2008): 435–50.

Bode, Katherine. *Reading by Numbers: Recalibrating the Literary Field.* London: Anthem Press, 2012.

Bode, Katherine. "Thousands of Titles without Authors: Digitized Newspapers, Serial Fiction, and the Challenges of Anonymity." *Book History* 18 (2016): 284–316.

Bode, Katherine, and Carol Hetherington. "Retrieving a World of Fiction: Building an Index—and an Archive—of Serialized Novels in Australian Newspapers, 1850–1914." *Script and Print* 38, no. 3 (2015): 197–211.

Boyd, Anne. "'What! Has She Got into the *Atlantic?*' Women Writers, the *Atlantic Monthly*, and the Formation of the American Canon." *American Studies* 39, no. 3 (1998): 5–36.

Brake, Laurel. "Lost and Found: Serial Supplements in the Nineteenth Century." *Victorian Periodicals Review* 43, no. 2 (2010): 111–18.

Brake, Laurel. *Print in Transition, 1850–1910: Studies in Media and Book History*. Basingstoke: Palgrave, 2001.

Brake, Laurel. "Writing, Cultural Production, and the Periodical Press in the Nineteenth Century." In *Writing and Victorianism*, edited by J. B. Bullen, 55–72. London: Longman, 1997.

Brantlinger, Patrick. *The Reading Lesson: The Threat of Mass Literacy in Nineteenth-Century Fiction*. Bloomington: Indiana University Press, 1998.

Brewer, David A. "Counting, Resonance, and Form: A Speculative Manifesto (with Notes)." *Eighteenth-Century Fiction* 24, no. 2 (2011–12): 161–70.

Brown, Susan. "Networking Feminist Literary History: Recovering Eliza Meteyard's Web." In *Virtual Victorians: Networks, Connections, Technologies*, edited by Veronica Alfano and Andrew Stauffer, 57–82. New York: Palgrave Macmillan, 2015.

Brown, Susan, Patricia Clements, and Isobel Grundy, eds. *The Orlando Project*. http://orlando.cambridge.org/

Burke, Tim. "Book Notes: Franco Moretti's *Graphs, Maps, Trees*." In *Reading "Graphs, Maps, Trees": Critical Responses to Franco Moretti*, edited by Jonathan Goodwin and John Holbo, 41–48. Anderson, SC: Parlor Press, 2011.

Buurma, Rachel Sanger. "The Fictionality of Topic Modeling: Machine Reading Anthony Trollope's Barsetshire Series." *Big Data & Society* (July–December 2015): 1–6.

Cain, William. "The Institutionalization of the New Criticism." *MLN* 97, no. 5 (1982): 1100–20.

Campbell, Ronald G. *The First Ninety Years: The Printing House of Massina, Melbourne, 1859 to 1949*. Melbourne: Massina, 1950.

Carter, David. "Critics, Writers, Intellectuals: Australian Literature and its Criticism." In *The Cambridge Companion to Australian Literature*, edited by Elizabeth Webby, 258–93. Cambridge: Cambridge University Press, 2000.

Carter, Paul. *The Road to Botany Bay: An Essay in Spatial History*. London: Faber, 1987.

Casey, Ellen Miller. "Edging Women Out? Reviews of Women Novelists in the *Athenaeum*, 1860–1900." *Victorian Studies* 39, no. 2 (1996): 151–71.

Clarke, Philip A. "Adelaide as an Aboriginal Landscape." In *Terrible Hard Biscuits: A Reader in Aboriginal History*, edited by Valerie Chapman and Peter Read, 54–72. Sydney: Allen and Unwin, 1996.

Cockroft, Steph. "The Basic Plots of Fiction: Professor Who Analysed 40,000 Novels Claims There Are Just SIX Possible Storylines." *Daily Mail* February 26, 2015. http://www.dailymail.co.uk/news/article-2969919/The-basic-plots-fiction-Professor-analysed-40–000-novels-claims-just-SIX-possible-storylines.html.

Colby, Robert A. "Tale Bearing in the 1890s: The Author and Fiction Syndicate." *Victorian Periodicals Review* 18, no. 1 (1985): 2–16.

Cordell, Ryan. "Reprinting, Circulation, and the Network Author in Antebellum Newspapers." *American Literary History* 27, no. 3 (August 2015): 417–45.

Cordell, Ryan. "Two (of Three) Ways of Looking at C19 Newspaper Exchange Networks." *Ryan Cordell* (blog). http://ryancordell.org/research/two-of-three/

Cordell, Ryan, and David Smith. "Viral Texts: Mapping Networks of Reprinting in 19th-Century Newspapers and Magazines." http://viraltexts.org/

Crittenden, Victor. *The Atlas. Sydney Weekly. Journal of Politics, Commerce and Literature: Index.* Canberra: Mulini Press, 2006.

Dalziell, Tanya. *Settler Romances and the Australian Girl.* Crawley: University of Western Australian Press, 2004.

Darnton, Robert. "What Is the History of Books?" *Daedalus* 111, no. 3 (1982): 65–83.

DeWitt, Anne. "Advances in the Visualization of Data: The Network of Genre in the Victorian Periodical Press." *Victorian Periodicals Review* 48, no. 2 (Summer 2015): 161–82.

DiMaggio, Paul, Manish Nag, and David Blei. "Exploiting Affinities between Topic Modeling and the Sociological Perspective on Culture: Application to Newspaper Coverage of U.S. Government Arts Funding." *Poetics* 41 (2013): 570–606.

Dinsman, Melissa. "The Digital in the Humanities: An Interview with Franco Moretti." *Los Angeles Review of Books* March 2, 2016. https://lareviewofbooks.org/interview/the-digital-in-the-humanities-an-interview-with-franco-moretti

Dixon, Robert. "Australian Literature–International Contexts." *Southerly* 67, no. 1–2 (2007): 15–27.

Dixon, Robert. "Before the Nation: Rolf Boldrewood and the Problem of Scale in National Literatures." *Australian Literary Studies* 30, no. 3 (2015). https://doi.org/10.20314/als.c93f1b250e

Dixon, Robert. *Writing the Colonial Adventure: Race, Gender and Nation in Anglo-Australian Popular Fiction, 1875–1914.* Cambridge: Cambridge University Press, 1995.

Docker, John. *The Nervous Nineties. Australian Cultural Life in the 1890s.* South Melbourne: Oxford University Press, 1991.

Dolin, Tim. "Fiction and the Australian Reading Public, 1888–1914." In *A Return to the Common Reader: Print Culture and the Novel, 1850–1900,* edited by Beth Palmer and Adelene Buckland, 151–74. Farnham: Ashgate, 2011.

Dolin, Tim. "First Steps toward a History of the Mid-Victorian Novel in Colonial Australia." *Australian Literary Studies* 22, no. 3 (2006): 273–93.

Dolin, Tim. "The Secret Reading Life of Us." In *Readers, Writers, Publishers: Essays and Poems*, edited by Brian Matthews, 115–33. Canberra: Australian Academy of the Humanities, 2004.

Donaldson, William. *Popular Fiction in Victorian Scotland: Language, Fiction and the Press*. Aberdeen: Aberdeen University Press, 1986.

Drucker, Johanna. "Distributed and Conditional Documents: Conceptualizing Bibliographical Alterities." *MATLIT: Materialidades da Literatura/ Materialities of Literature* 2, no. 1 (2014). iduc.uc.pt/index.php/matlit/ article/view/1891/1303

Drucker, Johanna. "Entity to Event: From Literal, Mechanistic Materiality to Probabilistic Materiality." *Parallax* 15, no. 4 (2009). http://dx.doi. org/10.1080/13534640903208834

Drucker, Johanna. "Humanities Approaches to Graphical Display." *Digital Humanities Quarterly* 5, no. 1 (2011). http://www.digitalhumanities.org/ dhq/vol/5/1/000091/000091.html

Easley, Alexis. *First-Person Anonymous: Women Writers and Victorian Print Media, 1830–1870*. Aldershot: Ashgate, 2004.

Easley, Alexis. *Literary Celebrity, Gender, and Victorian Authorship, 1850–1914*. Newark: University of Delaware Press, 2011.

Eggert, Paul. "Australian Classics and the Price of Books: The Puzzle of the 1890s." *The Colonial Present*. Spec. issue of *Journal of the Association for the Study of Australian Literature* (2008): 130–57.

Eggert, Paul. "The Book, Scholarly Editing and the Electronic Edition." In *Resourceful Reading: The New Empiricism, eResearch and Australian Literary Culture*, edited by Katherine Bode and Robert Dixon, 53–69. Sydney: Sydney University Press, 2009.

Eggert, Paul. "*Robbery Under Arms*: The Colonial Market, Imperial Publishers, and the Demise of the Three-Decker Novel." *Book History* 6 (2003): 127–45.

Eggert, Paul. *Securing the Past: Conservation in Art, Architecture and Literature*. Cambridge: Cambridge University Press, 2013.

Eggert, Paul, and Elizabeth Webby. Introduction. In *Robbery Under Arms*, by Rolf Boldrewood, edited by Paul Eggert and Elizabeth Webby, xxiii– lxxxix. St Lucia: University of Queensland Press, 2006.

Elliot, Simon. "Very Necessary but Not Quite Sufficient: A Personal View of Quantitative Analysis in Book History." *Book History* 5 (2002): 283–93.

English, James. "Everywhere and Nowhere: The Sociology of Literature after 'the Sociology of Literature.'" *New Literary History* 41, no. 2 (2010): v–xxiii.

Erlin, Matt, and Lynne Tatlock. "Introduction: 'Distant Reading' and the Historiography of Nineteenth-Century German Literature." In *Distant Readings: Topologies of German Culture in the Long Nineteenth Century*, edited by Matt Erlin and Lynne Tatlock, 1–26. Rochester, NY: Camden House, 2014.

Finkel, Jenny Rose, Trond Grenager, and Christopher Manning. "Incorporating Non-local Information into Information Extraction Systems by Gibbs Sampling." *Proceedings of the 43rd Annual Meeting of the Association for Computational Linguistics*, 2005. http://nlp.stanford.edu/~manning/papers/gibbscrf3.pdf

Finn, Ed. "The Social Lives of Books: Literary Networks in Contemporary American Fiction." PhD diss., Stanford University, 2011.

Folsom, Ed. "Database as Genre: The Epic Transformation of Archives." *PMLA* 122, no. 5 (2007): 1571–79.

Foucault, Michel "What Is an Author?" In *The Death and Resurrection of the Author?*, edited by William Irwin, 9–22. 1979. Westport, CT: Greenwood Press, 2002.

Freedman, Jonathan. "Whitman, Database, Information Culture." *PMLA* 122, no. 5 (2007): 1596–1602.

Frow, John. "Reading with Guns: Institutions of Interpretation and *District of Columbia v. Heller.*" *New Literary History* 47, no. 1 (2016): 83–107.

Frow, John. "Thinking the Novel: Review of *The Novel*, edited by Franco Moretti." *New Left Review* 49 (2008): 137–45.

Gelder, Ken. "Australian Gothic." In *The Routledge Companion to Gothic*, edited by Catherine Spooner and Emma McEvoy, 115–23. London: Routledge, 2007.

Gelder, Ken, and Jane Jacobs. *Uncanny Australia: Sacredness and Identity in a Postcolonial Nation.* Carlton: Melbourne University Press, 1998.

Gelder, Ken, and Rachael Weaver. *The Colonial Journals and the Emergence of Australian Literary Culture.* Crawley: University of Western Australia Press, 2014.

Gibbs, Frederick W., and Daniel J. Cohen. "A Conversation with Data: Prospecting Victorian Words and Ideas." *Victorian Studies* 54, no. 1 (2011): 69–77. http://muse.jhu.edu/journals/victorian_studies/v054/54.1.gibbs.pdf

Gilbert, Pamela K. *Disease, Desire, and the Body in Victorian Women's Popular Novels.* Cambridge: Cambridge University Press, 1997.

Gilbert, Sandra, and Susan Gubar. *The Madwoman in the Attic: The Woman Writer and the Nineteenth-Century Literary Imagination.* New Haven, CT: Yale University Press, 1979.

Giles, Paul. *The Global Remapping of American Literature.* Princeton, NJ: Princeton University Press, 2011.

Gitelman, Lisa, ed. *"Raw Data" Is an Oxymoron.* Cambridge, MA: MIT Press, 2013.

Goldstone, Andrew. "Distant Reading: More Work to Be Done." *Andrew Goldstone* (blog). http://andrewgoldstone.com/blog/2015/08/08/distant/

Goldstone, Andrew. "The Doxa of Reading." *PMLA*. Forthcoming in 2018. Preprint: https://andrewgoldstone.com/research/doxa-ms.pdf

Goldstone, Andrew. "From Reproducible to Productive." *Journal of Cultural Analytics* February 27, 2017. http://culturalanalytics.org/2017/02/from-reproducible-to-productive/

Goldstone, Andrew, and Ted Underwood. "The Quiet Transformations of Literary Studies: What Thirteen Thousand Scholars Could Tell Us." *New Literary History* 45, no. 3 (2014): 359–84.

Goldstone, Andrew, and Ted Underwood. "What Can Topic Models of *PMLA* Teach Us about the History of Literary Scholarship." *Journal of Digital Humanities* 2, no. 1 (2012). http://journalofdigitalhumanities.org/2-1/what-can-topic-models-of-pmla-teach-us-by-ted-underwood-and-andrew-goldstone/

Gordon & Gotch. *Australasian Newspaper Directory, 1886*. Melbourne: Gordon & Gotch, 1886.

Gordon & Gotch. *Australasian Newspaper Directory, 1888*. Melbourne: Gordon & Gotch, 1888.

Gordon & Gotch. *Australasian Newspaper Directory, 1892*. Melbourne: Gordon & Gotch, 1892.

Griffin, Robert J. Introduction. In *The Faces of Anonymity: Anonymous and Pseudonymous Publication from the Sixteenth to the Twentieth Century*, edited by Robert J. Griffin, 1–17. Basingstoke: Palgrave Macmillan, 2003.

Hack, Daniel. "Close Reading at a Distance: The African-Americanization of *Bleak House*." *Critical Inquiry* 34, no. 4 (2008): 729–53.

Hadgraft, Cecil. Introduction. In *The Australian Short Story before Lawson*, edited by Cecil Hadgraft, 1–56. Melbourne: Oxford University Press, 1986.

Harvey, Ross. "Sources of 'Literary' Copy for New Zealand Newspapers." *Bibliographical Society of Australia and New Zealand Bulletin* 27, no. 3–4 (2003): 83–93.

Hewitt, Martin. *The Dawn of the Cheap Press in Victorian Britain: The End of the "Taxes on Knowledge," 1849–1869*. London: Bloomsbury, 2014.

Hilliard, Christopher. "The Provincial Press and the Imperial Traffic in Fiction, 1870s to 1930s." *Journal of British Studies* 48, no. 3 (2009): 653–73.

Houston, Natalie M. "Visual Page." *Natalie M. Houston* (blog). http://nmhouston.com/visual-page/

Hughes, Linda K., and Michael Lund. "Textual/Sexual Pleasure and Serial Publication." In *Literature and the Marketplace: Nineteenth-Century British Publishing and Reading Practices*, edited by John O. Jordan and Robert L. Patten, 143–64. Cambridge: Cambridge University Press, 1995.

Hughes, Linda K., and Michael Lund. *Victorian Publishing and Mrs. Gaskell's Work*. Charlottesville: University Press of Virginia, 1999.

Inglis, Ken. "The Term 'Australian'." In *The Australian People: An Encyclopedia of the Nation, Its People and Their Origins*, edited by James Jupp, 755–57. Oakleigh: Cambridge University Press, 2001.

Jockers, Matthew L. "Confusion Matrices." *Matthew L. Jockers* (blog). http://www.matthewjockers.net/macroanalysisbook/confusion-matrices/

Jockers, Matthew L. "Expanded Stopwords List." *Matthew L. Jockers* (blog). http://www.matthewjockers.net/macroanalysisbook/expanded-stop-words-list/

Jockers, Matthew L. "500 Labelled Themes from a Corpus of 19th-Century Fiction." *Matthew L. Jockers* (blog). http://www.matthewjockers.net/macroanalysisbook/macro-themes/

Jockers, Matthew L. *Macroanalysis: Digital Methods and Literary History*. Champaign: University of Illinois Press, 2013.

Jockers, Matthew, and Gabi Kirilloff. "Understanding Gender and Character Agency in the 19th Century Novel." *Journal of Cultural Analytics*. Genre Cluster (2016). http://culturalanalytics.org/2016/12/understanding-gender-and-character-agency-in-the-19th-century-novel/.

Jockers, Matthew L., and David Mimno. "Significant Themes in 19th-Century Literature." *Poetics* 41 (2013): 750–69.

Johanningsmeier, Charles. "Determining How Readers Responded to Cather's Fiction: The Cultural Work of *The Professor's House* in *Collier's Weekly*." *American Periodicals* 20, no. 1 (2010): 68–96.

Johanningsmeier, Charles. *Fiction and the American Literary Marketplace*. Cambridge: Cambridge University Press, 1997.

Johanningsmeier, Charles. "Frank Norris's 'A Salvation Boom in Matabeleland': The Bibliographic Problems of Syndicated Fiction." *Text* 10 (1997): 283–96.

Johanson, Graeme. *A Study of Colonial Editions in Australia, 1843–1972*. Wellington: Elibank Press, 2000.

Johnson-Woods, Toni. *Index to Serials in Australian Periodicals and Newspapers: Nineteenth Century*. Canberra: Mulini Press, 2001.

Johnson-Woods, Toni. "Mary Elizabeth Braddon in Australia: Queen of the Colonies." In *Beyond Sensation: Mary Braddon in Context*, edited by Marlene Tromp, Pamela Gilbert, and Aeron Haynie, 111–25. New York: SUNY Press, 2000.

Jones, Aled. "Tillotson's Fiction Bureau: The Manchester Manuscripts." *Research Society for Victorian Periodicals* 17, no. 1–2 (1984): 43–49.

Judd, Catherine A. "Male Pseudonyms and Female Authority in Victorian England." In *Literature in the Marketplace: Nineteenth-Century British Publishing and Reading Practices*, 2nd ed., edited by John O. Jordan and Robert L. Patten, 250–68. Cambridge: Cambridge University Press, 1998.

Kirkpatrick, Rod. *Country Conscience: A History of the New South Wales Provincial Press, 1841 to 1995*. Canberra: Infinite Harvest, 2000.

Kirkpatrick, Rod. *Sworn to No Master: A History of the Provincial Press in Queensland to 1930*. Darling Heights: Darling Downs Institute Press, 1984.

Klein, Lauren. "The Image of Absence: Archival Silence, Data Visualization, and James Hemings." *American Literature* 85, no. 4 (2013): 661–88.

Knight, Stephen. *The Mysteries of the Cities: Urban Crime Fiction in the Nineteenth Century*. Jefferson, NC: McFarland, 2012.

Lake, Marilyn. "The Politics of Respectability: Identifying the Masculinist Context." *Historical Studies* 22, no. 86 (1986): 116–31.

Law, Graham. "Savouring of the Australian Soil? On the Sources and Affiliations of Colonial Newspaper Fiction." *Victorian Periodicals Review* 37, no. 4 (Winter 2004): 75–97.

Law, Graham. *Serialising Fiction in the Victorian Press*. Basingstoke: Palgrave, 2000.

Law, Graham, and Norimasa Morita. "The Newspaper Novel: Towards an International History." *Media History* 6, no. 1 (2000): 5–17.

Leighton, Mary Elizabeth, and Lisa Surridge. "The Transatlantic *Moonstone*: A Study of the Illustrated Serial in *Harper's Weekly*." *Victorian Periodicals Review* 42, no. 3 (2009): 207–43.

Lester, Alan "Imperial Circuits and Networks: Geographies of the British Empire." *History Compass* 4 (2006): 124–41.

Liddle, Dallas. "Reflections on 20,000 Victorian Newspapers: 'Distant Reading' *The Times* using *The Times Digital Archive*." *Journal of Victorian Culture* 17, no. 2 (2012): 230–37.

Liu, Alan. *Local Transcendence: Essays on Postmodern Historicism and the Database*. Chicago: University of Chicago Press, 2008.

Liu, Alan. "The Meaning of the Digital Humanities." *PMLA* 128, no. 2 (2013): 409–23.

Lohr, Steve. "Dickens, Austen and Twain, Through a Digital Lens." *New York Times*, January 26, 2013. http://www.nytimes.com/2013/01/27/technology/literary-history-seen-through-big-datas-lens.html?pagewanted=all&_r=0

Love, Heather. "Close but Not Deep: Literary Ethics and the Descriptive Turn." *New Literary History* 41, no. 2 (2010): 371–91.

Lovell, Terry. *Consuming Fiction*. London: Verso, 1987.

Lund, Michael. *America's Continuing Story: An Introduction to Fiction, 1850–1900*. Detroit: Wayne State University Press, 1993.

Lyons, Martyn. "Bush Readers, Factory Readers, Home Readers." In *A History of the Book in Australia, 1891–1945: A National Culture in a Colonised Market*, edited by Martyn Lyons and John Arnold, 17–23. St Lucia: University of Queensland Press, 2001.

Mak, Bonnie. "Archaeology of a Digitization." *Journal of the Association for Information Science and Technology* 65, no. 8 (2014): 1515–26.

Manoff, Marlene. "Theories of the Archive from Across the Disciplines." *Portal: Libraries and the Academy* 4, no. 1 (2004): 9–25.

Marche, Stephen. "Literature Is Not Data: Against Digital Humanities." *Los Angeles Review of Books*, October 28, 2012. https://lareviewofbooks.org/essay/literature-is-not-data-against-digital-humanities

Martin, Susan, and Kylie Mirmohamadi. Introduction. *Australian Literary Studies* 30, no. 3 (2015). https://doi.org/10.20314/als.2a0eedf0eb

Mays, Kelly. "The Disease of Reading and Victorian Periodicals." In *Literature and the Marketplace: Nineteenth-Century British Publishing and Reading Practices*, edited by John O. Jordan and Robert L. Patten, 165–94. Cambridge: Cambridge University Press, 1995.

McCallum, Andrew Kachites. "*Mallet*: A Machine Learning for Language Toolkit." 2002. http://mallet.cs.umass.edu

McCann, Andrew. *Marcus Clarke's Bohemia: Literature and Modernity in Colonial Melbourne*. Carlton: Melbourne University Press, 2004.

McCarty, Willard. *Humanities Computing*. Basingstoke: Palgrave Macmillan, 2005.

McGann, Jerome, ed. "The Complete Writings and Pictures of Dante Gabriel Rossetti." http://www.rossettiarchive.org/

McGann, Jerome. "Database, Interface, and Archive Fever." *PMLA* 122, no. 5 (2007): 1588–92.

McGann, Jerome. "From Text to Work: Digital Tools and the Emergence of the Social Text." In *The Book as Artefact: Text and Border*, edited by Anne Hansen, Roger Lüdeke, Wolfgang Streit, Cristina Urchueguía, and Peter Shillingsburg, 225–40. Amsterdam: Rodopi, 2005.

McGann, Jerome. *A New Republic of Letters: Memory and Scholarship in the Age of Digital Reproduction*. Princeton, NJ: Princeton University Press, 2014.

McGann, Jerome. "A Note on the Current State of Humanities Scholarship." *Critical Inquiry* 30, no. 2 (Winter 2004): 409–13.

McGann, Jerome. *The Textual Condition*. Princeton, NJ: Princeton University Press, 1991.

McGill, Meredith L. *American Literature and the Culture of Reprinting, 1834–1853*. Philadelphia: University of Pennsylvania Press, 2003.

McGill, Meredith L. "Copyright and Intellectual Property: The State of the Discipline." *Book History* 16 (2013): 387–427.

McGregor, Hannah, Faye Hammill, Paul Hjartarson, Clare Mulcahy, and Nick van Orden, eds. *Modern Magazine Project Canada*. http://modmag.ca/whm/

McKenzie, D. F. *Bibliography and the Sociology of Texts: The Panizzi Lectures*. 1986. London: British Library, 1999.

Meeks, Elijah, and Scott B. Weingart. "The Digital Humanities Contribution to Topic Modeling." *Journal of Digital Humanities* 2, no. 1 (2012).

http://journalofdigitalhumanities.org/2–1/dh-contribution-to-topic-modeling/

Michel, Jean-Baptiste, Yuan Kui Shen, Aviva Presser Aiden, Adrian Veres, Matthew K. Gray, the Google Books Team, Joseph P, Pickett, Dale Hoiberg, Dan Clancy, Peter Norvig, Jon Orwant, Steven Pinker, Martin A. Nowak, and Erez Lieberman Aiden. "Quantitative Analysis of Culture Using Millions of Digitized Books." *Science* 331, no. 6014 (2011): 176–82.

Mitchell, B. R., with Phyllis Deane. *Abstract of British Historical Statistics.* Cambridge: Cambridge University Press, 1971.

Moretti, Franco. "The Bourgeois: Between History and Literature; Review and Interview by Karen Shook." *Times Higher Education,* June 27, 2013. https://www.timeshighereducation.co.uk/books/the-bourgeois-between-history-and-literature-by-franco-moretti/2005020.article

Moretti, Franco. "Conjectures on World Literature." *New Left Review* 1 (2000): 54–68.

Moretti, Franco. *Distant Reading.* London: Verso, 2013.

Moretti, Franco. *Graphs, Maps, Trees: Abstract Models for a Literary History.* London: Verso, 2005.

Moretti, Franco. "Moretti Responds (II)." In *Reading "Graphs, Maps, Trees": Responses to Franco Moretti,* edited by Jonathan Goodwin and John Holbo, 73–75. Anderson: Parlor Press, 2011.

Moretti, Franco. "'Operationalizing': or, The Function of Measurement in Modern Literary Theory." *Stanford Literary Lab Pamphlet 6* (2013). https://litlab.stanford.edu/LiteraryLabPamphlet6.pdf

Morrison, Elizabeth. "The Archaeology of Australian Colonial Newspapers." In *Australasian Serials: Current Developments in Bibliography,* edited by Carol Mills and John Mills, 35–51. New York: Haworth Press, 1991.

Morrison, Elizabeth. "The Contribution of the Country Press to the Making of Victoria, 1840–1890." PhD diss., Monash University, 1991.

Morrison, Elizabeth. *Engines of Influence: Newspapers of Country Victoria, 1840–1890.* Carlton: Melbourne University Press, 2005.

Morrison, Elizabeth. Introduction. In *A Black Sheep,* by Ada Cambridge, edited by Elizabeth Morrison, xi–xvii. Canberra: Australian Defence Force Academy and Australian Scholarly Editions Centre, 2004.

Morrison, Elizabeth. "Retrieving Colonial Literary Culture: The Case for an Index to Fiction in Australian (or Australasian?) Newspapers." *Bibliographical Society of Australia and New Zealand Bulletin* 13, no. 1 (1989): 27–36.

Morrison, Elizabeth. "Serial Fiction in Australian Colonial Newspapers." In *Literature in the Marketplace: Nineteenth-Century British Publishing and Reading Practices,* 2nd ed., edited by John O. Jordan and Robert L. Patten, 306–24. Cambridge: Cambridge University Press, 1998.

Mullan, John. *Anonymity: A Secret History of English Literature*. London: Faber, 2008.

Mussell, James. "Elemental Forms." *Media History* 20, no. 1 (2014): 4–20.

Mussell, James. *The Nineteenth-Century Press in the Digital Age*. Basingstoke: Palgrave Macmillan, 2012.

Nicholas, S., and P. R. Shergold. "British and Irish Convicts." In *The Australian People: An Encyclopedia of the Nation, Its People and Their Origins*, edited by James Jupp, 16–22. Oakleigh: Cambridge University Press, 2001.

Nicholson, Bob. "Looming Large: America and the Late-Victorian Press, 1865–1902." PhD diss., University of Manchester, 2012.

Nicholson, Bob. "'You kick the bucket; we do the rest!': Jokes and the Culture of Reprinting in the Transatlantic Press." *Journal of Victorian Culture* 17, no. 3 (2012): 273–86.

Nile, Richard. Introduction. In *The Australian Legend and Its Discontents*, edited by Richard Nile, 1–7. St Lucia: University of Queensland Press, 2000.

Olsen, Mark. "*Ecriture feminine*: Searching for an Indefinable Practice?" *Literary and Linguistic Computing* 20 (2005): 147–65.

Pasquale, Frank. *The Black Box Society: The Secret Algorithms That Control Money and Information*. Cambridge, MA: Harvard University Press, 2015.

Pearson, Jacqueline. *Women's Reading in Britain, 1750–1834: A Dangerous Recreation*. Cambridge: Cambridge University Press, 1999.

Piepenbring, Dan. "Man in Hole: Turning Novels' Plots into Data Points." *Paris Review*, February 4, 2015. http://www.theparisreview.org/blog/2015/02/04/man-in-hole/

Pierce, Peter. *The Country of Lost Children: An Australian Anxiety*. Cambridge: Cambridge University Press, 1999.

Piper, Andrew, and Mark Algee-Hewitt. "The Werther Effect I: Goethe, Objecthood, and the Handling of Knowledge." In *Distant Readings: Topologies of German Culture in the Long Nineteenth Century*, edited by Matt Erlin and Lynn Tatlock, 155–84. Rochester, NY: Camden House, 2014.

Price, Kenneth M. "Edition, Project, Database, Archive, Thematic Research Collection: What's in a Name?" *Digital Humanities Quarterly* 3, no. 3 (2009). http://www.digitalhumanities.org/dhq/vol/3/3/000053/000053.html

Rhody, Lisa M. "Topic Modeling and Figurative Language." *Digital Humanities Quarterly* 2, no. 1 (2012). http://journalofdigitalhumanities.org/2-1/topic-modeling-and-figurative-language-by-lisa-m-rhody/

Robinson, Catherine. "How We Search Now: New and Old Ways of Digging Up Wolf's 'Sir John Moore.'" In *Virtual Victorians: Networks, Connections, Technologies*, edited by Veronica Alfano and Andrew Stauffer, 11–28. New York: Palgrave Macmillan, 2015.

Robinson, Julia. "Searching for Words." *National Library Magazine* 5, no. 2 (2013): 28–30.

Ross, Shawna. "In Praise of Overstating the Case," review of *Distant Reading,* by Franco Moretti. *Digital Humanities Quarterly* 8, no. 1 (2014). http://www.digitalhumanities.org/dhq/vol/8/1/000171/000171.html

Rothman, Joshua. "An Attempt to Discover the Laws of Literature." *New Yorker Magazine*, March 20, 2014. http://www.newyorker.com/books/pageturner/an-attempt-to-discover-the-laws-of-literature

Rubery, Matthew. *The Novelty of Newspapers: Victorian Fiction after the Invention of the News.* Oxford: Oxford University Press, 2009.

Rybicki, Jan. "*Vive la différence*: Tracing the (Authorial) Gender Signal by Multivariate Analysis of Word Frequencies." *Digital Scholarship in the Humanities* 31, no. 4 (2015): 746–61.

Schmidt, Benjamin M. "Words Alone: Dismantling Topic Models in the Humanities." *Journal of Digital Humanities* 2, no. 1 (2012). http://journalofdigitalhumanities.org/2-1/words-alone-by-benjamin-m-schmidt/

Schultz, Kathryn. "What Is Distant Reading?" *New York Times Sunday Book Review*, June 24, 2011. http://www.nytimes.com/2011/06/26/books/review/the-mechanic-muse-what-is-distant-reading.html?_r=0

Sheridan, Susan. *Along the Faultlines: Sex, Race and Nation in Australian Women's Writing, 1880s to 1930s.* Sydney: Allen and Unwin, 1995.

Sherratt, Tim. "Asking Better Questions: History, Trove and the Risks that Count." In *Copyfight*, edited by Phillipa McGuinness, 112–24. Sydney: NewSouth Books, 2015.

Sherratt, Tim. "4 Million Articles Later . . ." *discontents* (blog). http://discontents.com.au/4-million-articles-later/.

Shillingsburg, Peter. "How Literary Works Exist: Implied, Represented and Interpreted." In *Text and Genre in Reconstruction: Effects of Digitization on Ideas, Behaviours, Products and Institutions*, edited by Willard McCarty, 165–82. Cambridge: OpenBook, 2010.

Sinatra, Michael E. "Representing Leigh Hunt's *Autobiography*." In *Virtual Victorians: Networks, Connections, Technologies*, edited by Veronica Alfano and Andrew Stauffer, 107–20. New York: Palgrave Macmillan, 2015.

Smith, David A., Ryan Cordell, and Elizabeth Maddock Dillon. "Infectious Texts: Modeling Text Reuse in Nineteenth-Century Newspapers." *Proceedings of the 2013 IEEE International Conference on Big Data*, October 6–9, 2013, Silicon Valley, 86–94. http://www.viraltexts.org/infect-bighum-2013.pdf

Smith, David A., Ryan Cordell, and Abby Mullen. "Computational Methods for Uncovering Reprinted Texts in Antebellum Newspapers." *American Literary History* 27, no. 3 (2015): E1–E15.

So, Richard, and Hoyt Long. "Network Analysis and the Sociology of Modernism." *boundary2* 40, no. 2 (2013): 11–20.

Solberg, Janine. "Googling the Archive: Digital Tools and the Practice of History." *Advances in the History of Rhetoric* 15, no. 1 (2012): 53–78.

St Clair, William. *The Reading Nation in the Romantic Period*. Cambridge: Cambridge University Press, 2004.

Steele, Kathleen. "Fear and Loathing in the Australian Bush: Gothic Landscapes in *Bush Studies* and *Picnic at Hanging Rock*." *COLLOQUY text theory critique* 20 (2010): 33–56.

Stewart, Ken. *Investigations in Australian Literature*. Sydney: Sydney Studies Shoestring Press, 2000.

Stuart, Lurline. *Nineteenth-Century Australian Periodicals: An Annotated Bibliography*. Sydney: Hale & Iremonger, 1979.

Sunyer, John. "Big Data Meets the Bard." *Financial Times*, June 15, 2013. http://www.ft.com/cms/s/2/fb67c556-d36e-11e2-b3ff-00144feab7de.html

Sussex, Lucy. "'Bobbing around': James Skipp Borlase, Adam Lindsay Gordon, and Surviving in the Market of Australia, 1860s." *Victorian Periodicals Review* 37, no. 4 (2004): 98–110.

Sutherland, John. *Victorian Fiction: Writers, Publishers, Readers*. London: Macmillan, 1995.

Trigg, Stephanie. Introduction. In *Medievalism and the Gothic in Australian Culture*, edited by Stephanie Trigg, xi–xxiii. Carlton: Melbourne University Press, 2005.

Trumpener, Katie. "Paratext and Genre System: A Response to Franco Moretti." *Critical Inquiry* 36, no. 1 (2009): 159–71.

Tuchman, Gaye, with Nina E. Fortin. *Edging Women Out: Victorian Novelists, Publishers and Social Change*. New Haven, CT: Yale University Press, 1989.

Turner, Michael L. "Tillotson's Fiction Bureau." In *Studies in the Book Trade in Honour of Graham Pollard*, edited by R. W. Hunt, I. G. Philip, and R. J. Roberts, 351–78. Oxford: Oxford Bibliographical Society, 1975.

Underwood, Ted. "A Dataset for Distant-Reading Literature in English, 1700–1922." *The Stone and the Shell: Using Large Digital Libraries to Advance Literary History* (blog). http://tedunderwood.com/2015/08/07/a-dataset-for-distant-reading-literature-in-english-1700-1922/

Underwood, Ted. "Topic Modeling Made Just Simple Enough." *The Stone and the Shell: Using Large Digital Libraries to Advance Literary History* (blog). https://tedunderwood.com/2012/04/07/topic-modeling-made-just-simple-enough/

Underwood, Ted, and Jordan Sellers. Code and data to support the article "How Quickly Do Literary Standards Change?" *Github*. https://github.com/tedunderwood/paceofchange

Underwood, Ted, and Jordan Sellers. "How Quickly Do Literary Standards Change?" *Figshare*, May 19, 2015. https://figshare.com/articles/How_Quickly_Do_Literary_Standards_Change_/1418394

Underwood, Ted, and Jordan Sellers. "The *Longue Durée* of Literary Prestige." *Modern Language Quarterly* 77, no. 3 (2016): 321–44.

U.S. Bureau of Statistics. *Statistical Abstract of the United States, 1891.* 14th ed. Washington, DC: Government Printing Office, 1892.

Webby, Elizabeth. "Before the *Bulletin*: Nineteenth-Century Literary Journalism." In *Cross Currents: Magazines and Newspapers in Australian Literature,* edited by Bruce Bennett, 3–34. Melbourne: Longman Cheshire, 1981.

Webby, Elizabeth. "Colonial Writers and Readers." In *The Cambridge Companion to Australian Literature,* edited by Elizabeth Webby, 50–73. Cambridge: Cambridge University Press, 2000.

Webby, Elizabeth. *Early Australian Poetry: An Annotated Bibliography of Original Poems Published in Australian Newspapers, Magazines & Almanacks before 1850.* Sydney: Hale & Iremonger, 1982.

Webby, Elizabeth. "Journals in the Nineteenth Century." In *The Book in Australia: Towards a Cultural and Social History,* edited by D. H. Borchardt and W. Kirsop, 110–38. Melbourne: Australian Reference Publications in association with the Centre for Bibliographical and Textual Studies, Monash University, 1988.

Webby, Elizabeth. "Not Reading the Nation: Australian Readers of the 1890s." *Australian Literary Studies* 22, no. 3 (2006): 308–18.

Wilkens, Matthew. "The Geographic Imagination of Civil War–Era American Fiction." *American Literary History* 25, no. 4 (2013): 803–40.

Wright, Judith. *Preoccupations in Australian Poetry.* Melbourne: Oxford University Press, 1965.

Wynne, Emma. "Budget 2016: Cuts Force Online Archive Trove to Stop Adding to Collection." ABC *News Online,* May 5, 2016. http://www.abc.net.au/news/2016-05-05/national-library-trove-project-not-funded-to-add-to-collection/7377634

Index

Finn, Ed, 39, 40, 48–49
Foott, Mary Hannay, 115, 172, 175, 177, 194
Foucault, Michel, 85, 91, 162

Gaunt, Mary, 174, 193
Gelder, Ken, 62, 176
gender, as discussed literary histories, 93, 115, 146, 206; as an organising paradigm for nineteenth-century Australian newspaper fiction, 11, 86–87, 106; prediction of, 159, 161, 163, 165–170, 172, 225–226n9; trends in nineteenth-century Australian newspapers, 96, 98–100, 105–6, 108, 111, 113–15, 119–20, 194–96. *See also* American fiction in nineteenth-century Australian newspapers, prevalence of men's writing; American periodicals, dominance of women's fiction in; Australian colonial newspaper fiction, by men; Australian colonial newspaper fiction, by women; Australian colonial readers, interest in men's writing; authorial anonymity and pseudonymity, variation relating to gender; authorial inscription, of gender; British fiction in nineteenth-century Australian newspapers, prevalence of men's writing; British periodicals, dominance of women's fiction in; distant reading, and gender; feminist literary criticism; macroanalysis, and gender
George Robertson, 149
Gephi, 125, 129, 130. *See also* network analysis
Gibbs, Frederick, 32, 35
Giles, Paul, 97
mining fiction, 195–96
Goldstone, Andrew, 5, 57, 162–63
Google Books, 44, 47, 73
Gordon and Gotch, 69–72, 216n30
Goulburn Herald, 136, 145–46, 223n20
Gympie Miner, 120
Gympie Times, 146

Hardy, Thomas, 2
Harte, Bret, 110, 219n20

HathiTrust Digital Library, 40, 44, 51, 52, 54–56
Hawthorne, Julian, 110
Hay Standard, 146, 223n20
Hennessey, David, 117, 146, 196, 223n23
Hennessey and Harper, 146
Henty, G. A., 150
Hentz, Caroline Lee, 184
Hetherington, Carol, 73, 79, 87, 207
Hilliard, Christopher, 126, 132
Houlding, J. R., 114
Hugo, Victor, 2, 186

Illustrated Sydney News, 136, 143
Ingraham, Prentiss, 2

James, Henry, 2
Jocelyn, Mrs. Robert, 181
Jockers, Matthew L. *See* macroanalysis
Johanningsmeier, Charles, 70, 138, 141, 151, 224n28
Johnson-Woods, Toni, 65, 109, 131–32, 139, 211n2/3
Jones, Emma Garrison, 111
juvenile fiction, 159, 196, 226n13. *See also* popular fiction

Kingsley, Henry, 119
Kirkpatrick, Rod, 72, 216n31, 221n1

Lacie, Captain. *See* Wright, James Joseph
Lake, Marilyn, 157
Launceston Daily Telegraph, 136
Launceston Examiner, 136
Law, Graham, 106, 118–19, 132, 136, 138, 143
Lawson, Henry, 174–75, 220n26
Leader, 130, 134, 136, 142–43, 223n17
Lester, Alan, 127
Lewis, Harriet, 111
Lewis, Leon, 94
Libbey, Laura Jean, 2, 104, 111
libraries, 44, 85, 213n2; digital, 22, 40, 51–52, 68; public, 24, 51, 71–72, 149; university, 24, 51, 55, 91, 104. *See also* British Library; Google Books; HathiTrust Digital Library; Library of Congress; National Library of Australia